The Work of Forgetting

Philosophical Projections

Series Editor: Andrew Benjamin, Distinguished Professor of Philosophy and the Humanities, Kingston University, UK, and Professor of Philosophy and Jewish Thought, Monash University, Australia

Philosophical Projections represents the future of Modern European Philosophy. The series seeks to innovate by grounding the future in the work of the present, opening up the philosophical and allowing it to renew itself, while interrogating the continuity of the philosophical after the critique of metaphysics.

Titles in the Series

Foundations of the Everyday: Shock, Deferral, Repetition, by Eran Dorfman

The Thought of Matter: Materialism, Conceptuality and the Transcendence of Immanence, by Richard A. Lee

Nancy, Blanchot: A Serious Controversy, by Leslie Hill

The Work of Forgetting: Or, How Can We Make the Future Possible?, by Stéphane Symons

The Work of Forgetting

Or, How Can We Make the Future Possible?

Stéphane Symons

London • New York

Published by Rowman & Littlefield International, Ltd.
6 Tinworth Street, London SE11 5AL
www.rowmaninternational.com

Rowman & Littlefield International, Ltd. is an affiliate of
Rowman & Littlefield
4501 Forbes Boulevard, Suite 200, Lanham, Maryland 20706, USA
With additional offices in Boulder, New York, Toronto (Canada), and London (UK)
www.rowman.com

Copyright © 2019 by Stéphane Symons

All rights reserved. No part of this book may be reproduced in any form or by any electronic or mechanical means, including information storage and retrieval systems, without written permission from the publisher, except by a reviewer who may quote passages in a review.

British Library Cataloguing in Publication Information
A catalogue record for this book is available from the British Library

ISBN: HB 978-1-78552-323-6

Library of Congress Cataloging-in-Publication Data Available

ISBN: 978-1-78552-323-6 (cloth)
ISBN 978-1-5381-5827-2 (pbk)
ISBN: 978-1-78552-324-3 (electronic)

Contents

	PS-1
Acknowledgements	ix
Introduction: The Work of Forgetting. Or, How Can We Make the Future Possible?	1
A Note on Primo Levi	17
Notes	27
1 What Is Thought? And How Can We Bring It About?	33
'Dichtermut' and 'Blödigkeit'	34
The Concept of *Aufgabe*	38
The *Aufgabe* of Thought	45
The Turning of Time	49
Nihilism and Messianism in the 'Theological-Political Fragment'	53
A Note on Gershom Scholem	62
From Universal Forgetting to the Unforgettable	65
A Note on Theodor Adorno	76
Notes	81
2 What Is the Immemorial? And How Can We Make It Go Away?	89
Freud Contra Transience	93
Heidegger's Ground	100
A Note on Ernst Jünger	110
Benjamin and Experience	112
To Have Done with the Immemorial	117
A Note on Marcel, Albertine and Gilberte	130
Notes	134
3 What Is the Child? Or How Can We Begin Anew?	145
From Nietzsche to Arendt	147
A Note on Virgil and Augustine	153
Benjamin's Non-Metaphysics of Youth	160
Das Tagebuch	170
Notes	176

By Way of Conclusion: A Note on Shadows	181
Notes	186
Abbreviations and Translations	187
Bibliography	189
Index	201
About the Author	209
	PS-2

Acknowledgements

First, I would like to thank all my colleagues at the Institute of Philosophy, in particular Roland Breeur, Paul Cortois, Paul Moyaert and Steven Spileers.

I would also like to thank the colleagues from the Faculty of Arts, in particular Barbara Baert, Anneleen Masschelein, Bart Philipsen and Hilde Van Gelder, and Junji Hori, Takeshi Kadobayashi, Noriaki Kuwata and Yoshi Takemine.

For encouraging remarks along the way, I would like to thank Ulrich Baer, Colby Dickinson, Howard Eiland, Martin Jay, Nathan Ross and Dimitris Vardoulakis. I thank Andrew Benjamin for his support of this project and for his invitation to publish the book in the series Philosophical Projections.

Thanks are due to Willem Styfhals for his interesting remarks on the relation between Walter Benjamin and Gershom Scholem.

I thank Laura Smith and Jiha Kang for their help in preparing the manuscript and Hannah Fisher, Sarah Campbell, Rebecca Anastasi and their colleagues at Rowman & Littlefield International for their confidence in the project and their professionalism.

Though the argument has been modified, sections of the conclusion were published earlier in my article 'In Praise of Shadows: Commemorative Images and the Atomic Bomb', in *Image and Narrative* 14 (1) (2013): 19–34.

Infinitely more than thanks are due to my parents, my brother, sister, brother-in-law, family-in-law and friends.

This book, and its author, are dedicated to Tammy Lynn Castelein and Arthur Francis Symons.

Introduction

The Work of Forgetting.
Or, How Can We Make the Future Possible?

How to begin a book that considers the possibility to begin? Where to make a start when making a start, and the issue of natality, are among the main topics that this book will look into.

We could, for instance, begin with a reference to an ending. Or even the subject of death. For example, we could begin with the epilogue to a book of more than eight hundred pages, Tony Judt's monumental study *Postwar: A History of Europe since 1945*. In this epilogue, entitled 'From the House of the Dead: An Essay on Modern European Memory', the British historian mentions the often-heard idea that the first decades of the twenty-first century are still determined by some of the darkest events that occurred in the previous century. 'Extermination', writes Judt, is 'the pertinent European reference' and 'Holocaust recognition . . . our contemporary European entry ticket'.[1] For Judt, such an 'entry ticket' requires the assistance of *history* rather than *memory*, since memory is ultimately incapable of capturing the enormity of the horror that is under consideration. What makes Judt's epilogue remarkable is that his analysis of the limits of memory does not take recourse to the worn-out category of the 'unrepresentability' of the Holocaust and thus escapes the commonplace of the 'sublime' character of its atrocities. That the Nazi horrors confront the faculty of memory with its limits has less to do with their supposed 'unrepresentability' than with a characteristic that is believed to be *internal* to the faculty of memory itself. For memory 'confirms and reinforces itself': it enables us to experience the past as not wholly lost for the very reason that it can still be remembered.[2] If we can *commemorate* an event, we assume, it surely has not come to *nothing*. The remembrance of the past in books and in monuments, in thoughts and in images, may not necessarily work to make it meaningful but doesn't it affirm the human capacity to nevertheless somehow go *beyond* it? Because memory is ultimately wedded to such a belief in continuation and preservation, Judt suggests, it cannot in the end be trusted to testify to the extreme violence of the Holocaust.

In contrast to the confidence in the powers of memory, history starts from the sharp awareness that what ultimately matters the most has, to be sure, been lost. '[H]istory contributes to the disenchantment of the world'.[3] Judt therefore reminds us that the concept of history has in fact two different meanings: 'the professional study of the past' and 'the passage of time'.[4] In German, history can indeed be translated both as *Geschichte*, thereby referring to the past as the object of historiography (the second meaning of the word *Geschichte* is 'story') and *Vergangenheit*, referring to the past as something that has truly passed away (*'ist vergangen'*). This second meaning of the concept of history draws attention to a rather obvious fact: that it has *not* survived into the present is something that pertains to the essence of the past. This sets up the tension between history and memory that Judt refers to. When history is understood as a *succession* of events that pass away one by one, its rhythm is in fact much closer to *forgetting* than to memory, the latter being inseparable from a remarkable type of *simultaneity* between past and present. Of course, hardly anyone will still defend the old positivistic adage that either history or memory can bring back the past 'the way it has been'. Still, it is hard to deny that the faculty of memory is trusted to at least grant *something* a prolonged presence. Pitting the 'discomforting, even disruptive' nature of history against these preserving capacities of memory, Judt's epilogue touches upon one of the most important challenges of the years to come: how to remember the atrocities of the war when the forces of history are overpowering those of memory, when the generation that lived through the war will soon be extinct and, no less important, when their grandchildren are becoming less informed (and more indifferent) each year.[5] 'Europe's barbarous recent history, the dark "other" against which post-war Europe was laboriously constructed, is already beyond recall for young Europeans. Within a generation the memorials and museums will be gathering dust—visited, like the battlefields of the Western Front today, only by aficionados and relatives'.[6]

In the final paragraph of his epilogue, Judt suggests that the one true antidote against the disruptive pattern of history should be found within history itself, rather than in a counter-power such as memory. For Judt, the forgetting that is inscribed within the course of history (understood as the 'passage of time', history as *Vergangen-*

heit) cannot be countered by the conserving work of memory but only by the always interrupted and productive work of history itself (understood as 'the professional study of the past', history as *Geschichte*). While the attempt to save the horrors of the past from oblivion through historiography is no less threatened by oblivion than those horrors themselves, this attempt can and should nonetheless be ceaselessly renewed. It is therefore the very force of history, rather than memory, which will open into a process of learning and relearning—a process that will never be fully accomplished.

> Impossible to remember [the Nazi-evil] as it truly was, it is inherently vulnerable to being remembered as it wasn't. Against *this* challenge memory itself is helpless. . . . If in years to come we are to remember why it seemed so important to build a certain sort of Europe out of the crematoria of Auschwitz, only history can help us. . . . If Europeans are to maintain this vital link—if Europe's past is to continue to furnish Europe's present with admonitory meaning and moral purpose—then it will have to be *taught* afresh with each passing generation. 'European Union' may be a response to history, but it can never be its substitute.[7]

More than a decade after these words were written, Judt's argument that only history itself can counteract history has grown even more convincing and taken on a sudden sense of urgency. In spite of the enormous number of memorial sites, museums and monuments that are spread out across the globe, the preserving work of memory has suffered from serious blows in an era that thrives on acceleration and a ceaseless quest for renewal. Ours is a time that is reluctant to spend too much time with anything that cannot be made directly profitable, recently even aiming its arrows at the age-old concept of truth, memory's trusted companion since Plato's time. Hardly a surprise, therefore, that the idea that a common past of war and suffering ought to bring the nations of Europe together in a strong, political unity is now no longer a shared article of faith. Anti-EU feelings have not only spread deep into its border-regions of the West (the Brexit vote) and East (EU-bashing by political leaders in Eastern Europe) but even penetrated its inner core (populism and anti-European sentiments are rampant in the entire continent). Complex as these feelings may be, it is nevertheless clear that the process of political and historical commemoration that founded the EU (Judt's 'entry ticket') is ceaselessly exposed to criticism.[8]

Beyond an anticipation of these political and social conflicts, Judt's analysis coincides with the intellectual challenge to renew one of the most influential paradigms of the past decades, that is, the paradigm of *memory studies*. The recent literature on memory is enormous and it is impossible to summarize all of it in one common set of arguments. One idea, however, seems foundational to the field of memory studies at large. In contrast to Judt's text, the field of memory studies builds on the assumption that it is *not* history itself but first and foremost the faculty of *memory* that enables human beings to formulate a response to historical events. However diverse their works may be, scholars such as Maurice Halbwachs, Paul Ricoeur, Pierre Nora, Aleida Assman, Avishai Margalit, Andreas Huyssen, Tzvetan Todorov or Michael Rothberg share the conviction that the possibility of a re-negotiation of history is inseparable from the powers of memory. Having been released once and for all from the feeling that memory is but a subjective (and, as a consequence, unreliable) representation of past events and experiences, it has instead become manifest as a power that makes possible an active engagement with the realm of history at large. This gesture of turning the faculty of memory into the prime instrument to relate to history has brought the major proponents of the field of memory studies to look beyond the ties between memory and the past, equally emphasizing both its critical abilities vis-à-vis the present and its constructive potential for a joint future. Memory is thus believed to generate the possibility that history is encountered as more than a mere force of necessity: if events in history can be understood, acted upon and, who knows, in the end even worked through, this is first and foremost believed to be due to an intervention of memory. Scholars have made memory inseparable from a politics (Huyssen) and an ethics (Margalit) and presented it as the condition for a community in which even the commemoration of the 'thin' relations between strangers is deemed strong enough to build up a sense of belonging.[9] Other authors have rooted the argument that memory is a most fundamental faculty to relate to history in an analysis of its 'multidirectionality' (Rothberg): it is through memory-processes that are open, creative and heterogeneous that we overcome the 'zero-sum game' in which paying tribute to one particular past would automatically entail casting into oblivion another one.[10] In the past decades, memory has moved to the forefront of contemporary academia because it has been framed simultaneously as a reproductive and selective dynamic that blends elements from different contexts together in one multilayered complex. The field of memory studies has therefore pledged loyalty to a concept of memory that renders possible both a lived experience of one's own culture and a deep relationship with other ones. Memory is believed to yield the quintessential ingredient for human identities (both individual and collective) that are, on the one hand, stable enough to root our lives in a sense of belonging and, on the other, sufficiently *un*stable to allow for a genuine responsiveness to other ways of living and believing.

The background of the idea that memory is a privileged site to answer the many complexities of history is a multifaceted one and cannot be wholly captured in but a few paragraphs. The first impetus behind this relatively recent discourse on memory originated in the sixties in the wake of decolonization, the rise of identity-politics and the debate about race and gender. This first turn towards memory coincided with the independence of countries that were in the process of emancipating themselves from imperialism and with the struggle of minorities of various sorts to escape from the white, male and heterosexual discourse that dominated the West. Infused with insights that were borrowed from psychoanalysis, structuralist and post-structuralist philosophy, these movements took recourse to the category of memory in order to answer to the need for an identity that would match 'other' forms of thinking and, vice versa, would make it possible to think 'otherness'. The new discourse on memory, therefore, resulted not so much from a sudden interest in the past as from an urgent demand for a renewed *present*. In fact, the first exploration of the power of memory as the privileged capacity to deal with the challenges of history answered to a need to *break* with the past. These early stages of memory studies did not at all turn to the past as a *legitimation* of the present but, seeking to give a voice to various instantiations of the subaltern, it helped bring about a force of resistance against age-old strategies of domination.[11]

In the eighties, a second wave of memory studies also deployed the concept of memory as a response to historical challenges, but not without this time putting the *past* into the heart of the discussion. This second major moment of memory theory witnessed the publication of important texts on the relation between history and memory on both sides of the Atlantic (e.g., Yosef Hayim Yerushalmi's *Zakhor* [1982] and Pierre Nora's *Realms of Memory* [1984–1992]), but it was to a large extent colored by the famous *Historikerstreit* in Germany near the end of the decade. Indeed, the belief that it is primarily memory that enables a response to the many challenges of history had now become inspirational for a heated debate about the atrocities that were committed by the Nazi regime.[12] Beyond reaching a conclusive consensus on the facts of the war period, the *Historikerstreit* used the concept of memory to explore the issue whether the Nazi past has a unique status in history or whether it could be compared to other forms of violence, such as the crimes of the Soviet Union. This second moment marked an important shift with regard to the first one in that it coincided with experiences that had exhausted the earlier optimism about decolonization and the politics of identity, race and gender: the 'conservative revolution' in Britain and the United States, a crisis of Marxism, the Islamic Revolution in Iran, the Cambodian genocide and finally, of course, the fall of the Berlin Wall, which initiated a large-scale return to the dominant discourse of the West and a new stage of globalized and neoliberal capitalism.[13]

For about thirty years now, a third strand of memory studies has been using the category of memory as an answer to technological challenges of various sorts, thereby appealing more and more to widespread concerns about the *future*. In a world that is increasingly dominated by global technology, the speed of history has accelerated in ways that could not have been anticipated. This has led to a deeply felt sense of insecurity and the absence of any agreement about the direction in which the world is heading. This *condition informatique* requires a novel way of responding to history and it has sharpened the need to explore memory as an instrument to contemplate potential futures. Some of the impact of computers and information technology runs counter to the lived processes of memory and identity formation, making the borders between past, present and future seem much less rigid than ever before. After the example of Reinhart Koselleck's radical historicization of our experience of time and history, attention has been drawn to a deep transformation of the temporal structure of our lives, resulting from various, primarily technological evolutions that have reshaped our spheres of consumption, work and mobility.[14] Beyond an interest in the past and the present, both having been destabilized by informational and perceptual overload, memory has been cast as a 'reaction formation' against the speed and velocity of technical processes that are deeply impactful.[15]

With the concept of memory having thus gained a central position in a wide variety of contexts, it is hardly remarkable that the memory boom has affected not a few societal debates in the past decades. Memory studies moved to the forefront in some of the discussions that occupied scholars in intellectual history, cultural studies, literary studies, art history, human rights studies, political science, gender theory, race studies, philosophy and psychoanalysis. However, the field of memory studies at large rests on a paradox. For the view of memory that has been refined over years of research underscores both that the human faculty of memory belongs to the realm of history pure and proper *and* that it is a counterforce *to* history, capable of responding to its most fundamental conflicts. This tension cannot be easily resolved and it explains to no small degree why, as we will see, numerous scholars have questioned the belief that it is first and foremost memory that allows man to relate to history. This same paradox will also explain why the chapters that follow were written as a response to Judt's suggestion that it is history itself, rather than memory, that should be taken as the prime site to deal with the challenges of the past, present and future.

Let us begin with the first point, that is, with the emphasis that memory studies have made the human faculty of memory inseparable from history. The concept of memory that is central to memory studies bears the traces of the context in which it is being deployed, the sixties being marked by challenges (and, consequently, by a concept of memory) that differed in no small degree from those of the eighties and the turn of the century. This explains why the concept of memory has absorbed the contingencies and the possibility of change that mark the realm of history as such. By crafting a notion of 'historical memory', the turn to memory has made the openness of history fruitful for the endeavor to respond to its (i.e., history's) complexities.[16] In this way, the field of memory studies has managed to internalize its own *limitations*, turning them into a strength instead of a weakness. Rather than merely opposing memory and forgetting to each other, for instance, the main proponents of memory theory emphasize instead that, as Paul Ricoeur put it, forgetting is but 'the shadowy underside of the bright region of memory'.[17] A full recovery of the past is deemed both impossible and uncalled-for, little as one would be inclined to believe that the threat of forgetting the past can ever be really warded off. The rejection of the aims of positivistic historiography, where a factual past was still deemed retrievable, was therefore one of the founding moments of the memory boom. Following the lead of authors like Nietzsche, Benjamin, Foucault, Lyotard and Derrida, memory theory has exorcised the conviction that the present can wholly recover the past in a neutral and objective manner. Instead, it has replaced such a naïve belief in linear progress with the ideal of a lived interaction between past and present, and the quest for a genuine future.

As Enzo Traverso suggests, the position of memory studies is the one that Siegfried Kracauer, in his unfinished book *History: The Last Things Before the Last*, identified as that of 'exile'.[18] The space from which a researcher investigates the past is always, indeed, hovering in-between the present and the past: because the categories, ideas and tools of the researcher are colored by the needs and demands of his own situation, they will never fully match those of his object of research and forever stand in the way of a complete identification with the past. This gap between present and past, however, does not immediately result in anachronism. To the contrary, it is this caesura itself that helps memory theory to set up the interpretative distance from which historical events can be understood, compared, explained and, ultimately, be made meaningful beyond the narrow perspective of the past itself.[19]

This awareness that the work of memory is inevitably marked by the conflicts, lacunae and contingencies of history does not, of course, contradict the feeling that it can be made operational as a response *to* these very conflicts, lacunae and contingencies. Still, a deep-seated tension between both claims remains unanswered: How can memory be believed to make possible a lived reaction to the threats and challenges of history if it is at the same time deeply affected *by* these threats and challenges? The acknowledgement of this paradox has brought some of the main proponents of memory studies to emphasize that even a deeply *historical* memory is not fully *determined* by the course of history. In the first pages of Aleida Assman's groundbreaking study of cultural memory, where memory is associated with the age-old battle against death and oblivion and, more recently, in Jeffrey Andrew Barash's analysis of collective memory, we are reminded that the first credo of memory studies is as old as human society itself: the powers of memory are believed to *counter* potentially destructive forces that are at work within history.[20] For Andreas Huyssen, as well, 'we need to discriminate among memory practices in order to strengthen those that *counteract* the tendencies in our culture to foster uncreative forgetting'.[21] As we have seen, the confidence that memory can thus go against history has taken on many different guises over the years, focusing just as much on the struggle against the dominant and 'major' narratives of the West, as on the social, political and academic taboos after the Second World War or on the danger of a technologically induced amnesia.

Beyond the annihilating forces that can be identified in specific historical events or evolutions, some authors highlight that a capacity to destroy is present within the realm of history *at large*. In such cases, the appeal to memory as a prime site to face the conflicts of history rests on the assumption that a profound indifference pertains to the course of history *as such*. Theodor Adorno, for instance, describes the tension between memory and history as follows:

> As [the dead] are defenseless, at the mercy of our memory, so our memory is the only help that is left to them. They pass away into it, and if every deceased person is like someone who was murdered by the living, so he is also like someone whose life they must save, without knowing whether the effort will succeed. The rescue of what is possible, but has not yet been—this is the aim of remembrance.[22]

The hope that it is memory that grants man the capacity to somehow act *against* the course of history oftentimes goes hand in hand with the assumption that the course of history is in truth apathetic to human beings and their projects. With this, memory has become, in the formula of Tzvetan Todorov, a 'remedy for evil'.[23] It is believed to retain an operational layer that cannot be wholly subsumed by the potentially destructive forces of history. Herbert Marcuse, for example, stated that memory 'preserve[s] promises and potentialities which are betrayed and even outlawed by the mature, civilized individual'.[24] This identification of a potential violence within the realm of history at large, and the appeal to memory as a possible counterpower deployed against it, explains why the relationship between the past, present and future has been coined as a *dialectical* one. Rather than rigidly differentiating the dimensions of past, present and future from each other, the faculty of memory is deemed capable of somehow *dislocating* this very differentiation. Memory has been explored as a power that *interrupts* the otherwise irremediable course of history. In the canonized interpretation of Walter Benjamin's philosophy of history, for instance, 'remembrance' (the most common translation of the German term *Eingedenken*) is given the political and theological task to 'modify' the past and 'brush history against the grain' (AP, 471; SW 4, 392). While not of course capable of undoing the injustices that have been committed in earlier times, the power of remembrance is believed to nevertheless set these injustices right by 'blast[ing] [them] out of the continuum of history' (SW 4, 395). Memory is thus deemed capable of releasing the past from its original context of meaning and of somehow halting its forces of annihilation. The intervention by memory is 'a tiger's leap into the past' which can be likened to 'the dialectical leap Marx understood as revolution' (SW 4, 395). Beyond the aims of paying tribute to the losses of the past or actualizing a critical moment vis-à-vis the present, memory summons up a view of a radically different future. Benjamin is therefore often cited as a key source for the idea that it is the faculty of memory that conditions a glimpse of an improved universe: revolution is 'nourished by the image of enslaved ancestors rather than by the ideal of liberated grandchildren' (SW 4, 394). It was on a similar note that Benjamin's friend Ernst Bloch developed his notorious philosophy of utopianism and hope. Bloch, as well, rooted his affirmative view of an as yet undetermined future in the commemoration of ancient dreams about emancipation and in an anthropological optimism about universal equality that was inherited from the Enlightenment. Memory could thus be considered a crucial instrument for envisioning a philosophy of the future and a politics of 'anticipation' (*Vorschein*) that is wedded to the temporality of the 'not yet' (*noch nicht*).[25]

For a while now commentators have been suggesting that the potential of memory to somehow counteract the course of history has been exhausted. If this were true, the creative interaction between past, present and future would be increasingly hard to achieve. In the wake of the publication of Jacques Derrida's *Specters of Marx* (1993), the capacity of memory to actualize the wish-images of the past as anticipations of potential futures has indeed been divested of its utopian qualities. Published a few years after the fall of the Berlin Wall, Derrida's study was written against the backdrop of the recent implosion of the Soviet Union, once sparked by the utopian ideal of universal equality but subsequently having morphed into ideology and totalitarianism. It attacks Francis Fukuyama's apology of a neo-liberal 'end of history' that stubbornly holds fast to a belief in unilineal progress. In Derrida's view, memory's return to the past is confronted, first and foremost, with the ruins of unrealized dreams and it can no longer deliver images of a radically different and 'open' future. For Derrida, memory does not restore our optimism about the future but it conjures the melancholic afterlife of a lost and defeated past that refuses to be kept at bay. 'A messianic promise, even if it was not fulfilled . . . will have imprinted an inaugural and unique mark in history. And whether we like it or not, whatever consciousness we have of it, we cannot not be its heirs'.[26] In an important, more recent text, 'For a Left with No Future' (2012), the art historian T. J. Clark follows Derrida's lead to untie the dialectical threads through which the past, present and future can be put into motion. Clark's article is a 'sketch of what moderation might mean to revolutionaries' and polemically suggests that '[w]e moderns no longer provide the stuff from which a society might be constructed'. Clark tones down the urgency of anticipating the future and emphasizes the need to first of all recognize *and* resist the status quo. As a consequence, his call to politics shakes off any and all utopian tendencies ('Utopianism . . . is what the landlords have time for') and is founded in the awareness that the left will 'always [be] embattled and marginalized, always—proudly—a thing of the past'.[27] In line with these ideas, numerous scholars have pointed out that our times seem 'out of joint' in the sense that an ever expanding present (François Hartog's 'presentism') turns both the past and the future into unstable and inaccessible dimensions and blocks the 'prognostic' (Koselleck) value of historical time. In his recent study *Left-Wing Melancholia: Marxism, History, and Memory* (2016), Enzo Traverso joins this league of critics, affirming that 'the utopias of the past century have disappeared, leaving a present charged with memory but unable to project itself into the future'.[28] Traverso renders a succinct analysis of the most important causes of memory's incapacity to conjure images of a universe that is truly 'other'. For Traverso, as well, this has primarily to do with the world that we have inherited after 1989. Unlike the French and communist revolutions, the collapse of the Soviet Union has not been accompanied with an ideal of progress and an optimism about the future. Instead, the fall of the Berlin Wall has led to a neoliberal order that is fully tuned to the rhythm of the stock market, uprooting our identities, disciplining our bodies, controlling our thoughts and reifying our affects in the process. It was under the sign of such an unhinged, globalized and technologized form of capitalism that the twentieth century gave way to the twenty-first one. Increasingly successful at abolishing stable pasts and obfuscating alternative futures, our era seems characterized by a deep sense of disillusionment. As Traverso puts it, '[p]ositing oblivion as a possible destiny for communism means that its defeat at the end of the twentieth century could be more than a lost battle; it could be a lost war, a final defeat'.[29]

The upshot of this diagnosis is that the founding paradox of memory studies has ceased to be a productive one. That is, the confidence that our faculty of memory is at once the outcome of *and* a lived response to the many challenges of history has become increasingly difficult to maintain. Memory, it seems, can no longer creatively relate to the complexities and threats that are posed by the present. Our present world is marked by such a deeply rooted power to annihilate that the danger of amnesia that we are confronted with is incomparable to the threat of mere forgetfulness. While human beings have always been aware of the limits of their faculties of recollection, the fundamental type of oblivion that we are confronted with today is an entirely novel one. As Andreas Huyssen already put it more than twenty years ago, '[i]n th[e] dystopian vision of a high-tech future, amnesia would no longer be part of the dialectic of memory and forgetting. It will be its radical other. It will have sealed the very forgetting of memory itself: nothing to remember, nothing to forget'.[30] It would therefore be a mistake to understand the crisis of the dialectics between past, present and future as a token that the forces of memory have ultimately dominated over the power of history. In truth, the feeling that the past casts such a dark shadow over our present age that one cannot any longer intuit the future as truly 'open' signals a preponderance of historical forces over memory, rather than of memory over history. Our condition of being melancholically 'overcharged' with pastness is not the sign of excessively strong powers of memory but the symptom of radically *weakened* ones. No longer capable of adequately responding to the complexities of the current age, the faculties of memory that are at our disposal today are not merely affected by the conflicts, lacunae and contingencies of history but deeply invaded by them.

Taking seriously Judt's suggestion that only history itself can fully respond to the conflicts of history will require coming to terms with its second meaning, the 'passage of time' (history as *Vergangenheit*). As I suggested earlier, a dimension of forgetting is inseparable from the course of history as such. That they 'pass away' is one of the most fundamental features of historical events, and it is this aspect that most fundamentally sets apart the realm of history and the supposed counterforce of memory. While it is false to fully oppose memory and forgetting because memory is always a *selective* process, the functioning of memory does inevitably rest on a capacity to overcome the dynamic of disappearance that pertains to the realm of history at large. To be sure, as Plato and Aristotle already knew, memory does not make possible a full retrieval of past experiences. In the *Theaetetus*, Plato already has Socrates say that 'whatever is obliterated or cannot be impressed, we forget and do not know' and, in his important text on memory and recollection, Aristotle underscores that 'all memory implies a time elapsed'.[31] The preserving abilities of memory, in other words, cannot fully dismantle the transience that marks the temporal realm and the predisposition of historical events to 'fall away' one by one. Still, memory does perform a brief victory over transience and signals that past experiences have not altogether disappeared. 'Whatever is impressed upon the wax', Plato reminds us, 'we remember and know so long as the image remains in the wax'. Likewise, according to Aristotle, memory evidences the possibility to 'see or hear that which is not present'.[32]

This book is devoted to an analysis of a specific response to the realm of history that does not presuppose these interruptive faculties of memory. Rather than focus on the possibility that transience is overcome by an *external* counterforce such as memory, I will argue that the 'passage of time' that pertains to the realm of history at large can also be interrupted from *within*. This will involve a shift of focus, away from the capacities of memory and towards a process that Nietzsche has called 'creative' forgetting. Exploring the possibility that history counteracts its own rhythm of annihilation entails, first of all, discovering transience as a process that is not merely destructive. For the experience that historical events are marked by the propensity to fall away one by one does not necessarily result in an estrangement between past and present. The very confrontation with the *in*capacity of historical events to endure can set up a creative response to history. Such a response does not simply rest on any confidence in the decelerating counterpower of memory. The author who will figure most prominently in this book is Walter Benjamin. As has been mentioned, Benjamin's philosophy of history is often singled out as a key source of inspiration for the turn towards memory in academic debates. However, his views on the 'modifying' and even 'redemptive' qualities of memory are more layered than it might perhaps be assumed. With the notorious identification of a *'weak* messianic power' that sets up a responsibility of the present towards the past, Benjamin is not at all suggesting that the mere ability to somehow re-establish a connection with the past allows us to transcend its shortcomings (SW 4, 390). The idea that the past could be 'saved' or 'redeemed' by the sheer capacity to make it a part of the present would presuppose a belief in progress that is wholly at odds with Benjamin's way of thinking. For what would set our present age so distinctly apart from the past that it could be believed to set right the wrongdoings of earlier times and restore the injustices of previous generations? Why would our own times have been granted redemptive capacities while the past, for its part, is to be identified as a site of violence and struggle? In some of the sharpest passages of his writings, Benjamin emphasizes, instead, that the present suffers from the very same dangers that have also held sway over previous eras. Benjamin thereby goes beyond the view of history that underlies the field of memory studies: for him, the 'passing away' that is at work within history at large cannot be counteracted from without. The transience that he identifies within the core of history is described as 'eternal' and even our faculties of memory are ultimately rendered powerless by them: 'The true image of the past flits by. The past can be seized only as an image that flashes up at the moment of its recognizability, and is never seen again' (SW 4, 390).[33] Well surpassing the earlier mentioned view that history is marked with a deep-seated indifference vis-à-vis the human being and his projects, Benjamin's philosophy is in truth rooted in the view that the realm of history is hollowed out by an unceasing dynamic of obliteration. 'Redemption depends on the tiny fissure in the continuous catastrophe' (SW 4, 185). For Benjamin, 'the only historian capable of fanning the spark of hope in the past is the one who is firmly convinced that *even the dead* will not be safe from the enemy if he is victorious' (SW 4, 391). With this claim, Benjamin does not simply refer to the hope that cherishing the memory of our deceased loved ones can grant them a mental and emotional afterlife. Injecting an ability to annihilate deeply within the historical realm as such, Benjamin's writings are wholly unsuited as a source of solace. Benjamin's philosophy of history pushes to extremes the idea that transience is at work within the temporal realm. For him, there is nothing that is untouched by this impermanence and transience even becomes an all-encompassing force of annihilation: '[T]he enemy [for whom even the dead will not be safe] has never ceased to be victorious' (SW 4, 391). While, as we will see, Benjamin's philosophy has a deeply affirmative undercurrent, it lacks any and all ambition to be merely comforting. As Benjamin aptly describes it in his famous analysis of Paul Klee's 'angel of history', history can be perceived as 'one single catastrophe, which keeps piling wreckage upon wreckage'. This continuum of destruction is immune to the redemptive capacities of any external counterforce that 'would like to stay, awaken the dead, and make whole what has been smashed' (SW 4, 392).

Coining the concept of a 'natural history of destruction' (O, 166), to indicate a force of obliteration from which nothing is spared, Benjamin's philosophy departs from the paradigm of memory studies in an essential way. The violence that in his view dominates over history is not just to be taken for a *potential* force of destruction but it constitutes an *actual* one. The subsistence of a force of obliteration that is testified to in Benjamin's overall philosophy is of a deeply *structural* nature. 'There is no document of culture which is not at the same time a document of barbarism' (SW 4, 392). On account of this 'eternal' presence of a power to annihilate, Benjamin evacuates the faculty of memory of its preserving capacities. In spite of the multiple use of terms such as memory [*Gedächtnis*] and recollection [*Erinnerung*], Benjamin's philosophy of history is much more wedded to a theory of forgetting. Benjamin's statement that the writings of Marcel Proust can more accurately be described as a 'work of forgetting' [*Penelopewerk des Vergessens*] (SW 2, 238; GS II, 311) than as a 'work of remembering' matches his own writings as well. What Benjamin identified as the redemptive capacity of remembrance cannot be separated from an analysis of forgetting. The 'weak messianic power' that is endowed unto us 'like every generation that preceded us' does denote an ability to act upon the past but this intervention is not motivated by the belief in the possibility of preservation (SW 4, 390). Any analysis of Benjamin's description of the ability to make the past reappear should be accompanied with the claim that this moment of reappearance signals, in fact, a longed for distance. '[B]arbarism taints the manner in which [a document of culture] was transmitted from one hand to another. The historical materialist therefore dissociates himself from this process of transmission as far as possible' (SW 4, 392). For Benjamin, remembrance is not so much inspired by the belief that the past can become fully part of the present as by the hope that it might be *saved* from such a fate. The commemoration of the injustices of the past is in Benjamin's view inseparably entwined with forgetting because it above all entails the hope that these injustices are at least *protected* against those of the present.[34] Benjamin's suggestion that a specific type of forgetting thus precludes the past from fully entering into the present should not be confused with the claim that the present and past should be altogether separated from each other. To the contrary, when the past is protected from the injustices of the present, this entails nothing less than the restoration of an intimate contact between both. Such an experience *'with'* the past brings about an unexpected constellation of meaning in which the distance between the present and the past is made productive rather than overcome (SW 4, 396 [emphasis added]; see also AP, 462).

Benjamin's philosophy of history helps us to sharply distinguish such a process of creative forgetting from a mere 'working through' of the past. On a first level of analysis, creative forgetting is the sign of a specific re-establishment of the relation between the present and the past, and not a mere loosening of such ties.[35] Because it describes a specific intervention undertaken by the present, it is at odds, first of all, with amnesia, that is, with the mere antithesis of memory and recollection in which the past is simply left behind by the present. Moreover, in spite of Benjamin's affinities with avant-garde movements such as Dada and surrealism, his belief in creative forgetting is equally at odds with the futuristic drive to cut through all ties with the past. Creative forgetting is irreconcilable with such a belief in progress. It replaces the firm conviction that the present ought to immunize itself against the past with the precarious hope that, vice versa, the past can be immunized against the present. Creative forgetting brings about an interval that does not, however, wholly isolate the past from the present. Such an interval conditions, in Benjamin's own words, a 'secret agreement between past generations and the present one' (SW 4, 390).

This interval that protects the past from the continuum of violence that also holds sway over the present entails an unexpected disruption of what Benjamin terms 'mythic violence'. In spite of the term 'mythic', Benjamin describes such forms of violence as an otherwise ineradicable presence within the very heart of history. Mythic violence sets up an eternal repetition of the same in which mechanisms of domination and exclusion are built into the legal system of the state and thereby seek to perpetuate themselves in a seemingly automatic manner. Mythic violence is described as 'bloody power over mere life for its own sake' (SW 1, 248). As a sheer manifestation of power, it strives to modify the very potential to destroy into the sole thing that cannot be destroyed. As Derrida will comment years later, '[i]t belongs to the structure of fundamental violence that it calls for the repetition of itself'.[36] Benjamin's philosophy of history is dedicated to the possibility that such a deeply rooted mechanism of injustice and suffering can nevertheless be dislocated. However, in Benjamin's writings, this conviction that mythic violence can be overturned does not ultimately rest on any optimism about the existence of an external force of resistance, such as pacifism or humanism. Instead, Benjamin founds this possibility in the capacity to affirm and embrace the very transience of history at large: nothing but the experience that historical events can truly 'pass away' is capable of counteracting the mythic violence that strives for endless repetition. Even the intervention that Benjamin describes as 'divine violence' is not so much *external* to history as *expressive* of it, because it pushes to the fore the transience that holds sway over it. Such a divine intervention should not be confused with the sudden revelation of an absolute truth or an eternal value: it is not a fully fletched expression of transcendence but a momentary interruption of the seemingly endless or 'mythic' cycle of legal violence. The manifestations of divine violence are 'defined . . . not by miracles directly performed by God but by the expiating moment in them that strikes without bloodshed, and, finally, by the absence of all lawmaking' (SW 1, 250). Creative forgetting, I therefore argue, is the process that can expose the *internal* limits of mythic violence. In such a form of forgetting, the mythic drive to perpetuate violence is acted upon by an expression of the quality of impermanence that marks the realm of history in toto. Forgetting is made productive when such a deeply rooted impermanence is uncovered within the heart of a type of power that seeks to be all-encompassing.

A NOTE ON PRIMO LEVI

In *The Drowned and the Saved* (1986), one of the books about his past as a prisoner in a concentration camp, Italian author Primo Levi notoriously describes a recurring dream that he and his friends had when they were still inside. Though the dream conjured the option of a return to the family home and propelled them in the company of their loved ones, it was not at all a comforting one. It tormented the prisoners with the fear that their account of the horror would only be met with disbelief.

> Almost all the survivors, verbally or in their written memoirs, remember a dream which frequently recurred during the nights of imprisonment, varied in its detail but uniform in its substance: they had returned home and with passion and relief were describing their past sufferings, addressing themselves to a loved person, and were not believed, indeed were not even listened to.[37]

Levi's account makes palpable that being forgotten is chief amongst the acts of violence a person can undergo. The inability to testify about the horror he underwent is cast as its ultimate manifestation because such a type of oblivion would succeed in turning the violence of his guards into something ineradicable. If no prisoner would be capable of overcoming this inability to testify, this would proclaim an irrevocable victory on the part of the torturers. '[M]any survivors [. . .] remember that the SS militiamen cynically enjoyed admonishing the prisoners: "However this war may end, we have won the war against you; none of you will be left to bear witness, but even if someone were to survive, the world would not believe him"'.[38] In line with Benjamin's suggestion, it seems that the most extreme form of violence is indeed never but indicative of a specific event in time since it manages to somehow project itself onto the continuum of history at large. The deepest type of annihilation seeks to repeat itself infinitely and sets up a seemingly endless cycle of forgetting, thereby propelling itself into the future. This proclivity of extreme violence to go beyond its historical manifestations and become all-encompassing raises the stakes of Levi's testimony. Levi reworks the description of past horrors into a genuine counter-force that can reopen the future. The fact that he was capable of putting his experience into words indicates that at least the threat of a complete forgetting has been warded off. In the face of a violence that sought to eradicate the option of moving beyond the horrors of the past, the very act of testifying is modified into a power to dislodge the injustice. The sheer existence of Levi's writings evidences the possibility that the danger of 'mythic' violence, that is, a power to destroy that has seemingly become indestructible, can be halted in its tracks. These words bring about an openness of the future after a most fundamental force of annihilation had all but closed it off.

However, Levi's account is not built on the ambition to restore the *continuity* between the past and the present. Confronted with a form of violence that seeks to penetrate into the very course of history, Levi's work rests on the quest for a moment of *discontinuity*. His aim is to draw out a specific *break* between the past and present, rather than to establish a stable link between both. Levi's writings about the victims of the Holocaust are, in his own words, 'drenched in memory' but nothing seems further removed from his mind than the confidence that the distance between them and us can be foreshortened. Levi lets go of the belief that the horrors of Auschwitz can be enshrined in shareable memory. In the opening pages of *The Drowned and the Saved*, memory is termed a 'questionable source' that 'has to be protected from itself' because it fades with the passage of time and takes recourse to a whole series of reaction-formations to protect itself against trauma.[39] Even more crucial to understand why memory falls short to explain the importance of Levi's work is that he emphasizes the opposition between the 'drowned' (the dead) and the 'saved' (the survivors). The fact that one must survive in order to be capable of bearing witness distances these witnesses from all fellow prisoners who did not survive. In Levi's mind, therefore, the capacities of memory to bear witness to the horrors of Auschwitz are *inherently* limited. As he put it, every testimony to the injustice of the Holocaust will forever remain inseparable from a 'lacuna': 'We, the survivors are not the true witnesses . . . we survivors are not only an exiguous but also anomalous minority. We . . . did not touch bottom. Those who did so, who saw the Gorgon, have not returned to tell about it or have returned mute, but they are the 'Muslims', the submerged, the complete witnesses'.[40] Levi's writings are invaded by such fundamental voids and expressive of so many absences that it seems false to read them as a manifestation of the ability of *memory* to ward off the threat of forgetfulness. Levi, it can therefore be argued, did not pit this threat against the supposedly redemptive capacities of memory but against the possibility of a different, creative forgetting. Levi's writing is not a struggle *against* the many omissions that he identifies as unavoidable. It is an act of creation that *makes use of* these omissions. The 'lacuna' that makes manifest the incomplete nature of Levi's testimony is not constitutive of a mere 'outside' since it has entered into his writings. Levi's writings revolve *around* this absence and they allow this internal void to become an aid to his expressive abilities. Contrary to what might be assumed, Levi's work does *not* give us a direct view of the horror of a concentration camp. In crucial passages of his work he turns *away* from these atrocities and leaves room for scenes that seem *at odds* with them. In such passages, Levi diverts his gaze from the horror and draws attention to scenes that are even remindful of a 'normal' existence. Some of his most powerful passages include, for instance, descriptions of a persistent interest in intellectual endeavors. In the chapter 'The Canto of Ulysses', in *Survival in Auschwitz* (1947), Levi describes how he would have traded in his food for a few lines from Dante. Elsewhere, he writes: 'Culture was useful for me. Not always, and at times perhaps by subterranean and unforeseen paths, but it served me well and perhaps it saved me'.[41] With these descriptions of a precarious, intellectual life within the confines of the camp, Levi *dissociates* the description of his own life from the fate of the prisoners who did not survive the ordeal (the 'complete' witnesses). These scenes, however, do not at all mitigate Levi's rendering of the horrors of Auschwitz. To the contrary, they set up the one perspective vis-à-vis such suffering that deserves to be termed ethical. Levi does not just describe what he has seen but, because he at times turns *away* from the suffering, he also makes palpable that he would have preferred not to have seen what he has seen. The introduction of elements that seem at odds with the violence of the concentration camp state what should be obvious but is nevertheless absent from many books and films about pain and suffering: that the person who is showing us the violence would have preferred not to have shown us what he is showing us. A consequence of this is that Levi pushes to the front the fact that he cannot fully identify with the fate of those who 'drowned' and who, unlike him, did not have the option of turning elsewhere. Levi does not write from a place he has never been to himself, nor does he seek to bring the reader there.[42] The 'lacuna' that Levi articulates as an inevitable component of his writings should for this reason not be understood as the indication of the supposed 'unrepresentability' of the Holocaust. The inability to go into the depths of the horror makes the representation of life in a concentration camp both *possible* and *urgent* rather than that it would indicate the *im*possibility or *relativity* of such an endeavor. Only a certain type of distance allows Levi to sustain a relation with events that other prisoners have ended up being submerged by. Moreover, by including scenes that seem to contradict the descriptions of pain and suffering, Levi makes manifest the difference between *showing* the most extreme acts of violence and *pointing them* out.[43] While the former is a moral imperative, the latter is unethical: the gesture of zooming in on *nothing but* the atrocities themselves gives a false representation that does not touch upon these atrocities. By bringing to the fore the distance that separates him from the most extreme forms of violence, Levi avoids what Georges Didi-Huberman has called 'all images' (*images toutes*), that is, images that seek to 'absolutize' and even 'fetishize' the Shoah. Such 'all images' or 'images of all' run the risk of presenting these atrocities as indelible.[44] For the ambition to leave out everything that does not fit the picture of extreme horror is not always the one that testifies most to the perspective of the victim. It can even end up pushing one's position closer to that of the torturer since it is precisely he who, likewise, conjured images of a violence that would leave no space for anything else. Levi's juxtaposition of scenes of atrocities and 'normal' activities, to the contrary, demonstrates that these atrocities, though undeniable as historical facts, are bound to remain *unreal*. His writing is, to paraphrase Georges Didi-Huberman again, not a 'writing of all', but a 'writing *in spite of* all', that is, a writing *in spite of* the fact that he would have preferred not to have written. Making the 'lacuna' in his testimony visible as an aid to expression allows Levi to immunize the past against the longing of future generations to find closure. The voids and absences that break through his writings disqualify them from becoming wholly unified. These holes prevent the present from overwriting the past with meaning and they thereby preclude history from disintegrating into merely 'story'. The scenes that do not at all match the horrors of the concentration camps have no softening or relativizing effect on these horrors but a delegitimizing and a contesting one. Drawing out the internal contradictions of his life as a prisoner, Levi prohibits the horrors of the past from being inserted into a stable context of meaning, thereby making sure that they are never normalized.

The term 'forgetting' in the expression 'creative forgetting' does not only refer to the relation between the present and the past but also to a specific relation of the past with *itself*. With this, I mean that creative forgetting draws on a fissure that is situated primarily within the past itself. Creative forgetting builds on the visibility of elements that have somehow been saved from the otherwise irresistible force of disappearance with which the passage of time, and especially past episodes of violence, needs to be associated. However, such elements are marked by a distinct precariousness and fragility that makes them unsuited for the preserving work of memory. Rather than indicative of an overarching principle that would legitimate their ability to survive, their context of meaning cannot but be an unstable one. The Italian philosopher Giorgio Agamben has coined the term 'remnant' to indicate such a perplexing form of survival.[45] Prime examples are Levi's ongoing interest in poetry while he was held captive in a concentration camp or the shadows that have been transfixed by the flash that accompanied the explosion of the atomic bomb (I will return to these shadows in the epilogue to this book). Both of these phenomena have achieved, at most, a flimsy and insubstantial presence. They will always be 'at odds' with the context in which they are retrieved because an analysis of this context would only account for their *passing away* and not for their surprising endurance. If such elements can be called 'indestructible', this word, as Agamben suggests, 'does not mean something—an essence or human relation—that infinitely resists its own infinite destruction'.[46] Phenomena of this kind will never be fully anchored within a dynamic of continuity or resistance. They defy the attempts of memory to hold on to them, no less than the attempts to 'work through' the past. Everything about them seems ill-suited for a prolonged existence and expresses an inclination to fall away, a propensity to be forgotten and an inability to persist. *And still*, in spite of this predisposition to being left behind, they have indeed persisted. Their appearance is therefore forever a puzzling one, inseparable from a penchant to disappear.

The concept of a 'creative' forgetting that manages to somehow dislocate a dynamic of mere transience is, of course, indebted to Friedrich Nietzsche's great essay, 'On the Uses and Disadvantages of History for Life' (1874). As Harald Weinrich's study of forgetting, *Lethe: The Art and Critique of Forgetting* (1997), has shown, Nietzsche's essay is but one in a long line of texts that argue for a more positive understanding of this phenomenon.[47] Its originality does not so much lie in the idea that an 'active' forgetting can shake off an 'excess of history' as in the suggestion that such forgetting involves a type of forgetting that forgets *itself*.[48] Imagining a conversation between a man and an animal, Nietzsche introduces the phenomenon of 'active' forgetting by underscoring that an animal does not just forget but even forgets that he forgets. 'A human being may well ask an animal: "Why do you not speak to me of your happiness but only stand and gaze at me?" The animal would like to answer, and say: "The reason is I always forget what I was going to say" — but then he forgot this answer too, and stayed silent: so that the human being was left wondering'.[49] Man can at most remember that he forgets and thus pay heed to the overall ephemerality of events and experiences in an indirect manner. The animal, to the contrary, is capable of forgetting its own forgetting and, as a consequence, of truly *affirming* this principle of annihilation. Nietzsche argues that forgetting transmutes into a 'creative force' when it pushes itself to extremes and thereby voids the ability of memory to go against the passage of time. 'A leaf utters from the scroll of time, floats away — and suddenly floats back again and falls into the man's lap. Then the man says, "I remember" and envies the animal, who at once forgets and for whom every moment really dies, sinks back into night and fog and is extinguished forever'.[50] Nietzsche starts from the paradox that the transience of history can only be overcome when it is fully embraced. His notion of the unhistorical should not be regarded as a mere *counter*-power to history but as a 'plastic power' in its own right, dislodging the passage of time from *within*. In Nietzsche's account the forgetting that holds sway over the universe is capable of ultimately interrupting itself. What is unhistorical overcomes the becoming that marks all historical events but only because this dynamic of becoming is experienced as all-encompassing:

> Thus the animal lives unhistorically: for it is contained in the present, like a number without any awkward fraction left over; it does not know how to dissimulate, it conceals nothing and at every instant appears wholly as what it is; it can therefore never be anything but honest. Man, on the other hand, braces himself against the great and ever greater pressure of what is past: it pushes him down or bends him sideways, it encumbers his steps as a dark, invisible burden.[51]

Despite this seeming opposition between man and animal, Nietzsche's philosophy of forgetting revolves around the idea that man ought to move beyond the typically human recourse to memory and seek an affirmation of the rhythm of becoming that dominates over the universe at large. This entails that humans embrace a dynamic of forgetting that is *cosmic* and cannot for that reason be wholly *appropriated*. 'Creativity' is the most important concept to describe the possibility that human beings affirm a plasticity of life that cannot ever become completely *theirs*. In Nietzsche's view, the *activity of creation* allows man to overcome his propensity to either cling to what is stable and eternal or simply mourn the ephemerality and transience of life.

A large part of this book is devoted to the argument that Benjamin's philosophy of forgetting runs parallel to Nietzsche's in that it builds on the possibility that forgetting is not overcome by memory but by a forgetting that takes itself as object. Like Nietzsche, Benjamin takes the age-old possibility of an *ars oblivionalis* seriously.[52] Rather than designating a mere absence of memory and an involuntary process of disappearance, forgetting is in Benjamin's view an activity that can and should be learned, rooted in a faculty that can and ought to be cultivated. Not a few of Benjamin's most influential texts, ranging from his early essay on Hölderlin to his book on the German *Trauerspiel* or his theses 'On the Concept of History' focus on the possibility of what is called a 'turning of time' (*Wende der Zeit*) (SW 1, 31; GS II, 120 [translation modified]), 'about-turn' (*Umschwung*) (O, 232; GS I, 406) or 'arrest of happening' (*Stillstellung des Geschehens*) (SW 4, 396; GS I, 703). When such moments of sudden reversal are brought about, the transience that is deemed universal is brought to interrupt *itself*, and this, as we will see, *for the very reason* that it *is* universal. Like Nietzsche's forgetting of forgetting, Benjamin's concepts of 'thought', 'nihilism', 'messianism' and 'allegory' indicate the paradox that forgetting becomes creative by turning towards itself. In the absence of any genuine *counter*-principle to forgetting, forgetting is overcome by way of an expression of its own, *internal* limits.

However, Benjamin's philosophy of forgetting does *differ* in an important manner from Nietzsche's in that he rejects the presuppositions of Nietzsche's *Lebensphilosophie*. Benjamin dismisses the concept of an inherent creativity that pertains to life as such. In Benjamin's view, life does *not* ceaselessly regenerate itself in a spontaneous manner. For this reason, creative forgetting cannot in his view be considered as a 'plastic force' that is built into life as such, waiting to be embraced by the life-affirming activities of man. For Benjamin, forgetting can indeed be brought to forget *itself*, but this possibility does not refer to the recovery of a vitalist process of infinite renewal or an *ontologized* becoming. In Benjamin's view, life itself is not at all a 'plastic force' but a continuum of endless repetition that is immune to change. It is at this moment that the concept of 'work' comes into play. The forgetting of forgetting cannot in Benjamin's view be released from a 'construction', 'image' or 'constellation' that results from an activity on the part of man. As we will see, Benjamin's own conception of a creative 'forgetting of forgetting' does therefore not so much rest on a direct *expression* of life in any Nietzschean sense as on the creation of an 'interval' (*Abstand*) vis-à-vis life and even an 'active negation' of the transience that holds sway over it.

In the first chapter, Benjamin's concept of 'thought' (*Denken, Eingedenken*) is the starting point for a reinterpretation of Benjamin's essay on Hölderlin and his philosophy of history. In the essay on Hölderlin, thought is likened to 'a gift that is added to' life to indicate that only thought is capable of interrupting the eternal repetition that evacuates life of meaning. In this text, Benjamin makes clear that the interruptive and redemptive intervention by thought is conditioned by the creation of an added and purely 'spiritual' reality that differs inherently from the world in which we live. This surplus reality, produced by the powers of thought, is constituted by the unity of the poem itself. Benjamin believes thought to both share in *and* neutralize the 'passing-away' that dominates over life. In Benjamin's view, it is precisely the universalization of transience that conditions the possibility that it is dislodged. Consequently, in thought, the all-encompassing forgetting that characterizes life is not counteracted but amplified. In the essay on Hölderlin, moreover, Benjamin discovers thought as a capacity to neutralize the main oppositions in history, including the opposition between men and God, history and transcendence. This is an argument that we will rediscover as the crux of Benjamin's philosophy of history. In spite of his multiple references to concepts such as 'recollection' [*Erinnerung*] (e.g., GS II, 311; VII, 1255) or 'memory' [*Gedächtnis*] (e.g., GS I, 608–13; GS II, 453), Benjamin's philosophy of history is inseparable from his analysis of thought. When he describes the '*Aufgabe*' of politics as a 'strive for . . . a passing away' (SW 3, 306), this entails an appeal to a nihilism that is complete and a 'restitutio' that is purely 'spiritual'. Understanding the *Aufgabe* of thought as a nihilistic negation of everything that negates change, we will analyze Benjamin's puzzling connection between nihilism and messianism and recast his philosophy of history as a philosophy of forgetting and a philosophy of the future.

The second chapter revolves around the concept of the 'immemorial' and the paradox that forgetting can enable a specific type of memory. It starts off with an analysis of Sigmund Freud's essay on the mystical writing pad. Freud is most of all fascinated with the mystical writing pad's combination of two capacities that are usually believed to be mutually exclusive: the reception and the preservation of stimuli. According to Freud, the receptive surface and the preserving material of the mystical writing pad operate *independently*. For this reason, the wax slab is in fact an illustration of a type of memory that preserves stimuli that have always already been forgotten. Freud's suggestions about the presence of an immemorial past are situated in the context of his discussion of the death drive. Because Freud highlights the 'conservative' nature of the death drive, and the persistence of a fundamental 'inertia', the concept of the death drive is wholly unsuited to understand Benjamin's concept of nihilism as the 'strive for a passing away'. Nihilism being a concept that Freud mentions only once in the entirety of his *oeuvre*, Freud's conceptual framework is incapable of coming to terms with the possibility of a productive forgetting that overcomes the persistent presence of an immemorial past. In spite of radically different interests, Martin Heidegger's concept of the 'forgetting of Being' [*Seinsvergessenheit*] opens up a similar argument about the relationship between forgetting and memory. Heidegger's concept of the 'abandonment of Being' [*Seinsverlassenheit*] refers to 'a unique era in the history of the truth of beyng' and, as a consequence, not to an overall disappearance.[53] Of greatest importance in this discussion is Heidegger's emphasis that the 'forgetting of Being' entails a form of 'nihilism'.[54] Drawing on the discussion with Ernst Jünger, I argue that Heidegger cannot come to terms with a *complete* nihilism along Benjamin's lines because he presupposes an ontological ground that cannot be wholly obliterated. In the final part of this chapter, Freud and Heidegger's views are opposed to Benjamin's own concept of the immemorial. Though his concept of a 'deep' or 'long' experience [*Erfahrung*] and the emphasis on the importance of tradition bear a resemblance to the concept of the immemorial as laid out by both Freud and Heidegger, the philosophical stakes of his writing are ultimately much higher. I argue that Benjamin's philosophy of history revolves around a forgetting that does not in any way condition a type of memory. Even though the concept of *'correspondances'* (in Benjamin's essays on Baudelaire) and the concept of *'souvenir involontaire'* (in his essay on Proust) can both illustrate a 'deep' memory that is formed by forgetting, Benjamin's philosophy is ultimately founded on two altogether different concepts: the *'poverty* of experience', and allegory. Unlike Heidegger, Benjamin's thought does come to terms with a 'nihilism' that 'strives for a passing-away [that is] eternal and total' and can even be called a 'task of world politics' (SW 3, 306). This complex argument is illustrated with a close reading of Baudelaire's poem 'Une Martyre' and the penultimate volume of Proust's *À la recherche du temps perdu*, *Albertine Disparue*.

The last chapter revolves around the figure of the child in the works of Friedrich Nietzsche, Hannah Arendt and Benjamin. All three thinkers consider the child and childhood an illustration of the capacity to begin anew, but each of them adds a different emphasis. In Nietzsche's writings the child embodies the principle of a 'creative' forgetting. Such a principle evidences a 'plastic power' and an 'artistic facility' that allows for a selective, productive and critical attitude towards the past.[55] Nietzsche moves beyond a humanistic worldview because active forgetfulness refers to a force that is at work within the universe at large and cannot be simply appropriated by man. If forgetfulness is believed to be 'salutary and fruitful for the future' this is because it is nourished by the inherent creativity of life itself.[56] It is only by virtue of this *cosmic* foundation that forgetfulness can reinvigorate the confidence in the human capacity to change and be changed. In Arendt's writings, the child also stands for a capacity to begin anew. However, for Arendt, this capacity is 'rooted in *natality*, and by no means in creativity'.[57] Arendt and Nietzsche part ways when she introduces the suggestion that there might not in fact exist such a thing as a *cosmic* principle of change. In spite of her reference to 'natality' as an *'ontological* root',

Arendt's conceptual framework runs counter to Nietzsche's.[58] Rather than discovering life as a 'plastic force' that is marked by an inherent capacity for self-renewal, Arendt emphasizes that mortality and death are the 'only reliable law of . . . life'.[59] For this reason, she associates the child with the faculty of memory, and not with any type of forgetting. Retracing Arendt's interpretations of Virgil and Augustine, this part of the chapter analyzes how Arendt's view of memory rests on a humanistic worldview, and on the confidence that the passage of time can be overcome with the help of an external counterpower. In an essay that was written on the eve of the First World War, 'The Metaphysics of Youth', Benjamin does not only associate the child with the possibility to begin anew, but also with the necessity to end. Disappointed with the youth movements of his time and steeped in despairing prospects about the future, Benjamin detaches the figure of the child from any cosmic principle of change that is supposed to be built into life as such. However, in the essay's section on the *Tagebuch* (diary) Benjamin analyzes the concept of *ent-sinnen* (de-thinking) as the proof that this emptiness and groundlessness of history can be dislodged from within (SW 1, 11). This ability to embrace the passage of time in pure thought is neither associated with a humanistic worldview, nor with the confidence in the (counter-)powers of memory but with an 'obliviousness' and the unexpected creation of an 'interval' in time (SW 1, 11). For Benjamin, the child is ultimately associated with a forgetting that enables the production of an 'immortality' in which the transience of history is interrupted. In the *Passagen-Werk* and his autobiographical writings as well, Benjamin returns to the topic of 'childhood' to argue for the presence of a similar, *internal* counterforce to the passage of time.

NOTES

1. Tony Judt, *Postwar: A History of Europe Since 1945* (New York: Penguin Books, 2005), 803.
2. Ibid.
3. Ibid.
4. Ibid.
5. The quoted words come from ibid., 830.
6. Ibid., 830. David Rieff's book on forgetting is equally concerned with this issue, revolving around the following suggestion: 'What if, over the long-term, forgetfulness is inevitable, while even in the comparatively short-term the memory of an instance of radical evil, up to and including the Shoah itself, does nothing to protect society from future instances of it?' Rieff even goes further than this when he asks himself, 'What if, instead of heralding the end of mean-

ing, a decent measure of communal forgetting is actually the sine qua non of a peaceful and decent society, while remembering is the politically, socially, and morally risky pursuit?' in David Rieff, *In Praise of Forgetting: Historical Memory and Its Ironies* (New Haven, CT: Yale University Press, 2016), 56–57.

7. Tony Judt, *Postwar*, 830–31.

8. For a more optimistic perspective on the same issue, see Aleida Assmann, 'Die Zukunft der Erinnerung an den Holocaust' and 'Europa als Erinnerungsgemeinschaft', in *Der lange Schatten der Vergangenheit. Erinnerungskultur und Geschichtspolitik* (München: C. H. Beck, 2006), 235–49, 250–71.

9. See Andreas Huyssen, *Present Pasts. Urban Palimpsests and the Politics of Memory* (Stanford, CA: Stanford University Press, 2005), 11–29 and Avishai Margalit, *The Ethics of Memory* (Cambridge and London: Harvard University Press, 2004), 6–15.

10. Michael Rothberg, *Multidirectional Memory. Remembering the Holocaust in the Age of Decolonization* (Stanford, CA: Stanford University Press, 2009), 1–29. The reference to the 'zero-sum game' of memory can be found on p. 11.

11. See Andreas Huyssen, 'The Search for Tradition' and 'Mapping the Postmodern', in *After the Great Divide: Modernism, Mass Culture, Postmodernism* (Bloomington: Indiana University Press, 1986), 160–78, 179–221.

12. See, e.g., *New German Critique* 44 (Spring/Summer 1988), special issue on the *Historikerstreit*.

13. See also Enzo Traverso, *Left-Wing Melancholia. Marxism, History, and Memory* (New York: Columbia University Press, 2016), 54–84.

14. For the historicization of our experience of time and history, see Reinhart Koselleck, *Futures Past: On the Semantics of Historical Time*, transl. with introduction by Keith Tribe (New York: Columbia University Press, 2004), esp. 255–75. See also Huyssen's reference to 'an ever-shrinking present—the present of short-term recycling for profit, the present of in-time production, instant entertainment, and placebos for our sense of dread and insecurity', in Huyssen, *Present Pasts*, 21.

15. Andreas Huyssen, *Twilight Memories. Marking Time in a Culture of Amnesia* (New York and London: Routledge, 1995), 7: 'I would argue that our obsessions with memory function as a reaction formation against the accelerating technical processes that are transforming our *Lebenswelt* (life-world) in quite distinct ways. Memory is no longer primarily a vital and energizing antidote to capitalist reification via the commodity form, a rejection of the iron cage homogeneity of an earlier culture industry and its consumer markets. It rather represents the attempt to slow down information processing, to resist the dissolution of time in the synchronicity of the archive, to recover a mode of contemplation outside the universe of simulation and fast-speed information and cable networks, to claim some anchoring space in a world of puzzling and often threatening heterogeneity, non-synchronicity, and information overload'.

16. See Enzo Traverso, *Left-Wing Melancholia*, 10.

17. Paul Ricoeur, *Memory, History, Forgetting*, transl. by Kathleen Blamey and David Pellauer (Chicago and London: The University of Chicago Press, 2004), 21.

18. Siegfried Kracauer, *History: The Last Things Before the Last*, completed after the death of the author by Paul Oskar Kristeller (Princeton: Markus Wiener Publishers, 1995), 83–84: 'The exile's true mode of existence is that of the stranger. So he may look at his previous existence with the eyes of one "who does not belong to the house"'. The reference to Kracauer in Enzo Traverso's *Left-Wing Melancholia* is on p. 11.

19. See for instance the emphasis on the disparity between the immediate life-world (the original experience of the past when it was still a present) and its transfiguration in a symbolic order in Jeffrey Andrew Barash, *Collective Memory and the Historical Past* (Chicago and London: The University of Chicago Press, 2016). A prime example of such a productive use of the *interval* between past and present is Rothberg's concept of 'multidirectional' memory ('The logic of comparison explored here does not stand or fall on connections that can be empirically validated for historical accuracy; nor can we ensure that all such connections will be politically palatable to all concerned parties', in Michael Rothberg, *Multidirectional Memory*, 18).

20. Aleida Assman, *Cultural Memory and Western Civilization. Arts of Memory* (Cambridge: Cambridge University Press, 2011), 8–9: 'Unlike the ceaselessly effective continuity of tradition, the workings of memory are sporadic, fractured, and enervated under the impact of trauma. Memory always needs a stimulus, and, according to Heiner Müller, begins with a shock'. See also Assman's use of Aby Warburg's term *Leidschatz* further in the book ('Memory as *Leidschatz*', ibid., 358–68). For Barash, 'the twentieth century witnessed a widespread questioning of all-encompassing spiritual or natural principles in their capacity to account for human historical development as an overall process. Parallel to the unprecedented transformation of the conditions of human life, beginning in Europe and North America, and a wide experience of discontinuity with the past, the preoccupation with collective memory reflected a shift in the modes of interpreting the phenomenon of social cohesion and human historical development'. In Jeffrey Andrew Barash, *Collective Memory and the Historical Past*, 39.

21. Andreas Huyssen, *Present Pasts*, 10 (emphasis added).

22. Theodor Adorno, *Essays on Music*, ed. by Richard Leppert, transl. by Susan H. Gillespie (Berkeley and Los Angeles: University of California Press, 2002), 612.

23. Tzvetan Todorov, *Memory as a Remedy for Evil*, transl. by Gila Walker (London: Seagull Books, 2010). See also Margalit's statement that '[e]ven remembering the gloomiest of memories is a hopeful project [because] it ultimately rejects the pessimist[ic] thought that all will be forgotten, as expressed by Ecclesiastes'. In Avishai Margalit, *The Ethics of Memory*, 82.

24. Herbert Marcuse, *Eros and Civilization. A Philosophical Inquiry into Freud* (Boston: Beacon Press, 1966), 19.

25. Ernst Bloch, 'The Shape of the Inconstruable Question', in *The Spirit of Utopia*, transl. by Anthony A. Nassar (Stanford, CA: Stanford University Press, 2000), 165–229, e.g., 204: 'Every object of moral-metaphysical expression is . . . simultaneously the reality that has not yet been fully achieved, that nonetheless already compelling, essential, utopian, ultimately sole "real" reality'. See also Ernst Bloch, 'Anticipatory Consciousness', in *The Principle of Hope. Volume 1*, transl. by Neville Plaice, Stephen Plaice and Paul Knight (Cambridge, MA: The MIT Press, 1995), 45–336, e.g., 309: 'The Not as *processive Not-Yet* thus turns utopia into the real condition of unfinishedness, of only fragmentary essential being in all objects. Hence the world as process is itself the enormous testing of its satisfied solution, that is, of the realm of its satisfaction'.

26. Jacques Derrida, *Specters of Marx. The State of the Debt, the Work of Mourning, and the New International*, transl. by Peggy Kamuf (New York and London: Routledge, 1994), 91.

27. T. J. Clark, 'For a Left With No Future', in *New Left Review* 74 (March–April 2012): 53–75. The four quotes come from 68, 67, 68 and 75.

28. Enzo Traverso, *Left-Wing Melancholia*, 7.

29. Ibid., 32.

30. Andreas Huyssen, *Twilight Memories*, 9.

31. Plato, *Theaetetus*, transl. by M. J. Levett, revised by Myles Burnyeat, ed. and introduced by Bernard Williams (Indianapolis, Cambridge: Hackett Publishing Company, 1992), 325 (191e) and Aristotle, 'De Memoria et Reminiscentia (On Memory and Reminiscence)', in *The Basic Works of Aristotle*, ed. Richard McKeon, trans. J. I. Beare (New York: Random House, 1941), 607 (449b).

32. Plato, *Theaetetus*, 67 (190d); Aristotle, 'De Memoria et Reminiscentia (On Memory and Reminiscence)', 610 (450b).

33. See, e.g., the reference to 'eternal transience' (*ewige Vergängnis*) in O, 179; GS I, 355 and similar metaphors in GS I, 935 and SW 4, 392. For a more elaborate discussion of this concept, see my *More Than Life: Georg Simmel and Walter Benjamin on Art* (Evanston, IL: Northwestern University Press, 2017).

34. For this reason, Benjamin establishes an 'indissolubl[e]' connection between 'the idea of redemption', the concept of 'transience' and the 'idea of happiness' (SW 4, 389). The introduction of a desired distance between the past and the present installs the possibility that a dimension of lived happiness is shielded against violence and injustice. For Benjamin, such an intervention entails a 'mindfulness' that modifies 'happiness' from something 'incomplete' into something 'complete' (AP, 471). Rather than 'determining' or eternalizing the moments of joy and bliss, this process of completion indicates that they have been returned to the passage of time and thus allowed to fully run their course. '[I]n happiness, all that is earthly seeks its downfall, and only in happiness is its downfall destined to find it. . . . The rhythm of th[e] eternally transient worldly existence, transient in its totality, . . . the rhythm of messianic nature, is happiness' (SW 3, 305–6). See also chapter 1.

35. In an important text, 'The Meaning of Working Through the Past' (1960), Adorno, as well, is very skeptical about such a process. Referring to the Nazi era, Adorno finishes his essay as follows: 'The past will have been worked through only when the causes of what happened then have been eliminated. Only because the causes continue to exist does the captivating spell of the past remain to this day unbroken'. In Theodor W. Adorno, 'The Meaning of Working Through the Past', in *Critical Models: Interventions and Catchwords*, transl. by Henry W. Pickford, introduced by Lydia Goehr (New York: Columbia University Press, 2005), 103.

36. Jacques Derrida, *Force de loi: le fondement mystique de l'autorité / Force of Law: The Mystical Foundation of Authority*, transl. by Mary Quaintance (New York: Cardozo Law Review, 1990), 997.

37. Primo Levi, *The Drowned and the Saved*, transl. by Raymond Rosenthal, (New York: Simon and Schuster, 2017), 2. See also Primo Levi, *Survival in Auschwitz. The Nazi Assault on Humanity*, transl. by Stuart Woolf (New York: Collier, 1993), 60.

38. Primo Levi, *The Drowned and the Saved*, 1.

39. Ibid., 24.

40. Primo Levi, *The Drowned and the Saved*, 63.

41. Ibid., 124.

42. For a similar argument in the context of film theory, see Serge Daney's criticism of Gillo Pontecorvo's aestheticization of the Holocaust (in his 1959 film *Kapò*), 'The Tracking Shot in *Kapò*', transl. by Laurent Kretzschmar, *Senses of Cinema* 30 (January–March 2004), http://sensesofcinema.com/2004/feature-articles/kapo_daney/.

43. See also Daney's opposition between 'showing with the gaze' and 'pointing with the finger' in 'The Tracking Shot in *Kapò*'.

44. Georges Didi-Huberman, *Images in Spite of All: Four Photographs from Auschwitz*, transl. by Shane B. Lillis (Chicago and London: The University of Chicago Press, 2008), esp. 51–88.

45. See, e.g., Giorgio Agamben, *Remnants of Auschwitz*, transl. by Daniel Heller-Roazen (New York: Zone Books, 2000), 133-34: '[T]*he human being is the inhuman; the one whose humanity is completely destroyed is the one who is truly human.* The paradox here is that if the only one bearing witness to the human is the one whose humanity has been wholly destroyed, this means that the identity between human and inhuman is never perfect and that it is not truly possible to destroy the human, that something always *remains. The witness is this remnant*'.

46. Ibid., 134.

47. Harald Weinrich, *Lethe: The Art and Critique of Forgetting*, transl. by Steven Rendall (Ithaca, NY: Cornell University Press, 2004).

48. The reference to 'excess of history' is in Friedrich Nietzsche, 'On the Uses and Disadvantages of History for Life', in *Untimely Meditations*, transl. by R. J. Hollingdale, ed. by Daniel Breazeale (Cambridge: Cambridge University Press, 1997), 64.

49. Ibid., 60–61.

50. Ibid., 61.

51. Ibid.

52. For a positive account of the concept of an *ars oblivionalis*, see Weinrich, *Lethe: The Art and Critique of Forgetting*, 11–12. Umberto Eco, however, dismisses this possibility on semiotic grounds, that is, because signs and symbols always necessarily produce presence, see his 'An *Ars Oblivionalis*? Forget It', *PMLA* 103 (1988): 254–61.

53. Martin Heidegger, *Contributions to Philosophy (Of the Event)*, transl. Richard Rojcewicz and Daniela Vallega-Neu (Bloomington and Indianapolis: Indiana University Press, 2012), 95.

54. Ibid., 95.

55. Friedrich Nietzsche, 'On the Uses and Disadvantages of History for Life', 93.

56. Ibid., 67.

57. Hannah Arendt, *The Life of the Mind / Willing* (San Diego, New York, London: Harcourt, Inc., 1978), 217.

58. The reference to 'the fact of natality, in which the faculty of action is ontologically rooted' can be found in Hannah Arendt, *The Human Condition* (Chicago and London: The University of Chicago Press, 1998), 247.

59. Ibid., 246.

ONE

What Is Thought? And How Can We Bring It About?

In his essay on Robert Walser, Benjamin describes how the Swiss author modifies Friedrich Schiller's line 'Along this narrow pathway must he come' into 'Along this narrow pathway must he come, *I think*' (SW 2, 258 [emphasis added]). This first chapter revolves around an analysis of what happens in this seemingly insignificant subordinate clause, 'I think'. Throughout his *oeuvre*, Benjamin develops a unique concept of 'thought' [*Denken, Eingedenken*] and 'spirit' [*Geist*] that is unrelated to the quest for absolute truths or a principle of sufficient ground. In Benjamin's *oeuvre*, thought is a force of interruption that *releases* the phenomenon that is being thought from any reference to an underlying legitimation. In the shift from Schiller to Walser the formula 'I think' unhinges the original meaning of Schiller's sentence, in which the moment of change and salvation was presented as a certainty ('he *must* come'). Because of the added formula 'I think', Walser is believed to have asserted a possibility of change that is much more radical than whatever type of predetermination. The insertion of the formula 'I think' exposes that the world in which we live remains radically *un*determined. For Benjamin, it is precisely this lack of determination on the part of history at large that replenishes the hope that it can be changed. Walser's protagonists have lost all faith in transcendent and suprahistorical principles of salvation, as they 'come from insanity and nowhere else'. However, most important of all *'they have all been healed'* [*sie sind alle geheilt*] (SW 2, 259).

In what follows, the concepts of thought and spirit are used as the focal point for a reconsideration of Benjamin's early essay on Hölderlin and his philosophy of history. Because thought and spirit indicate a capacity to assert a fundamental *absence* of meaning, an analysis of Benjamin's use of these terms opens towards a better understanding of his concept of nihilism. With reference to Gilles Deleuze's notion of a *productive* but *'complete'* nihilism, Benjamin's philosophy of history will be read as an affirmation of the irremediable emptiness that pertains to history and, as a consequence, as a philosophy of creative forgetting. In his essay on Hölderlin already, and later in his texts on history, Benjamin describes how only the confrontation with history's groundlessness can motivate the belief that the world can become truly different from what it currently is. Benjamin's affirmation of the radical transformability of history is wedded to the idea that both the work of the poet and the historian can neutralize the main categories and hierarchies that streamline our reception of the actual world. These suggestions about art and history reinstall the possibility of a true 'redemption' that is called 'messianic' and 'utopian'.

'DICHTERMUT' AND 'BLÖDIGKEIT'

In his early analysis of Friedrich Hölderlin's poems 'Dichtermut' and 'Blödigkeit', Benjamin introduces one of the main tropes of his philosophical *oeuvre*, that is, the question of how a literary construction can simultaneously bring to expression *and* overcome a lack that is located within the structure of life itself. Understanding 'Dichtermut' and 'Blödigkeit' as 'different versions' of one literary idea, Benjamin interprets the second installment, 'Blödigkeit', as a 'dislocation of the mythological' (SW 1, 28) that no longer takes recourse to the formative foundation of an atemporal and absolute truth. Benjamin criticizes the first version of Hölderlin's poem, 'Dichtermut', for its overblown appeal to a form-giving 'sun god' and a profoundly ambivalent 'affinity' with the assumed purity of a People [*Volksverwandtschaft*] (SW 1, 23; GS II, 109 [translation modified]). He criticizes the idea that the poet has a 'sacred-natural existence' that 'approximate[s] [him] to God' (SW 1, 33) and takes Hölderlin to task for using the first version of his poem as the apology of a deeply suspicious concept of courage. In 'Dichtermut' [*The Poet's Courage*], that is, courage is a 'quality' through which the poet can 'mediat[e]' with God and thus overcome the danger of death

(SW 1, 33). In Benjamin's view, this appeal to the legitimacy of a suprahistorical power, be it a god or a People, inevitably fails and results in a poem that lacks coherence. In fact, 'Dichtermut' is not convincing as an *artwork* with a *unity of its own* because it suffers from an 'all too great proximity to life' (SW 1, 24). The longed-for connection with life weakens the internal structure of the poem since 'the feeling for life' burdens the poem with something 'extended and undetermined' [*ausgebreiteten und unbestimmten Lebens*] (SW 1, 24; GS II, 110 [translation modified]). While artistic creation requires a novel construction that reworks life into something *different*, 'Dichtermut' is incapable of going beyond the perception of life as 'an undoubted facticity' (SW 1, 24 [translation modified]). Because the reference to both a form-giving 'sun god' and the 'affinity' with a People remains unconvincing, the process of creating life anew in and as a work of art cannot fully come to pass. 'Dichtermut' ends up with an 'isolation of form and a lack of relation between events' (SW 1, 24) that drastically weakens the inner consistency of the poem. Rather than bringing about the longed-for connection between the poet on the one hand, and the foundational legitimacy of a god or People on the other, 'Dichtermut' marks an unwelcome gap between both that plunges the poem into an artless and spiritless obscurity. It falls short in setting up a novel, artistic unity and instead conjures up a universe that is 'but weakly constructed' [*eine nur schwach gefügte Welt*]: 'The ... indeterminacy [*Unbestimmtheit*] of the formative principle ... threatens the entire poem' (SW 1, 23; GS II, 110 [translation modified]).

The title of the second version of the poem, 'Blödigkeit', for its part, can best be translated into English as 'bashfulness' or 'unintrusiveness' but can also be associated with 'stupidity' [*Blödheit*] and 'lack of experience'. Here, the suspicious profundity of 'Dichtermut' has been replaced with the ideal of a 'matter-of-factness' or 'sobriety' [*Nüchternheit*] that considers truth to be a 'surface' that one 'can stride upon' (SW 1, 27; GS II, 113 [translation modified]). Benjamin argues that 'Blödigkeit' has done away with the Greek concept of a 'foundational form' [*Gestalt*] that, in 'Dichtermut', was put forward as the ultimate legitimation for the truth of the poet's words. In 'Blödigkeit', instead, an 'Oriental, mystical principle' (SW 1, 34) inserts the necessary distance between the position of the poet on the one hand, and the supposedly absolute nature of a god or People on the other. Due to its distance from the absolute, 'Blödigkeit' forecloses all claims to a foundational and formative, atemporal truth and 'transpose[s]' the poet smack 'in the middle of life' (SW 1, 34).

Instead of a pseudo-transcendent truth that conjures the false belief in an all-determining force of Destiny (SW 1, 34), 'Blödigkeit' submits to the view that life can be actively engaged with and needs to be acted upon. In this context, Benjamin follows Hölderlin's intuition that 'what is true' should be imagined as a 'carpet' that is meant for 'your foot [to] stride [upon]' (Hölderlin, quoted on SW 1, 22). When truth is conceptualized as but a mere 'surface' that one 'can stride upon' it invites an active response on the part of man rather than an obscure and intuitive recovery of a supposedly absolute origin.[1] For the second version of Hölderlin's poem rejects the belief in 'ultimate elements' (SW 1, 32) and recasts the experience of truth as a specific commitment to the world that surrounds us. Instead of referring to atemporal essences, 'Blödigkeit' opens the sphere of history pure and proper and brings to expression the 'supreme sovereignty of relationship' (SW, 34). With this concept of 'relationship' [*Beziehung*] Benjamin formulates his belief in the ability to create new contexts of meaning in the world that go beyond the original and overarching context of mere life. In contrast to 'Dichtermut', 'Blödigkeit' avoids being burdened by an overwhelming lack of determination because the poem does not just refer to life as a facticity. Replacing the quest for an ultimate ground with the construction of hitherto non-existent 'relationships', the poem actively intervenes *within* life and '*seizes hold* of the living' [*ergreift . . . die Lebendigen*] (SW 1, 34; GS II, 125 [emphasis added]). The concept of courage that underlies 'Blödigkeit' therefore differs from the one that was developed in 'Dichtermut' in that the supposed intimate mediation between the poet and a god or People has here retreated in favour of a rejuvenated engagement with our immediate surroundings. Courage now no longer refers to a 'quality' that enables man to *transcend* history but instead refers to a 'relation of man to world and of world to man' (SW 1, 33).

Benjamin's concept *Gedichtete* [poeticized] helps us to further elucidate his argument that 'Blödigkeit' can create hitherto non-existent relationships that rejuvenate our commitment to the world. The *Gedichtete* is Benjamin's term for what makes visible the relationship between the poem on the one hand, and the sphere of life on the other.[2] It 'can no longer be compared with the poem' because it marks the '*transition* [*Übergang*] from the functional unity of life to that of the poem' (SW 1, 18 and 19–20). Rather than referring to the poem itself, the *Gedichtete* is understood as the 'truth of the poem' [*Wahrheit der Dichtung*] which serves as the basis of the evaluation of the poem (SW 1, 19). With each specific poem being characterized by a specific *Gedichtete*, it is only by way of this 'fundamental aesthetic unity' (SW 1, 19) that we can assess why some poems, like 'Blödigkeit', are endowed with the ability to uncover a potential of renewal, while others, like 'Dichtermut', succumb to the view that the fundamentals of life are immune to change. For, in Benjamin's view, it is vital that the *Gedichtete* is a 'limit concept' between the poem and life and, consequentially, that it is not *subsumed* by life (SW 1, 19). A poem can only express the possibility that life can be *changed* when its *Gedichtete* retains a certain *autonomy* vis-à-vis the realm of life in general. '[T]he more the poet tries to convert without transformation the unity of life into a unity of art, the plainer it is that he is a bungler' (SW 1, 20). In Benjamin's reading, 'Blödigkeit' retains a distance vis-à-vis life because the poem gives shape to an extra layer of meaning, and even a novel *reality*, that is of a purely *artistic* nature. 'Blödigkeit' expresses a potential for change because 'the identity of each individual being is a function of an infinite chain of series in which the *Gedichtete* unfolds' (SW 1, 25). In 'Blödigkeit', as we will see, certain details resonate with an inexhaustibility, which suggests that these details can be used to set up the *poetic*; a quality of the work that was hitherto non-existent and cannot be derived from elemental, pre-artistic relationships. In 'Dichtermut', to the contrary, life is made visible as something that is complete in itself because 'reflection . . . reveals a considerable indeterminacy of the perceptual and an incoherence of detail' (SW 1, 22). Here, the *Gedichtete* no longer functions as a genuine '*transition*' of the sphere of life into an artistic construction pure and proper. The reference to an *extra*-artistic and supposedly absolute ground conjures up the false belief that the ultimate truth of the poem is located elsewhere than in the poem itself. This continuous effort to legitimise the significance of the poem in an extra-poetic and even divine truth voids it of both the capacity to create novel interactions between its various elements and the concomitant replenishment of our feeling that life can be altered.

For Benjamin, the specific *Gedichtete* of a poem is always dependent on a *practice* on the part of the reader, in this case the activity of analyzing the specific relationships that are set up between various elements and details within the poem. Benjamin describes such an active response as the 'product' [*Erzeugnis*] of the *Gedichtete* (SW 1, 18; GS II, 105). Because this response *brings about* relationships that did not exist prior to the activity of reading, the *Gedichtete* refers to a reality that is *added* to the poem. Still, the *Gedichtete* is at once the 'product' and the 'subject' of a specific 'investigation' [*Untersu-*

chung] of the poem because the *added* reality is in fact the actualization of a dimension that was already present within the poem, albeit in a merely *virtual* manner. Benjamin describes the *Gedichtete* as the recovery of a dimension of meaningfulness that pertains to the poem but goes beyond the concepts and associations that are 'actually present in the poem' [*im Gedicht aktuell vorhanden*] (SW 1, 19; GS II, 106 [translation modified]).[3] The *Gedichtete* reinvigorates a layer of meaning that has remained 'other' [*andrer*] with regard to the meanings that are readily accessible within the poem. As Benjamin puts it, the 'production' of the *Gedichtete* requires 'a loosening up of the firm functional coherence that reigns in the poem itself' [*eine Auflockerung der festen funktionellen Verbundenheit, die im Gedichte selbst waltet*] (SW 1, 19; GS II, 106). In the poem itself, the 'other' meanings that are actualized by the production of the *Gedichtete* have a mere 'potential existence' [*potentielle Dasein*] (SW 1, 19; GS II, 106). Therefore, when the production of the *Gedichtete adds* a novel reality to the poem, it does so by *retrieving* a level of 'determinability' [*Bestimmbarkeit*] that had not yet been fully exhausted. The production of the *Gedichtete* entails that the original and 'actual' meaning of the original poem has been opened up towards a process of unexpected renewal.

THE CONCEPT OF *AUFGABE*

In Benjamin's view, the belief in the transformability of the world can be restored by way of an active consideration of specific artworks. He makes this retrieval and consideration dependent on a specific *Aufgabe*. The German word *Aufgabe* needs, first of all, to be translated as 'task'. Because the *Gedichtete* modifies the original and 'actual' meaning of the poem, Benjamin describes the *Gedichtete* as 'the fulfillment of the artistic task' [*die Erfüllung der jeweiligen künstlerischen Aufgabe*] and as the 'concept/understanding' [*Begriff*] of the task of the poem (SW 1, 19; GS II, 105–6). Throughout the years, Benjamin analyses a variety of such tasks that can all be understood as activities that add extra layers of meaning to a given work of art and thereby uncover an unexpected possibility of change within the world. Critique, translation or reproduction, for instance, enable the reader or spectator to go beyond the context of meaning that was 'actually present' within the artwork itself.[4] The task of the critic, translator or photographer/filmmaker is dependent on the presence of virtual layers of meaning that had remained unexhausted. As such, the 'task' of the critic, translator or photographer/filmmaker cannot be believed to pre-exist the works under consideration or, as Benjamin puts it, 'task and solution [*Lösung*] can be separated only in the abstract' (SW 1, 19). In Benjamin's view, the work of the critic, translator or photographer/filmmaker evidences that the works of art that are brought under consideration did indeed already enclose a higher degree of 'determinability' than had been assumed so far. This dimension of unexhausted 'determinability', residing within works of art in a merely *virtual* manner, is described as, respectively, their 'criticizability', 'translatability' or 'reproducibility'. In the essay on art criticism, for instance, Benjamin describes how the very 'fact of critique' evidences the presence of a layer of meaning within the artwork that had not yet been uncovered before. The fact that critique can make such virtual layers of meaning visible provides proof that the artwork was worthy of being evaluated in the first place.

> The criticizability of a work demonstrates on its own the positive value judgment made concerning it; and this judgment can be rendered not through an isolated inquiry but only by the fact of critique itself, because there is no other standard, no other criterion for the presence of a reflection than the possibility of its fruitful unfolding, which is called criticism. (SW 1, 160)

The task of the critic is to reveal a newly established unity of meaning as the token of a potential for renewal that has not yet fully run its course. By actualizing a virtual dimension of determinability, criticism enables an artwork to grow beyond the dominant views of the era from which it results or the intentions of the artist who created it. In Benjamin's view, criticism confirms that artworks can be reworked from a *product* or *result* of a process of artistic creation into the *beginning* or *origin* of something altogether *new*. Criticism is thus believed to replenish a deeply rooted longing for change. 'Criticism', writes Benjamin, 'fulfills its task insofar as, with greater closure of reflection and more rigorous form in the work, it drives these the more manifoldly and intensively out of itself, dissolves the original reflection in one higher, and so continues' (SW 1, 156). In the same vein, Benjamin takes the translation of a text to be an *addition* to the original work of art. The translation exemplifies the fact that the original was capable of acquiring a renewed significance that was not readily at hand before the translation itself was made. 'Translatability is an essential quality of certain works'. This means 'that a specific significance inherent in the original manifests itself in its translatability' (SW 1, 254). Like the task of the critic, the task of the translator is to *transform* the original work by fashioning an 'afterlife' [*Fortleben*] (GS IV, 11) for it. In Benjamin's view, the translator similarly replenishes our belief in the potential for change. By establishing a 'vital' connection between the original text and its translation, he provides proof for a 'perpetually renewed' or 'eternal life' that installs the possibility of meaningful rejuvenation (SW 1, 257). Alongside criticism and translation, the phenomenon of technological reproduction is framed as a *rebirth* rather than as a *loss* of meaning. By reproducing a given work of art, an 'exhibition value' is added to original works of art, renewing their initial meaning and endowing them with hitherto non-existent capacities.

> [T]echnological reproduction can place the copy of the original in situations which the original itself cannot attain. Above all, it enables the original to meet the recipient halfway, whether in the form of a photograph or in that of a gramophone record. The cathedral leaves its site to be received in the studio of an art lover; the choral work performed in an auditorium or in the open air is enjoyed in a private room. (SW 4, 254)

In this sense, the task of the photographer or filmmaker, like that of the critic and translator, consists of restoring our belief in the possibility of genuine transformation. Because technological reproduction grants us a new perspective on our surroundings, it discloses a non-depleted potential for renewal. Film 'manages to assure us of a vast and unsuspected field of action. Our bars and city streets, our offices and furnished rooms, our railroad stations and our factories seemed to close relentlessly around us. Then came film and explored this prison-world with the dynamite of the split second, so that now we can set off calmly on journeys of adventure among its far-flung debris' (SW 4, 265).

In addition to the translation of the word *Aufgabe* as 'task', a second, and more literal translation is called for. The prefix '*Auf-*' can be translated as 'away from' while the main root of the word, '*Gabe*' can be rendered as 'gift'. In the earlier mentioned essays on art-criticism, translation and reproduction, and, as we will see, in his philosophy of history and writings on youth and childhood, Benjamin's use of the word *Aufgabe* draws attention to the necessity to come to terms with the fact that the world that surrounds us can no longer be considered a Gift from God. Despite the references to a 'higher reflection' or 'eternal life', Benjamin's descriptions of the *Aufgabe* of the critic, translator and photographer/filmmaker part with the belief that an absolute truth reveals itself to man. This second, more literal meaning of *Aufgabe* derives from the verb *aufgeben* which is the German word for 'giving up'. In Benjamin's view, discovering a work of art as an expression of the possibility of change entails that man *gives up* the quest for 'ultimate elements'. Benjamin criticizes the search for absolute truths because this search negates the belief that a principle of change can be recovered from *within* our immediate surroundings. With the term *Aufgabe* Benjamin conceptualizes the need to give up this negation or, as we will see, the importance of negating this negation. The urgency of such a giving-up is stressed explicitly in the essay on Hölderlin when Benjamin states that the *Gedichtete* of a poem 'cannot arise otherwise than by disregarding certain determinations' [*kann nicht anders entstehen als durch ein Absehen von gewissen Bestimmungen*] (SW 1, 19; GS II, 106).[5] In other words, when a poem presents absolute truths and ultimate essences as a suprahistorical ground for our world, as is the case in 'Dichtermut', this negation of the sphere of immanence precludes the active response that replenishes the belief in the possibility of true, historical change. The longing for ultimate essences and divine truths brings with it a disavowal of the confidence that human beings can intervene within their surroundings. Moreover, such longing installs an illusionary opposition between human beings on the one hand and gods on the other. In the Hölderlin essay, Benjamin illustrates the danger of such views when he analyzes the difference between the line 'Whatever happens, let everything be a blessing for you', (in 'Dichtermut') and its second version 'Whatever happens, let it all be opportune for you!' (in 'Blödigkeit'). With the substitution of the word '*gesegnet*' [blessed] by '*gelegen*' [opportune], the belief in a divine force of determination and intervention is renounced and the world is reopened as a realm that can be altered by human beings. The 'ancestor' or 'sun god' who, in 'Dichtermut', 'grants the joyful day to poor and rich' has, in 'Blödigkeit', 'cease[d] to determine the cosmos of the poem' (SW 1, 32). According to Benjamin, 'Blödigkeit' therefore parts with the mythological belief that 'destiny determined life' and replaces it with the expression of a spiritual world where 'every function of life is destiny' (SW 1, 34). The difference between both worldviews is unmistakable. While the former surrenders life fully to the all-determining and predetermining forces of Fate, the latter brings with it the expression of a multiplicity of historical and worldly fates that resonate with a necessity of their own but can nonetheless be actively engaged with.

Similarly, in 'The Task of the Translator', Benjamin does not build his optimism about the chance to 'release [*erlösen*] in [one's] own language that pure language which is exiled [*gebannt*] among alien tongues' (SW 1, 261; GS IV, 19) on any potential *restoration* of the pure, paradisiacal language that makes divine truths accessible to man. Benjamin's term 'translatability' describes the experience that the original language of the text that is to be translated *falls short* in bringing back the lost language of divine essences. Such a language of absolute truths should not be considered as an object of intention, that is, as a target-language that one can present directly. The 'task' of the translator is to *give up* the belief that such a hidden, perfect language still *gives* itself to man. '[A]ll translation is only a somewhat provisional way of coming to terms with the foreignness of languages' (SW 1, 257). Rather than seeking to retrieve the lost, paradisiacal language of absolute truths, the translator is to dislodge his own 'fallen' language even further by 'allowing his language to be powerfully affected by the foreign tongue' (SW 1, 262). The work of the translator is therefore not a work of memory in which the founding, Adametic language of absolute truths can be retrieved. Translation does not restore a lost ground, but it hollows out the target language in such a manner that it can resonate with the language of the original text, however remote both languages may be. The text that results from this process brings to expression the disparity of merely human languages *and* allows these languages to somehow reverberate with each other. 'The task of the translator consists in finding the particular intention toward the target language which produces in that language the echo of the original' (SW 1, 258).[6] For such a dynamic work of language to arise, no prior experience of any underlying ground or formative foundation is required. The belief in what Benjamin calls the 'very nucleus of the pure language' (SW 1, 261), can only be maintained when the ultimate *groundlessness* of all human languages is asserted. The translator's task is to restore the belief in a life that can be 'perpetually renewed' precisely by fully affirming that all human languages are but in a state of 'becoming' [*Werden*] (SW 1, 261; GS IV, 19). In Benjamin's view, it is thus not the case that the belief in the existence of a pure, divine language *underlies* the act of translation. It is, vice versa, the prolonged confrontation with the impurities of human language that keeps alive the hope that this language continues to partake in a dynamic of transformation and might at some point yield to something altogether different.[7]

Likewise, in Benjamin's essay on mechanical reproduction the concept *Aufgabe* is used to draw attention to the importance of overcoming the mythological account of ultimate essences and absolute foundations. In a footnote to the essay, Benjamin writes that '[the] compact mass with its unmediated reactions [*unvermittelten Reaktionen*], forms the antithesis of the proletarian cadre, whose actions are mediated by an *Aufgabe*, however momentary' (SW 3, 129; GS VII, 370). Benjamin thus makes a distinction between the 'petit-bourgeois' and 'fascist', 'compact' 'mass', on the one hand, and the 'revolutionary' and 'proletarian', 'open' 'public' 'cadre' or 'class', on the other. He criticizes Gustave Le Bon's *The Crowd: A Study of the Popular Mind* (and, implicitly, also Sigmund Freud's *Group Psychology and the Analysis of the Ego*) because it clings to the idea that a collective is formed on the basis of a set of internalized, suprahistorical characteristics. These characteristics enable a clear opposition between the members of a collective and individuals who cannot belong to it. Benjamin argues that individuals can only come together in a politically empowered collective if they remain *immune* to the belief in suprahistorical qualities that are believed to be common to all members of the collective. Only in this manner will the allure of a dictator with an extraordinary status be warded off (SW 3, 129). The unity of a class does not require the controlling powers of a leader and it is wholly unrelated to the mythology of absolute truths or unspoiled identities (exemplified by, for instance, a shared language, history, nationality or religion). The unity of a true collective is, in other words, a *historical* construction. A class retains an essential openness towards the people who do not belong to it, and the difference between the members of a class and other people can never be fixated into a genuine opposition. It is important to 'abolish the undialectical opposition between individual and mass' (SW 3, 129) since a mass is a changeable unity that can always absorb new individuals coming from outside.[8]

Benjamin suggests that artworks and literary texts can replenish the hope for genuine change because they are instrumental in the task of giving up the belief in absolute or divine truths. This argument that renouncing the belief in predetermination can reopen a space of 'opportunity' should not be confused with the assertion that moments of meaningful alteration arise in a spontaneous manner. In Benjamin's view, the recovery of a possibility of change remains dependent on *human constructions* such as, in the abovementioned cases, artworks and literary texts. Criticism, translation or reproduction evidence a non-exhausted dynamic of renewal and regeneration, but this dynamic is conditioned by the active response to a *work* and it cannot be projected onto the sphere of life *as such*. For this reason, Benjamin's use of the concept *Aufgabe* comes together with a third meaning. *Aufgabe* does not only refer to the 'task' of retrieving a hitherto non-depleted dimension of 'determinability' within works of art, nor only to the importance of 'giving up' the idea that the world that surrounds us can be considered a *Gift* from God, but also to the view that life itself should not be treated as a dynamic that *gives*. If the second meaning of the word *Aufgabe* indicated the need to give up the belief that only a transcendent ground or divine intervention can bring about change, this third meaning warns against the belief that meaningful renewal is *built into life*. Life is not a field of hitherto non-actualized possibilities that partake in a natural process of actualization. Benjamin rejects both the attitude that *negates* immanence by considering it immune to change *and* the attitude that *affirms* immanence directly by considering it to be a realm of internal innovation. The earlier mentioned warning that the poet should refrain from an 'all too great proximity to life' is rooted in this awareness that life does not generate change on its own account. On numerous occasions Benjamin associates 'mere life' precisely with an *in*ability to change, an *in*capacity of transforming itself and an *absence* of possibilities. Life is chief amongst the illustrations of the 'eternal repetition of the same' that Benjamin associates with 'myth' and 'false totalities'.[9] It designates a sphere of existence that *lacks* any and all redemptive qualities and does *not* open a sphere of possibility. Unlike *Lebensphilosophen* like Stefan George, Georg Simmel and Ludwig Klages, Benjamin refuses to *ontologize* the process of renewal.[10] This is the reason why an all too direct association between the work of art on the one hand, and the sphere of life on the other poses the threat of 'indetermination'. In opposition with later phenomenologists like Maurice Merleau-Ponty or Henri Maldiney, Benjamin does not consider the proximity between art and life a longed-for quality that increases the artwork's expressiveness and vitality. For Benjamin, neither nature nor history is marked by an experiential richness that can subsequently be recaptured in artistic creation. Because an excessive proximity between art and life weakens the artwork's ability to express a potential for change, the task of the artist should never be confused with the aim of restoring an immediate connection between man and life.

THE *AUFGABE* OF THOUGHT

The emphasis of a longed-for *interval* or *distance* between life and art explains why Benjamin ends his Hölderlin essay with a reference to *Nüchternheit*. The word *Nüchternheit* needs to be translated as 'sobriety' or 'down-to-earthness'. This term, first of all, indicates that, in poems such as 'Blödigkeit', Hölderlin forecloses the reference to a supposedly divine foundation for life. These poems have cast aside the negation of the sphere of immanence that, in a poem such as 'Dichtermut', resulted in false assumptions about 'ultimate' and 'divine' essences. As Benjamin puts it, a poem such as 'Blödigkeit' 'stand[s] beyond all exaltation in the sublime' (SW 1, 35). However, the *Nüchternheit* of such poems also serves Benjamin to highlight that they reject the view that life is *itself* a dynamic that spontaneously gives. Benjamin's concept of *Nüchternheit* illustrates the twofold renunciation or *Aufgabe* that motivated some of Hölderlin's later works. These works give up both the belief that there is an ultimate ground *to* life and the belief that life can *itself* be considered a foundational principle. In the Hölderlin essay, the concept of *Nüchternheit* frames an analysis of 'thought' and 'spirit'. Since life can neither be believed to share in a suprahistorical truth nor bring about meaningful change on its own, Benjamin understands the activity of thinking as a process that is *external* to life. Because of this irreducible difference between the spheres of life and thought, thought is granted the capacity to *dislodge* life's immunity to change. Life is neither a Gift from God to man nor a dynamic that freely gives itself to human thought but, vice versa, thought is 'a gift that is added to' life [*es wird . . . die Gabe beigelegt*] (SW 1, 30; GS II, 119 [translation modified]). Only thought or spirit is capable of opening life up to a process of meaningful renewal. This intervention of thought and spirit within life is tantamount to a supplement *to* life since it fashions works and constructs that cannot possibly be absorbed by the sphere of life itself. A line from Hölderlin's poem 'Chiron' that is quoted by Benjamin references the 'thinking one, that must always / Go to one side at times' [*Nachdenkliches, das immer muß / Zur Seite gehn zu Zeiten*] (Hölderlin quoted on SW 1, 30–1; GS II, 119 [translation modified]). Benjamin's own concept of thought similarly refers to a process that inevitably comes *after* life: thought is always *after*-thought [*Nach-denkliches*]. Thinking neither indicates that something is 'characterized in its essence' [*in seiner Eigenschaft gekennzeichnet*] (SW 1, 30; GS II, 119 [translation modified]) nor that a given phenomenon is delivered back to an originary dynamic of regeneration and differentiation. It neither reaches the formative ground or ultimate essence of a given phenomenon, nor does it reconnect this phenomenon to any supposed stream of life or flux of becoming. Instead, thought is understood as an act that brings out an unexpected potential for transformation by *voiding* the phenomenon under consideration of the reference to anything absolute, be it a suprahistorical ground or an immanent force of renewal. In Benjamin's view, life can only be delivered to thought and thereby express the possibility of renewal when it is *emptied* of all suprahistorical qualities. This replenishment is due to the way in which thought and spirit enforce a moment of 'objectification' [*Versachlichung*] that lays bare the very *in*completeness of life itself. Life can indeed express 'something spiritual' [*das Geistige*] (see e.g., SW 1, 30; GS II, 119 [translation modified]) but such surfacing of 'an idea' always signals that life has been *reworked into something else.*[11]

The argument that thought and spirit make visible both the incompleteness *and* the changeability of life underlies Benjamin's reading of the opposition between the line 'Who grants the *joyful* day to poor and rich' (from 'Dichtermut', referring to the 'sun god') and the corresponding line 'Who grants the *thinking* day to poor and rich' (from 'Blödigkeit', referring to the 'god of heaven'). While the former version conjures the fullness of a foundational truth that gives meaning to history and can always be recovered within it, the latter version empties history from the reference to a formative ground, but not without establishing the possibility of its transmutation. Due to this qualification of 'thinking', the second version needs to be 'distinguished very rigorously' from the first version (SW 1, 30). The first version testifies to 'traditional mythology, which lets the day be given as a gift' (SW 1, 30). The second version, however, deposes the gods and renders them incapable of doing more than either 'concede [*gönnen*] or not concede the day' (SW 1, 30; GS II, 119 [translation modified]). In 'Blödigkeit', the 'day' has been cut loose from absolute truths that can only be 'intuited' and are assumed to have always remained in place. When history has become the object of thought, this provides proof for the possibility of a truly 'spiritual life' that is forever to begin anew. The 'thinking day' that is mentioned in 'Blödigkeit' can only be considered 'conceded' to man and no longer 'given' by God. For this very reason, however, it no longer signals an enduring essence but an ongoing potential for alteration. Instead of enabling a process of ultimate determination, thought dislodges the seeming immutability of life by exposing that a given phenomenon is *as yet non-determined*.

Thought, in other words, reopens life as a sphere that can still be *made* meaningful in spite of its otherwise irrevocable incompleteness. It thus entails a neutralization of the sphere of life that is *being* thought. The incompleteness of life now no longer merely indicates a *lack* since, when it is reworked into an object of thought, the day 'appears to the highest degree formed, at rest, at one with itself in its consciousness' [*erscheint . . . auf das höchste gestaltet, ruhend, mit sich selbst einstimmend im Bewußtsein*] (SW 1, 30; GS II, 119).

In this context, Benjamin returns to the argument that only a *construct* or *work* is capable of expressing a non-exhausted potential *to be* determined. Benjamin mentions 'a life that is in itself sacred [*in sich heilig*]' (SW 1, 35; GS II, 125), but this 'sacredness' does not refer to life *as such* but only to the independent unity of some of Hölderlin's late poems themselves: only in and as a literary text can the sphere of history be 'thought' and, hence, become visible as a realm that has not depleted its potential to be made meaningful. Benjamin connects Hölderlin's poem 'Blödigkeit' to a 'sacred sobriety' because it rejects absolute claims without succumbing to an overall sense of randomness. To the contrary, such works constitute a reality of their own and testify to an 'intensified certainty [*innigen Sicherheit*]' (SW 1, 35: GS II, 125 [translation modified]). This sense of autonomy exemplifies the truly 'spiritual life' that has done away with the need for underlying grounds or absolute foundations.

Hölderlin's poem 'Blödigkeit' is a work of thought and spirit along these lines because the sustained confrontation with the absence of an ultimate determination has here been transmuted into the creation of a novel, artistic reality that sets up an experience of determin*ability*. 'Blödigkeit' no longer conjures the image of a god who is supposed to provide legitimation for the words of the poem since, vice versa, this god is being made visible as the *product* of nothing but the poem itself. In the final stanza of the poem, Hölderlin presents the possibility of a god who no longer *brings* life *to* man but '*is brought*' *by* man, and this by way of the 'spiritual life' that is at work within art itself. In the line 'When we come, with art, and bring one / From among the heavenly beings' Benjamin rediscovers God itself as the outcome of man's work. A god that exists nowhere but in the poem itself can of course no longer lay claim to absolute powers. 'Transform[ed] . . . into a dead form', such a god has been evicted from the realm of ultimate essences and suprahistorical truths (SW 1, 32). 'The formation [*Gestaltung*], the internal plastic principle, is so intensified [*gesteigert*] that the fate of the dead form breaks over the god [*das Verhängnis der toten Form über den Gott* *hereingebrochen ist]*, so that . . . the plastic dimension is turned inside out, and now the god becomes wholly an object [*die Plastik von innen nach außen umschlug und nun völlig der Gott zum Gegenstande wurde*]' (SW 1, 32; GS II, 121 [translation modified]). However, this gesture of transforming the god into an object is far from annihilating or iconoclastic. The deflation of the divine pretenses of the poet exemplifies Benjamin's concept of a poetic *Aufgabe* and marks the poem's capacity to think for itself. The poetic expression of a god-turned-object is instrumental in *giving up* at once the belief in a suprahistorical principle of predetermination and the belief that life gives itself in a meaningful manner. A god who no longer brings but *is brought* in and by the poem exemplifies that no element of history, *not even the very distinction between the historical realm and the divine*, can be considered an immutable given. 'Blödigkeit' is a work of thought because it exposes that, while there is no ultimate ground that legitimises the obliteration of the distinction between man and God, this distinction should not be considered an unchangeable given either. As Benjamin puts it, in 'Blödigkeit', the orders of men and God are 'like two scales' that 'are left in their opposing positions' but they are 'lifted off the scale beam' (SW 1, 25).

The reproduction of the formative distinction between man and God in and as a work of thought renders this distinction inoperative and reveals it to be as yet undetermined. However, when the distinction between mortals and gods is dislodged, this does not result in the feeling that both are actually quite 'similar'. Benjamin's statement that, in 'Blödigkeit', 'the orders of gods and men are curiously raised up toward and against each other' (SW 1, 25), should not be confused with the claim that gods are, in truth, not all that different from mortals or that men should aspire to be like gods. As we have seen, one of the foremost arguments of the Hölderlin essay comes under the form of a warning to all artists (and philosophers) who do indeed claim an ambiguous and intuited intimacy with a god or People that is supposed to legitimise their work. With the suggestion that the newly fashioned reality of the poem itself ties man and God together in one and the same poetic 'chain of series' [*Kette von Reihen*], Benjamin is not arguing for the possibility that the opposition between both can be overcome. Instead of a historical possibility, this 'sublat[ion] within a single vision' indicates but a *'poetic destiny [dichterischen Schicksals]'* (SW 1, 25–6; GS II, 113). The novel context of meaning in which gods and men can switch sides signals a historical *im*possibility and a deeply-seated incompleteness on the part of life as such. The 'Law of Identity' [*Identitätsgesetz*] that neutralises the opposition between God and man applies to the 'spiritual life' of the artwork alone. As an object of thought, and *only* as an object of thought, what had initially been deemed Fated or Destined [*geschickt*] is suddenly shot through with a precariousness that brings it down to the level of mortal beings. Vice versa, when it has entered into the sphere of thought, the most seemingly unworthy phenomenon can evoke an unsuspected layer of significance and urgency.

THE TURNING OF TIME

This capacity of the poem to unhinge the foundational hierarchies of life comes with a specific relevance for the issue of forgetting. An important key to understand how 'Blödigkeit' dislodges the seeming immutability of life is Hölderlin's reference to the 'passing away' of temporal events. According to Benjamin, Hölderlin's poem has not only unhinged the apparently irrevocable opposition between mortals and gods but also the equally ineradicable passing-away that marks the temporal flow. Like the formative opposition between man and God that conjures a false belief in predetermination, the forgetting that voids the temporal realm of any genuine creativity has somehow been neutralized in and by the autonomous unity of the poem itself. 'Blödigkeit' is believed to reveal that not even the transience that holds sway over life is immune to being changed. In 'Blödigkeit', the search for the murky ground of an atemporal truth has been replaced with the feeling that even transience can be transmuted into a *creative* force.

On a first level of analysis, Benjamin's argument that 'Blödigkeit' expresses a productivity *within* transience rather than an *external* counterpower *to* it revolves around his interpretation of the second line of the fifth verse of both poems. In 'Dichtermut', this line runs as follows: 'Who in fleeting time holds us, the ephemeral ones' [*Der in flüchtiger Zeit uns, die Vergänglichen / hält*]. In 'Blödigkeit', it has been changed into: 'Who, at the turning of time, holds us, who pass away in sleep' [*Der, zur Wende der Zeit, uns die Entschlafenden / hält*]. In the first version, the possibility of a suspension of 'fleeting' and 'ephemeral' time remains dependent on something that is untouched by the transience of history, that is, the absolute nature of '[o]ur ancestor, the sun god' (mentioned in the final line of the fourth verse). The second version entails an 'opposition' to the first version and even a 'refine[ment] to the highest degree' (SW 1, 31). In

'Blödigkeit', the suspension of the passage of time is made dependent on a 'turning of time' [*Wende der Zeit*] that is brought about by 'sleep'. Benjamin associates this suspension of transience through sleep with a genuine 'turning of time' because sleep is, itself, described as a 'passing away'. As we will see in the second and third chapters, in numerous places in his work, Benjamin introduces a 'turning of time' or 'about-turn' that fashions a capacity to persist from within the very dynamic of passing away. In the essay on Hölderlin, as well, the reference to the 'passing away' in 'sleep' illustrates the possibility of such a redemptive 'turning of time' because it is read alongside Heraclitus's words: 'Waking, we indeed see death—but in sleep we see sleep' (Heraclitus, quoted on SW 1, 31). Sleep is believed to somehow dislodge an experience of irrevocable loss but, as an exemplification of 'passing away', this dislocation of the experience of loss by way of sleep is disconnected from any supposed ability to *withstand* transience. As is expressed by the negative prefix '*ent-*' (de-) in the German word for sleeping *entschlafen* (literally: de-sleeping), sleeping is believed to be indicative of a 'movement away' and not of a 'being drawn to'. Sleep refers to the ability to keep the 'fleetingness' of time at a distance but it should not at all be confused with an ability to recover experiences from the past or regain access to mental strata that had been preserved all along. The concept of sleep is framed as the neutralization of an irrevocable forgetting (death) but it neither exemplifies a process of *recollection* nor the workings of *memory*. Since sleep is itself a 'passing away' and thus believed to *share in* a process of disappearance, its deactivating abilities exemplify for Benjamin that the very process of disappearance that dominates life can somehow be neutralized. Benjamin suggests that the 'turning of time' that is brought about by a 'passing away' in 'sleep' entails a dislocation of the passage of time, and this precisely because we surrender ourselves *to* the passage of time. Sleep has here become the foremost mark of a 'forgetting of forgetting' that has become productive. Rather than exemplifying the powers of recollection or memory, sleep illustrates a forgetting that takes as its object the forgetting that is inscribed within the passage of time itself. Because 'in sleep we see sleep' and no longer 'death', the passing away that marks the temporal flow has itself been made to pass away.

On a second level of analysis, Benjamin's argument that 'Blödigkeit' retrieves a creative force within the passage of time itself no longer revolves around a specific *thematic trope* or *content*, such as the phenomenon of sleep and its connection with a productive 'passing away'. 'Blödigkeit' *makes use of* transience. In doing away with the mythological account of an underlying, suprahistorical ground that motivated 'Dichtermut,' 'Blödigkeit' injects an interval into the passage of time and reworks it into a *novel*, purely *artistic* reality. According to Benjamin, 'Blödigkeit' overcomes the excessive proximity to life by setting up the 'utmost, internal cohesion of a *poetic* world' [*innerster Zusammenhang jener dichterischen Welt*]: 'the second version produces [*ergibt*]' a 'structured center [with] a structuring movement [that] necessarily forces its way from verse to verse' (SW 1, 24; GS II, 111 [translation modified, emphasis added]). This entails a 'sublat[ion] [of] the difference between form and the formless' (SW 1, 31) that is exemplified by the fact that the reference to a 'sun-god' (in 'Dichtermut') has been replaced with the image of 'heaven' (in 'Blödigkeit'). The 'architectonic significance of the heavens' embodies a plentitude of realities that cannot be wholly encompassed by whatever suprahistorical ground or foundation (SW 1, 31). The poet now no longer jumps *beyond* the world that surrounds us but 'he is a hero because he lives in the center of all relations' (SW 1, 34). In Benjamin's view, therefore, it is the '*lawfulness*' of the poem itself which makes possible a creative use of the transience of life. 'Blödigkeit' can only give shape to a redemptive 'turning of time' because the poem has fashioned a succinct 'temporal plasticity' [*zeitliche Plastik*] of its own (see, e.g., SW 1, 31; GS II, 120). With this concept, Benjamin argues that 'Blödigkeit' does not only *refer* to the possibility of a 'turning of time' that renders the passage of time productive, for instance through the description of the phenomenon of sleep as a productive passing away. Instead, the 'temporal plasticity' of 'Blödigkeit' indicates that the poem's very *structure* is inseparable from such a passing away. 'Blödigkeit' *embodies* a dynamic of transience and simultaneously transmutes it into a *surplus* unity of meaning that is not simply reducible to the *content* of the poem. For Benjamin connects the 'temporal plasticity' of 'Blödigkeit' to the poem's 'intensification of intention in the domain of pure sound' [*die Steigerung der Absicht im rein Lautlichen*] (SW 1, 30; GS II, 119). With this, he draws attention to the importance of effects within the poem that are of a merely *aesthetic* nature, that is, 'rhyme' and 'alliteration'. Because the sound of a word is almost always unrelated to its content, it is to be regarded as a deeply contingent element that can be used to create extra layers of meaning or, indeed, 'relationships' that did not pre-exist the poem itself. These relationships of 'pure sound' pertain to the *materiality* of words and exemplify the process of 'objectification' that opens the poem's capacity to 'think'. They are realities that are *added* to the original meaning of words, evidencing the dimension of non-exhausted determinability that signals the 'spiritual life' of a given artwork. Moreover, these qualities of words only become manifest when the poem is *read* and thus *surrendered* to the flow of time. Benjamin gives us the example of Hölderlin's line 'Where are you the thinking one (literally: 'after-thinking'), that must always / Go to one side at times? Where are you, Light?' [*Wo bist du, Nachdenkliches! das immer muß / Zur Seite gehn zu Zeiten, wo bist du Licht?*] (Hölderlin quoted on SW 1, 30–1; GS II, 119 [translation modified]) from the poem *Chiron* to indicate the rhyming effect of the words *Seite* [side] and *Zeiten* [times]. These two words refer to very different things. However, since they *sound* more or less alike, their juxtaposition introduces a new idea that *results from* the passage of time and goes beyond the initial meaning of both terms. Benjamin connects the phrase '*Zur Seite gehn zu Zeiten*' with the above mentioned 'turning of time/time that switches sides' [*Wende der Zeit*] (SW 1, 31; GS II, 120 [translation modified]) that is referred to in 'Blödigkeit', and even with the possibility that this poetic *use* of the passage of time can yield an unexpected 'instant of persistence' [*den Augenblick der Beharrung*]. Because this transmutation of 'fleeting time' into something that 'persists' is conditioned by relationships of 'pure sound' and a specific 'temporal plasticity', it should be considered the utmost proof of an *internal* dislocation of transience. What persists here is no longer *antithetical* to what passes away, let alone that it would restore our confidence in the powers of memory or recollection. The 'instant of persistence' exists nowhere else but within the newly shaped reality of the poem itself and cannot therefore be separated from a process of passing away. This 'instant of persistence', as a consequence, is first and foremost expressive of forgetting. But, in 'Blödigkeit', we could say, forgetting has been *put to work*. While the 'temporal plasticity' of this poem bespeaks no faculty of memory or recollection, it does not *succumb* to the transience of life either.

Before I leave behind the analysis of Benjamin's essay on Hölderlin and move to his philosophy of history, it bears repeating that, with the conception of a poetic construction that *makes use of* the passage of time, Benjamin does not introduce the idea that the flow of time can be interrupted *in actual life*. The poem constitutes a novel *reality* and no historical *possibility*. This novel reality of the poem is *added* to history, but it retains a non-actual and purely artistic status. This novel poetic reality expresses the *im*possibility to fully overcome life's rhythm of passing away. Still, the internal coherence and strength of this poetic reality reveals that not even the transience of life is *predetermined*. As a novel reality and work of *thought*, and only as such, the poem releases the passage of time from any ultimate ground or absolute power. The 'inner certainty' of 'Blödigkeit''s 'spiritual life' exposes that even the otherwise irremediable passage of time ultimately lacks determination, but it cannot altogether *undo* life's necessities.

NIHILISM AND MESSIANISM IN THE 'THEOLOGICAL-POLITICAL FRAGMENT'

Three posthumously published texts jointly constitute Benjamin's philosophy of history: his 'Theological-Political Fragment', the 'Convolute N' from the *Passagen-Werk* ('On the Theory of Knowledge, Theory of Progress') and the theses 'On the Concept of History'. These texts surely belong to the most commented upon sources of twentieth-century continental thought. While they are most often situated in the final decade of Benjamin's life, the date of origin for the 'Theological-Political Fragment' is still a point of dispute. Benjamin's friend and philosophical interlocutor Gershom Scholem insisted on dating it back to the early twenties, while Theodor Adorno situated it in the late thirties. If we take into consideration the temporal gap that separates the early essay on Hölderlin from the later texts on history, it is remarkable that reading them alongside each other brings out strong conceptual parallels and a shared philosophical framework that revolves around the concepts of *Aufgabe*, transience and thought or spirit. For, in the final paragraph of the 'Theological-Political Fragment', all three of the concerns that have been introduced in the analysis of the Hölderlin essay are put into play once more. Benjamin famously mentions the '*Aufgabe*' to 'strive for . . . an eternal and total passing away [*ewigen und totalen Vergängnis*]' and he connects this to the possibility of a 'spiritual [*geistlichen*] *restitutio in integrum*' (SW 3, 305–6; GS II, 204). Returning to the earlier idea that human existence is 'fleeting' and 'ephemeral', Benjamin now even goes as far as to describe an 'eternally transient worldly existence, transient in its totality [*ewig vergehenden, in seiner Totalität vergehenden*]' (SW 3, 306; GS II, 204). Moreover, Benjamin again suggests that, for all its universality, the transience that thus holds sway over our lives can indeed be transmuted into a moment of 'persistence': while a 'worldly restitution' only 'leads to an eternity of downfall' this all-encompassing transience should nonetheless be associated with a 'spiritual *restitutio in integrum*, which introduces immortality [*Unsterblichkeit*]' (SW 3, 305–6; GS II, 204).[12] In other words, both the essay on Hölderlin and the 'Theological-Political Fragment' revolve around the possibility that the forgetting that hollows out our actual existence can somehow be dislodged in and by a 'spiritual' or 'thinking' life. In both texts, this 'spiritual restitutio' is disconnected from the workings of memory or recollection since it 'corresponds to' [*entspricht*] and does not counteract the 'rhythm of th[e] eternally transient worldly existence'. However, what is new to the 'Theological-Political Fragment' and requires further analysis, is that Benjamin's description of a redemptive 'turning of time' has now taken recourse to two concepts with an enormous philosophical and theological weight, nihilism and messianism. The connection between both concepts is a very puzzling one. How can (messianic) redemption be possible when the entire realm of history is first emptied of meaning (nihilism)? In the 'Theological-Political Fragment' Benjamin argues that the 'method' of the *Aufgabe* of politics to 'strive for such a passing away' is 'nihilism'. In a surprising twist, the possibility that this method of nihilism is fruitful, and that the very affirmation of transience can result in its neutralization, is framed with a reference to 'messianism'.

In his book on Nietzsche, Gilles Deleuze distinguishes three conceptions of nihilism that help gain a more precise grasp of Benjamin's own use of this term. The first form of nihilism refers to a 'negation' of life. In Deleuze's view, Nietzsche uses the term 'negation' to describe the 'becoming-reactive' of a force.[13] The notion 'reactive force' designates what is 'separated from what [it] can do, [and] den[ies] or turns against [itself]'.[14] The main illustrations of this first type of nihilism are resentment, bad conscience and the ascetic ideal since all three of these attitudes testify to the 'triumph' of reactive forces that merely 'obey' other forces. This first type of nihilism is most clearly revealed by the possibility that 'active' forces are brought down by reactive forces. Now no longer capable of 'commanding' other forces, nihilism turns active forces into reactive ones and contaminates them with an overall 'will to nothingness'. This first type of nihilism corresponds to the concept of an 'eternal return' that empties the experience of life from any belief in change and differentiation. This concept of an eternal return of the same is in Deleuze's reading of Nietzsche's *Will to Power* 'nauseating and difficult to bear'. In this first type of nihilism, therefore, the eternal return 'becomes an object of anguish, repulsion and disgust. Even if active forces return they will again become reactive, eternally reactive'.[15]

While the first conception of nihilism that is mentioned by Deleuze is an attitude of negation, the second one is a wholehearted *affirmation*. In an affirming will, forces become active: '[a]ffirmation [is] becoming active personified'.[16] Deleuze defines active forces as forces 'which go to the limit of their consequences' and 'command' other forces.[17] This second type of nihilism is therefore associated with the figure of the Overman [*Übermensch*] and with the discovery of a rule that enables us to determine what an affirming will truly is. This rule stipulates that something only deserves to be called willed when we also will its eternal return. 'The eternal return gives the will a rule as rigorous as the Kantian one'.[18] This second type of nihilism overthrows the first one since the concept of eternal return is now no longer indicative of an eternal return of the same. The eternal return has instead been discovered as a criterion to establish whether a given will embraces *becoming* and *change*. Deleuze connects this second type of nihilism to a 'thought' [*pensée*] because the eternal return initially only motivates an affirming will as an *idea*, and not as a physical reality. 'How does the eternal return perform the selection here? It is the thought of the eternal return that selects'.[19] The second type of nihilism marks the becoming active of a force because it subsequently enables the projection of the *thought* of an eternal return onto the dynamic of *life*. For in this type of nihilism, the thought of the eternal return ultimately results in the exploration of an *ontological* principle of continual change and becoming. The eternal return is then no longer a thought but a process of differentiation that is ontologized. The second type of nihilism is indicative of Nietzsche's view of life as a field of hitherto non-actualized possibilities and it replenishes the trust in a natural and spontaneous dynamic of renewal. The thought of the eternal return 'makes willing something whole. The thought of the eternal return eliminates from willing everything which falls outside the eternal return, it makes willing a creation, it brings about the equation "willing = creating"'.[20]

The third conception of nihilism is the most complex and intriguing one. According to Deleuze, it draws attention to 'the most obscure parts of Nietzsche's philosophy' and 'an almost esoteric element in the doctrine of the eternal return'.[21] Only this third conception can be called a 'complete nihilism' [*nihilisme complet*]. Unlike the first conception of nihilism, this third type of nihilism *affirms* the changeability of history. Contrary to the negating nihilism of resentment, bad faith and the ascetic life, complete nihilism indicates an affinity for transformation and action. It does not jump beyond this world in search for an absolute and suprahistorical ground but, rather, it embraces history as a realm that can be altered. Unlike the second conception of nihilism, however, this third conception does not *ontologize* this potential for change. It rejects the concept of an eternal return that spontaneously produces difference, refusing to project creation and regeneration directly onto life itself. Complete nihilism is indeed rooted in an eternal return, but what is believed to return is a principle of 'destruction' and not 'creation'. Deleuze founds his conception of a complete nihilism in Nietzsche's description of a 'will to destruction [*volonté de détruire*] as the will of a still deeper instinct, the instinct of self-destruction [*volonté de se détruire*], the will for nothingness [*volonté du néant*]'.[22] This passage from Nietzsche's *Will to Power* singles out the presence of an all-encompassing force of passing-away. This instinctive 'perishing' [*disparition*] and 'will to destruction' cannot be reconciled with the Overman's affirmation of an eternal return that is inherently creative. The reason why complete nihilism nonetheless reconciles this instinctive and unceasing 'perishing' with an *affirming* will is that it signals a *'transmutation'*. Complete nihilism evidences an 'eternal return [that] mak[es] something come into being which cannot do so without changing nature'.[23] In complete nihilism, the assertion that life can be changed has nothing to do with the retrieval of a force of production or becoming that is built into life itself. The belief in change that underlies complete nihilism results from the 'instinct of self-destruction' itself but this process of infinite destruction has been made productive. In complete nihilism, the changeability of life is not considered a *given* but it results from the belief that an all-encompassing 'perishing' can be *transformed* into a source of creation. Complete nihilism is not the nihilism that embraces the supposed activity of life as such, but the nihilism of reactive forces that have *become* active by *negating themselves*. In complete nihilism 'strong spirits... destroy the reactive in themselves, submitting it to the test of the eternal return and submitting themselves to this test even if it entails willing their own decline [*vouloir leur déclin*]'.[24] The affirmation that belongs to the heart of complete nihilism is therefore not associated with a regenerating dynamic of life, but with the possibility that the process of infinite destruction *takes itself as object*. Nowhere in life can complete nihilism discover a productivity that can be directly embraced. Based in the feeling that life is in truth *depleted* of such productivity, complete nihilism only recovers the possibility of change through the destruction of its own inclination to destroy. As a consequence, affirmation is here first and foremost the result of a *negation of negation*. Deleuze puts it as follows:

> What happens when the will to nothingness is related to the eternal return? This is the only place where it breaks its alliance with reactive forces. Only the eternal return can complete nihilism because it makes negation a negation of reactive forces themselves. By and in the eternal return nihilism no longer expresses itself as the conservation and victory of the weak but as their destruction, their self-destruction.[25]

In complete nihilism, 'negation, by making itself the negation of reactive forces themselves, is not only active but is, as it were, transmuted [*elle est comme transmuée*]'.[26] Complete nihilism is rooted in a process of negation and destruction, yet this process is pushed to such limits that it destroys itself and leads to a 'negation transformed into a power of affirmation [*la négation transformée en puissance d'affirmation*]'.[27]

In crucial places of his *oeuvre*, Benjamin turns to this third type of nihilism and the suggestion that an infinite power of destruction and negation can be transmuted into a force of affirmation.[28] His concept of a 'destructive character' [*destruktive Charakter*], for instance, is a prime example of complete nihilism since it knows 'only one activity: clearing away'. 'The only work he avoids is creative' (SW 2, 541–2).[29] The destructive character is framed as an attitude that embraces the possibility of change, but it has done away with the belief in any supposed creativity on the part of life as such. Benjamin's concept of an infinite will to destroy cannot be understood with the categories of *Lebensphilosophie*. Moreover, it cannot be understood with the phenomenological category of intentionality either.[30] Such a will to destroy is not just a mental state that is directed to the outside world, rooted in the feeling that the latter is unworthy of being preserved. It does not seek to legitimate itself through the projection of qualities on an external sphere. In the destructive character, the will to destroy *precedes* any firm orientation in the world and it does not require any ground beyond itself. The will to destroy has here taken on such acuity that it becomes an overwhelming presence in itself, annihilating precisely our supposed, lived experience of the world. Still, this 'destroying rejuvenates'. The destructive character replenishes the belief in the possibility of transformation and innovation, but only because its power to negate and destroy has been universalized and taken itself as object: destroying 'cheers, because everything cleared away means to the destroyer a complete reduction, indeed a rooting out, of his own condition' (SW 2, 541).

The 'messianism' that is mentioned in the 'Theological-Political Fragment' is much less hyperbolic than this concept of a 'destructive character'. It is more intimately linked with the 'sacred sobriety' that was mentioned in the Hölderlin essay. Nonetheless, it should equally be read as an instantation of the complete nihilism that transmutes infinite negation and destruction into a productive power. Benjamin frames messianism as a belief in radical change, conceptualized with the term 'redemption' [*Erlösung*]. This possibility of true, messianic change should firstly be opposed to the belief in a suprahistorical or divine force of intervention. Benjamin's reference to nihilism in the 'Theological-Political Fragment' is fully at odds with Deleuze's first conception of nihilism. For Benjamin, the 'method' of politics is nihilism precisely because it runs counter to the negation of life that characterizes Deleuze's first conception. Benjamin's nihilism targets the very 'will to nothingness' that voids our experience of the world from the feeling that it can be changed. It rejects the impulse to bring down our 'affinity of action and affirmation' and it is a radical antidote *against* the 'becoming-reactive' of active forces. Like the concept of *Aufgabe* that was put into play in the Hölderlin essay, the '*Aufgabe* of world-politics' that is mentioned in the 'Theological-Political Fragment' requires that one *give up* the belief that life is a divine *Gift*: '[T]he secular order cannot be built on the idea of the Divine Kingdom, and theocracy has no political but only a religious meaning' (SW 3, 305). Benjamin's messianism, in other words, releases life from any direct connection with the transcendent. The belief that a *supra*historical ground gives meaning to our world stands in the way of the feeling that *historical* change is possible. Making change dependent on a divine force with absolute qualities runs counter to everything that is worthy of being called 'politics'.

Benjamin's messianism simultaneously rejects the concept of an entirely immanent principle of change. 'Only the Messiah himself completes all history, in the sense that he alone redeems, completes, creates [*erlöst, vollendet, schafft*] its relation to the messianic' (SW 3, 305; GS II, 203). For this reason, Benjamin's use of the concept of nihilism in the 'Theological-Political Fragment' does not correspond to Deleuze's second conception either. With his emphasis of an 'eternally transient worldly existence, transient in its totality' Benjamin dismisses the view of life as continuous creation. Benjamin's reference to such a total transience forms an obstacle to the Overman's affirming will and the becoming active of his forces. For, in his 'Theological-Political Fragment' Benjamin reiterates the suggestion from the Hölderlin essay that an 'all too great proximity to life' *precludes* the belief in change and becoming. In the 'Theological-Political Fragment' as well, the concept of *Aufgabe* serves to formulate the need to give up both the view of life as a divine Gift, *and* the idea that life is *itself* a dynamic that *gives*. The *Aufgabe* of 'world-politics' refers precisely to the relentless *passing away* that holds sway over life. Politics, moreover, ought 'to *strive for* such a passing away' (SW 3, 306 [emphasis added]). Benjamin's concept of 'eternal transience' cannot therefore be squared with the 'thought of the eternal return' that motivates Nietzsche's Overman. Benjamin's conception of an unceasing *disappearance* and an *absence* of possibilities is at odds with the Overman's affirmation of an *ontologized* becoming and renewal. According to Benjamin, in and of itself, life cannot at all be believed to rejuvenate or produce difference: mere life is but an eternal repetition of the *same*, and it is *at odds with* a rhythm of natural innovation.[31]

In Benjamin's view, neither a transcendent nor an immanent dynamic of transformation can be used to support the belief in messianic change. The reason for this is that he makes the possibility of redemption dependent on a complete nihilism. Benjamin's messianism presupposes a universalized power to *negate* and *destroy*: '[N]ature is messianic by reason of its eternal and total passing away' (SW 3, 306). As a consequence, the 'spiritual restitutio', 'immortality' and even 'happiness' that mark the moment of redemption do not signal the recovery of a process of infinite productivity. Messianic restitution 'corresponds' precisely to a principle of destruction and negation that has become complete: 'In happiness all that is earthly seeks its downfall, and only in happiness is its downfall destined to find it' (SW 3, 305). This suggestion that the moment of redemption attests to a completion of negation instead of a direct affirmation of creation casts light on one of Benjamin's most complex hypotheses. 'If one arrow points to the goal toward which the secular dynamic acts', Benjamin famously writes, 'and another marks the direction of messianic intensity [*messianischen Intensität*], then certainly the quest of free humanity for happiness runs counter to the messianic direction. But just as a force, by virtue of the path it is moving along, can augment another force on the opposite path, so the secular order—because of its nature as secular—promotes [*befördern*] the coming of the Messianic Kingdom' (SW 3, 305; GS II, 203–4). Benjamin's metaphor of the two arrows that go in different directions but can nevertheless 'augment [each other's] force' functions in the same manner as the suggestion, made in the Hölderlin essay, that the orders of men and God are 'like two scales' that 'are left in their opposing positions' but can be 'lifted off the scale beam' and thereby 'raised up toward and against each other'. Both of these passages introduce the possibility that the opposition between the secular and the divine is neutralized. This neutralization illustrates what Deleuze calls a 'negation transformed into a power of affirmation'. For the opposition between the orders of men and God is a foremost illustration of the reactive, first type of nihilism that was laid out above. The opposition between the secular and the messianic is rooted in the mythological account of a suprahistorical, divine foundation for history and it *negates* the possibility of historical change. With the image of 'the secular order promot[ing] the coming of the Messianic Kingdom', Benjamin recasts the opposition between both as something that lacks an ultimate form of determination. The metaphor of two opposing forces augmenting each other opens the possibility that the negation of history, which is otherwise an inherent element of the belief in transcendence, can *itself be negated*. It is such a 'negation of negation' that conditions the process of radical renewal and rejuvenation that is termed 'redemption'. As Benjamin mentions in the theses 'On the Concept of History', the messianic is first and foremost a 'force'. The messianic, we now know, is a reactive force that has *become* active on account of its ability to negate everything that is reactive within history, *first and foremost the very opposition between history and transcendence*. Benjamin's messianism affirms change because it upsets precisely those historical oppositions that negate history. The belief that even the reactive opposition between the secular and the divine can be rendered inoperative epitomises the belief that true change is indeed possible.

Messianic change pushes history beyond itself, though neither in the direction of a suprahistorical intervention nor back towards the supposed flux of life. Benjamin's messianism exposes the ultimate *groundlessness* of life but it simultaneously designates the belief that a 'spiritual' realm can be *added* to life. This messianic supplement to life cannot be projected back onto history and its affirmation of change resists being absorbed by life itself. Despite Benjamin's suggestion that 'we have been endowed with a *weak* messianic force' (SW 4, 390), this messianic force is not a category of history. Messianic change *interrupts* history and opens it up towards a dynamic of renewal that cannot be internalized by history itself. Therefore, like Hölderlin's reference to a god that does not 'bring' but 'is brought', the image of the arrival of the divine as 'promoted' by secular events is in no way indicative of a *historical possibility*. Along with the purely *artistic* universe of Hölderlin's late poems, the messianic realm should be considered a *reality of its own*, non-actual and 'spiritual'. This type of messianic redemption, like Hölderlin's poem 'Blödigkeit', attests to an 'intensified certainty' and even a 'sacred life', but such a life is the outcome of a *transmutation*. The belief in a 'spiritual' life that is testified to by Benjamin's messianism does not at all adhere to any sacredness on the part of life *as such*. '[T]he dogma of the sacredness of life', writes Benjamin in his essay on violence, 'is indeed probably . . . relatively recent' but it constitutes 'the last mistaken attempt of the weakened Western tradition to seek the saint it has lost in cosmological impenetrability' (SW 1, 251). Benjamin grounds his messianism in the idea that life itself is incomplete but that it can be *produced anew*. It is unrelated to the idea that life is inhabited by an ultimate force, and at odds with the belief that divine actions can be assisted by human ones. It *affirms* true, radical change but it *rejects* the conception that human actions can prepare a divine intervention. His messianism does not restore our belief that history is a domain replete with hitherto non-actualized possibilities, let alone the belief that historical action can lay claim to absolute qualities. To the contrary, Benjamin's messianism exposes that no historical process can resist a universal force of negation and destruction. It thus highlights a profound *im*possibility that lies at the heart of history. As an 'active negation' Benjamin's messianism creates an additional and purely 'spiritual' reality that exposes that the opposition between the secular and the divine lacks an ultimate foundation. Still, this affirming, 'complete' nihilism does not abolish the difference between human beings and gods altogether. It is, according to Benjamin, only in a purely 'spiritual' life that human beings and god can be believed to switch sides. Only in this added and non-actual reality, can the opposition between the profane and the divine be revealed as something that is as yet non-determined.

A NOTE ON GERSHOM SCHOLEM

The discussion about an 'active negation' casts light on the relation between Benjamin and Gershom Scholem. Like Benjamin's messianism, Scholem's philosophy is built on the renunciation of the reactive, first type of nihilism that negates the sphere of history proper. Scholem, too, rejects the belief in a suprahistorical ground that establishes a firm connection between history on the one hand, and the realm of ultimate and divine essences on the other. In Scholem's view, 'it is one of the most important characteristics of Messianism that to the minds of a great many there was an abyss here'.[32] In words that resonate strongly with Benjamin's claim that 'the secular order cannot be built on the idea of the Divine Kingdom', Scholem emphasizes that '[t]here can be no preparation for the Messiah. He comes suddenly, unannounced, and precisely when he is least expected or when hope has long been abandoned'.[33] Like Benjamin, moreover, Scholem equally rejects the second type of nihilism that affirms the changeability of life in a direct manner. Scholem is mostly drawn to forms of messianism that have a Gnostic and apocalyptic undercurrent. Such types of messianic religion are at odds with the belief that life is a realm of non-actualized possibilities, animated by an absolute force of creation. In the essay 'Redemption Through Sin', for instance, Scholem famously turns to the case of the Sabbatians, a mystical sect that was led by the self-proclaimed messiah Sabbatai Zevi (1626–1676). According to the Sabbatians, history is at such distance from the absolute that it is only worthy of being negated. '[T]he way to Life is not easy', writes Scholem, 'for it is the way of nihilism and it means to free oneself of all laws, conventions, and religions, to adopt every conceivable attitude and to reject it, and to follow one's leader step for step into the abyss'.[34]

However, unlike Benjamin's messianism, Scholem's 'active negation' cannot be identified with the 'complete nihilism' that Deleuze associates with a 'negation of negation'. For Scholem describes the transgressive and subversive attitude of Sabbatian messianism as an *obligation*. He introduces concepts such as 'the potential holiness of sin' or the 'duty to violate' and frames the messianic negation of history as a distinctly *religious* attitude.[35] This explains why he goes through pains to analyse even the heretic movement of the Sabbatians as 'an integral part of Jewish history', ultimately identifying Zevi's conversion to Islam as 'a religious mystery of the utmost importance'.[36] 'Through a revolution of values', he writes 'what was formerly sacred has now become profane and what was formerly profane has become sacred. . . . [T]he violation of the Torah is now its true fulfillment'.[37] For this reason, Scholem's philosophy is steeped in a dialectics that runs counter to Benjamin's complete nihilism.[38] In Scholem's messianism, the inaccessibility of transcendence can be taken up by an antinomian attitude towards this world and thereby result in a paradoxical reinvestment of history. While such a dialectic sublation of the inaccessibility of transcendence does lead to a nihilistic 'return to immanence', this very return can lay claim to a 'true fulfillment of the Torah'.[39] In Benjamin's view, to the contrary, the inaccessibility of transcendence cannot at all be considered a legitimating ground for our attitude vis-à-vis history. While the awareness of this inaccessibility of transcendence does inspire an *Aufgabe*, this 'task' of politics consists precisely in *giving up* [*auf-geben*] the belief that our commitment to the world can in any way be reconnected to a religious or moral truth. Benjamin's complete nihilism rejects dialectics since it is not wedded to a philosophy of *opposition* but to a philosophy of *difference*. His argument does not start from the (Gnostic) opposition between history and transcendence but from the (completely nihilistic) awareness that *even this opposition lacks an ultimate ground of determination*. Key to Benjamin's messianism is that the affirmation of genuine change results from the negation of precisely the reactive attitude that Scholem describes in his examples of apocalyptic messianism. As a consequence, Benjamin's messianism does not argue for any religious or moral 'duty' to counteract history but for the political *Aufgabe* to neutralize even this antinomian attitude and thereby release it from any suprahistorical claims. While Benjamin calls for a revolutionary overthrow of the mythic violence of the law, he importantly adds that 'only mythic violence, not divine, will be recognizable as such with certainty, unless it be in incomparable effects, because the expiatory power of violence is invisible to men' (SW 1, 252). The upshot of Benjamin's messianism is the belief that history should not simply be opposed but *reworked* into a reality that is truly *other*. Benjamin's messianism does not at all result in the belief that the opposition between history and transcendence can be overcome in an (antinomian) affirmation of history. His complete nihilism is not a nihilism of 'subversion' or 'reversal' but a nihilism of *reproduction*. It does not seek to unceasingly 'violate' history but to create it anew as something different.

A handful of references to Kafka in the works of Scholem and Benjamin illustrate this difference of perspective with regard to the issue of messianism. In Scholem's interpretation, Kafka's work revolves around 'a world . . . in which redemption cannot be anticipated'.[40] Kafka's *oeuvre* is rooted in an awareness of the 'nothingness of revelation [*Das Nichts der Offenbarung*]'.[41] It derives its relevancy from the ability to ceaselessly express this gap between history and the beyond. From this point of view, Kafka's nihilism is dialectical: the experience of the inaccessibility of transcendent and absolute truths has here been sublated into the source of an exceptionally rich literary *oeuvre* that unceasingly affirms the unredeemed state of history at large. In line with his interpretation of Sabbatian antinomianism, Scholem emphasizes that it is precisely this relentless affirmation of the opposition between history and transcendence that vouchsafes Kafka's 'position in the continuum of Jewish literature'. 'It would be an enigma to me how . . . [one could] go about saying something about [Kafka's] world without placing the *Lehre* [teaching], called *Gesetz* [law] in Kafka's work, at the center'.[42] Like Scholem, Benjamin reads Kafka as a messianic author, albeit as a *completely* nihilistic one who negates even the very negation of history. For Benjamin, Kafka's work revolves around a 'fail[ure] . . . to convert poetry into teachings [*Lehre*, doctrine]' (SW 2, 808; GS II, 427). Unlike Scholem's reference to a 'nothingness of revelation', Benjamin's reference to Kafka's 'failure' to reach 'teaching' releases his work from the belief in an absolute truth, including the supposedly unshakeable claim that history and transcendence are irrevocably opposed to each other. In Kafka's work, the sustained awareness that no ultimate truth can be recovered within history does not lead to a 'duty' to unceasingly articulate the unredeemed state of history. For the experience of an empty and negative revelation is ultimately as non-determined and unfounded as the experience of a full and positive one. It is for this reason that Benjamin highlights that Kafka's universe is not just opposed to history but wholly different from it. Some of Kafka's protagonists are 'mist-bound creatures, beings in an unfinished state [*unfertige Geschöpfe*][,] . . . neither members of, nor strangers to, any of the other groups of figures, but, rather, messengers [*Boten*] busy moving between them' (SW 2, 798). These protagonists are so deeply *'ungeschickt'* [unsuited, un-sent (by Fate)] that even the experience that this world is at odds with the divine is revealed to be deeply inaccurate. Like the 'two scales' that are 'raised up toward and against each other' and the opposing arrows that nonetheless 'augment each other's force', these creatures conjure the presence of an *additional reality*. They can neither be grasped with the help of historical categories nor be considered to simply 'subvert' or 'reverse' them. Instead, these creatures give rise to a *non-actual* and purely *imaginary* realm in which even the opposition between men and god no longer holds. 'There are two ways to miss the point of Kafka's works', Benjamin writes, 'One is to interpret them naturally [*natürliche Auslegung*]; the other is to interpret them from a supernatural [*übernatürliche*] perspective' (SW 2, 806; GS II, 425). It is because Kafka's complete nihilism thus enables him to vouchsafe a (non-) place which is uncontaminated by the shortcomings and oppositions of history, that Benjamin associates his *oeuvre* with a type of hope that is one with despair. '*An infinite amount of hope*', as Kafka himself put it, '*but not for us*' (Kafka quoted on SW 2, 798).

FROM UNIVERSAL FORGETTING TO THE UNFORGETTABLE

Like Benjamin's early essay on Hölderlin and the 'Theological-Political Fragment', his writings on history from the late thirties are built on the suggestion that too much proximity to life depletes our belief in genuine change. His critique of the 'myth of progress', for instance, rests on the rejection of both a theological and a secularized eschatology that projects redemptive qualities directly onto the sphere of life. The well-known image of history as 'one single catastrophe, which keeps piling wreckage upon wreckage' (SW 4, 392) serves Benjamin to revisit his suggestion that it presents nothing but an eternal return of the same. Moreover, in the theses on 'The Concept of History' and the *Passagen-Werk* as well, the possibility of radical change is analyzed with the help of three familiar concepts: *Aufgabe*, transience and thought. The philosophy of history that is being developed in the thirties revolves around a like-minded plea for a redemptive interval vis-à-vis life, now described as a 'now-time' [*Jetzt-Zeit*] or 'messianic arrest of happening' (SW 4, 396). What is new, however, is an analysis of the possibility of the *future*. Near the end of his theses on 'The Concept of History', Benjamin writes that 'we know that the Jews were prohibited from inquiring into the future: the Torah and the prayers instructed them in *Eingedenken*. This disenchanted the future' (SW 4, 397; GS I, 704). A close reading of Benjamin's late writings will result in the suggestion that his philosophy of history is ultimately not wedded to a philosophy of the past or present, but to the conception of a future that does replenish our hope for change.

In line with the '*Aufgabe* of world-politics' to 'strive for' a 'passing away' that is 'total', the *Aufgabe* of historiography is described as a nihilistic completion of the transience that is inscribed within history at large. Benjamin's statement that 'historical materialism supplies a unique experience *with* the past/passage of time [*Vergangenheit*]' (SW 4, 396 [translation modified, emphasis added]) should be read as a clear-cut renunciation of the capacity to *go against* the passage of time. While historicism is motivated by the quest for suprahistorical essences or an 'eternal' image of the past, historical materialism gives up the belief in the preserving work of memory or recollection altogether. Like poetry and 'world-politics', historiography must replace the ideal of a recollected past with the reality of a redemptive 'arrest' of time (SW 4, 396). It is with such a 'turning of time' in mind that Benjamin reintroduces the concept of 'thought' and a 'spiritual' life. In his late writings on history, as well, these concepts describe an *internal* dislocation of transience.

Most often the German term *Eingedenken* is translated as remembrance or commemoration. The word then highlights the possibility that something from the past can be brought back to the present. In a revealing note, the English translators write that '*Eingedenken* is Benjamin's coinage from the preposition *eingedenk* ('mindful of') and the verb *gedenken* ('recollect', 'remember'). The resultant term has a more active sense than *erinnern* ('remember') and often verges on the notion of commemoration' (SW 4, 345). However, this association between the concept *Eingedenken* and the faculties of memory and recollection is misleading. 'The notion that the historian's *Aufgabe* is to make the past 'present' [*das Vergangene zu 'vergegenwartigen'*]', writes Benjamin, 'is guilty of ... fraudulence' (SW 4, 401). The term *Ein-gedenken* should be translated literally as 'thinking-in'. In contrast to the (Heideggerian) concepts *Andenken* or *Gedächtnis*, *Eingedenken* refers to the capacity to *enter fully within* the passage of time and not at all to a faculty that *counteracts* it. Instead of the ability of memory and recollection to *preserve* or *recover* the past, *Eingedenken* embodies the 'temporal plasticity' of thought, dislodging forgetting precisely by surrendering itself fully to it. In the Hölderlin essay, the concept *Denken* was already opposed to the ambition to 'characterize [something] in its essence'. Likewise, in the thirties, the concept *Eingedenken* serves Benjamin to reject the quest for the past 'the way it really was' (SW 4, 391). *Ein-gedenken* is the antithesis of *Ein-fühlung* (empathy, literally 'feeling-in'), the ideal of a positivist historiography that seeks to re-establish a direct connection with a lived past, using intuition to weave the past into a continuum with the present. *Eingedenken*, to the contrary, transmutes forgetting into a power that pushes a given moment in time beyond the confines of history proper. While *Einfühlung* is but an instrument to legitimate the status quo and 'sympathize[e] with the victor' (SW 4, 391 [translation modified]), *Eingedenken* opens life up to a process of radical change. In a letter to Horkheimer, Benjamin formulates it as follows: 'History is not simply a science but also and not least a form of *Eingedenken*. What science has "determined", *Eingedenken* can modify. Such an *Eingedenken* can make the incomplete (happiness) into something complete, and the complete (suffering) into something incomplete' (AP, 471). Like the 'thinking' and 'spiritual' life that is described in the Hölderlin essay and the 'Theological-Political Fragment', *Eingedenken* refers to a neutralization of the main categories of history. It testifies to Benjamin's 'complete nihilism' because it calls for an active affirmation of the powers of forgetting in order to dispel precisely those forces that are an obstacle to change. It therefore comes as no surprise that Benjamin's analysis of *Eingedenken* in the thirties hinges on the same tension that can be found in his earlier metaphors of the two opposing scales and arrows that nonetheless work together and his insistence, in the Kafka essay, that the opposition between a 'natural' and a 'supernatural perspective' can be neutralized. 'In *Eingedenken*', he writes, 'we have an experience that forbids us to conceive of history as fundamentally atheological [*grundsätzlich atheologisch*], little as it may be granted us to try to write it with immediately theological concepts [*unmittelbar theologischen Begriffen*]' (AP, 471; GS V, 589). Like the *Aufgabe* of poetry and politics, the *Aufgabe* of historiography is to negate the very opposition between history and transcendence and thereby replenish our belief in radical renewal. Historiography is founded in neither a theological nor an immanent principle of rejuvenation, but it makes the affirmation of change inseparable from the awareness that the realm of history at-large lacks an ultimate sense of determination. While it cannot recover a principle of spontaneous productivity, historiography uses thought to negate precisely those forces that negate history.

The historian's negation of everything that negates history requires the creation of a specific set of 'images of thought' [*Denkbilder*]. 'History is the subject of a construction' (SW 4, 395; see also AP, 461). Like the distinctly 'poetic' destiny of Hölderlin's 'Blödigkeit', and the purely 'spiritual' realm of a messianic 'restitutio ad integrum', these 'constellations', 'dialectical images', 'historical images', 'dream images', 'wish-images' or even 'historical objects' (for just a few references, see AP, 461, 464, 474, 893) set up a novel and distinctly non-actual world that enables the passing away of those forces in history that are an obstacle to change. These images and constructions are a supplement *to* history, with a unity and coherence of their own. 'It is not that what is past casts its light on what is present, or what is present its light on what is past; rather, image is that wherein what has been comes together in a flash with the now to form a constellation' (AP, 463). The becoming-'imagistic' (AP, 463; GS V, 578 [translation modified]) of history creates history anew as a non-actual, purely 'spiritual' entity. Because the continuum of history is in itself immune to change, these 'constellations' do not refer to a realm of historical possibilities that either will or will not *become* real. Although they are 'constructions', these 'constellations' are a *reality in and of themselves*, having let go of the direct reference to whatever possibility in history. It is for this reason that Benjamin's philosophy of history is no philosophy of memory or recollection and does not ultimately revolve around the preservation or recovery of the past. It is a philosophy of forgetting that revolves around the construction of a genuine future. In contrast to the phenomenologists of his generation, the future is for Benjamin not at all a dimension that is always already at work within the present. It is not posited in and by the present by means of protention and anticipation. When the future becomes real, this indicates that a moment in history, either past or present, has been reworked into something truly *different*. Therefore, when Benjamin concludes his theses on 'The Concept of History' with the line that 'every second was the small gateway [*die kleine Pforte*] in time through which the Messiah might enter' (SW 4, 397; GS I, 704), he is not at all making a prediction for the fate of mankind. The arrival of the Messiah is not an event that can be projected onto history.[43] It presents an element of hope that is rendered irreducibly real precisely because it was pushed *outside of* history. The coming of the Messiah is not what *inspires* the *Aufgabe* of historiography to create redemptive 'images of thought' but, vice versa, it *is* an 'image of thought' and it *results from* this *Aufgabe*. While Benjamin connects the creation of such 'images of thought' to the 'rescue' of history, they do not express a 'timeless truth' [*zeitlosen Wahrheit*] (AP, 463; GS V, 578), let alone that they anticipate the divine fulfillment of history. Their affirmation of radical change testifies to the historian's ability to negate everything that negates history, first and foremost the very opposition between historical events and a divine intervention. For that very reason, these 'images of thought' do not recover an ultimate essence that *legitimises* the belief in the final fulfillment of mankind.

While not at all a messianic thinker, Deleuze has developed a concept of 'thought' [*pensée*] that illuminates Benjamin's own suggestions about *Eingedenken*. In two important studies from the late sixties, *Difference and Repetition* (1968) and *Logic of Sense* (1969), Deleuze clarifies why only 'thought' affirms true change and thereby opens the dimension of the future. In Deleuze's view, thought needs to be distinguished from the faculty of memory because the latter is conditioned by the spontaneous survival of the past. Deleuze's view of memory is based on Bergson's conception of a 'pure' past [*passé pur*]. This 'pure' or 'immemorial' past constitutes the 'ground' [*fondement*] of time. It manages to persist over time because it was never consciously experienced or fully lived. 'The past . . . neither passes nor comes forth [*le passé . . . ne passe ni n'advient*]'.[44] External to and unaffected by the passage of time that makes each present instant go away, the 'pure' past sets up a dynamic of continuity and repetition. It signals a 'virtual' surplus or excess vis-à-vis the present and refuses to succumb together with it. 'The present exists, but the past alone insists'.[45] Deleuze turns to Bergson to understand why this emphasis on continuity and repetition is not at all antithetical to the possibility of change and difference. By granting the 'pure' past the capacity to endure, Bergson injects heterogeneity within the stream of time itself. Due to the survival of a 'mirror-image' or 'shadow' for each present moment, the stream of time includes a dimension that is real but inevitably eludes the grasp of our consciousness.[46] For that reason, difference is not the opposite of repetition. Difference is believed to always already be 'included in' repetition and to even be spontaneously produced by it.[47] Like the affirming, second type of nihilism that Deleuze analyses in his book on Nietzsche, Bergson's philosophy of memory rests on a philosophy of becoming. Because the *élan* of life is endowed with the capacity to retain a 'pure' and 'virtual' dynamic that is wholly distinct from the present, it ceaselessly renews itself. Such vitalism *ontologizes* change and renewal and projects differentiation and transformation directly onto life.

In Deleuze's view, thought is a counterpower to memory because it cuts through all ties with a supposedly 'pure' past that withstands the passage of time. Deleuze's concept of thought presupposes an 'event' [*événement*] or 'cesura' that is fully at odds with the belief that the past can somehow endure over time.[48] By way of such a moment of interruption, time is 'liberated from its overly simple circular figure, freed from the events which made up its content, its relation to movement overturned; in short, time presenting itself as an empty and pure form. Time itself unfolds (that is, apparently ceases to be a circle) instead of things unfolding within it (following the overly simple circular figure)'.[49] Thought is conceptualized as the affirmation of an *'effondement'*. This French term brings together the terms *'fondement'* [ground] and *'effondrement'* [collapse] to indicate how thought can come to terms with the collapse of the ground of time. Deleuze describes such an 'ungrounding' with the same terms as his third concept of a complete nihilism. Like all instantiations of complete nihilism, the 'ungrounding' that is embraced by thought endows only the power to destroy and negate with the capacity to return. Deleuze describes such a 'universal ungrounding' as an 'eternal return, affirmed in all its power, [that] allows no installation of a foundation-ground. . . . By "ungrounding" we should understand the freedom of the non-mediated ground, the discovery of a ground behind every other ground, the relation between the groundless and the ungrounded, the immediate reflection of the formless and the superior form which constitutes the eternal return'.[50] Thought incarnates a 'death instinct' that leaves nothing intact. It can be likened to 'a great amnesiac' because it incarnates a forgetting that has become all-encompassing.[51] In Deleuze's view, therefore, thought gives up the idea that life is characterized by spontaneous productivity and regeneration. The belief in the powers of thought is at odds with the vitalist conception of an *ontologized* principle of change. Like all instantiations of complete nihilism, thought testifies to reactive forces that *have become* active. Thought replenishes the belief in radical renewal because it transmutes the power to destroy and negate into a principle of affirmation and creation. In thought, destruction and negation have become so universal that they turn towards themselves and obliterate everything that negates the possibility of change. In Deleuze's view, thought no longer shies away from the radical emptiness of time but brings about a remarkable repetition of this emptiness. In thought a 'universal ungrounding . . . turns upon itself and causes only the yet-to-come to return'.[52] This repetition neither rests on an underlying 'duration' nor recovers an originary fullness. However, the fact that thought installs a capacity to return signals the possibility that the emptiness of time has been dislodged, even though it is the very experience of a lack of ground which returns. It is for this reason that only thought is capable of opening up the dimension of a future that is truly *other*. Having given up the belief in the spontaneous generation of change, thought is rooted in the awareness that genuine difference needs to be produced again and again. This explains why Deleuze emphasizes that thought cannot exist without the construction of a 'work' (*oeuvre*). It is only with the creation of a 'work of thought' that thought manages to extract something truly new from the very affirmation of an overall groundlessness. When thought embraces the eternal return of a dynamic of destruction and negation, 'it is properly called a belief of the future, a belief in the future. Eternal return affects only the new, what is produced under the condition of default and by the intermediary of metamorphosis. . . . It constitutes the autonomy of the product, the independence of the work [*l'autonomie du produit, l'indépendance de l'oeuvre*]'.[53]

Time and again Deleuze comes back to this idea that thought entails an 'ungrounding' that is concomitant with the construction of a 'work'. It underlies, for instance, the chapter 'Thought and Cinema' of his book on the *Time-Image* (1989). Deleuze underscores that 'thought has no other reason to function than its own birth, always the repetition of its own birth, secret and profound'.[54] His analysis of a cinema that 'thinks' establishes a firm connection between the powers of thought and a profound 'impower of thought' [*impouvoir de la pensée*] or 'powerlessness to think' [*impuissance à penser*] that can only be neutralized by the creation of a specific type of product.[55] For, with Artaud and Blanchot, Deleuze stresses that 'the impossibility of thinking' can and should actually be thought, and this by way of the production of images that present a 'fissure, a crack'.[56] In contrast to the dialectical montage of Eisenstein, which conjures a sense of wholeness and an ultimate, foundational truth (ideology), genuine thought goes hand in hand with images that have '"a dissociative force" which would introduce a "figure of nothingness" [*figure de néant*], a "hole in appearances"'.[57] From this very confrontation with a radical groundlessness, thought draws the capacity to reopen the world and 'a higher power or birth [*une plus haute puissance ou naissance*]'.[58] In such 'images of thought', the world is reshaped into 'purely visual situations' that cannot be confused with an actual event or moment in time. Such a 'suspension of the world' neutralizes the foundational hierarchies and distinctions through which we orient ourselves in daily life.[59] It affirms the most profound type of change for the very reason that it has moved beyond an exploration of the mere possibilities of this world. For Deleuze, it enables us instead to believe 'in the impossible, the unthinkable, which nonetheless cannot but be thought'.[60] In the films of Dreyer and Rossellini, for instance, Deleuze discovers a universe that is so much at odds with our usual experience of the world that it should be taken for an added and novel reality in its own right. This truly other and non-actual world has been rendered so internally coherent and unified that it, paradoxically, exposes the world in its current state as lacking in reality. In comparison with the intensity of Dreyer and Rossellini's 'thinking' images, our lives are so utterly 'banal' and even 'intolerable' that we have lost the means to truly believe. 'The modern fact is that we no longer believe in this world [*Le fait moderne, c'est que nous ne croyons plus en ce monde*]'.[61]

The cinema of thought makes use of 'ungrounding' to replenish our belief in radical change.[62] It is, therefore, no exaggeration to state that the 'thought' produced in the films of Dreyer and Rossellini is an instantiation of complete nihilism. This is the case, firstly, because their work gives up the concept of a transcendent ground to history, in spite of being inspired by Catholic beliefs. According to Deleuze, the religious convictions of Dreyer and Rossellini are in no way the legitimating ground of their unwavering affirmation of change. Vice versa, the religious qualities of their work are, at most, the *result of* an unshakeable affirmation of change. Dreyer and Rossellini do not jump beyond the world as it is, but only for the reason that its current and deplorable state reinvigorates the belief that it can be transformed. Therefore, their films are not at all exemplary for our own lives. Their protagonists are 'fossilized' and 'mummified', engaged in actions that do much more than simply show us what is possible in the world.[63] The second reason why their work can be labelled *completely* nihilistic is that they give up the idea that differentiation and transformation can be projected directly onto life. The cinema of Dreyer and Rossellini is a 'thinking' cinema because it produces images that do not shrink back from the intolerability of the world in its actual state. In their *oeuvre*, it is precisely this intolerability which shows that the world as we know it can and needs to be changed. Rossellini, for instance, starts from the idea that 'the less human the world is, the more it is the artist's duty to believe and produce belief in a relation between man and the world, because the world is made by men'.[64] In the films of Dreyer and Rossellini, the belief in change can never be considered a given. It remains dependent on a work that is always to be restarted, again and again.

> The link between man and the world is broken. Henceforth, this link must become an object of belief: it is the impossible which can only be restored within a faith. . . . Whether we are Christians or atheists, in our universal schizophrenia, *we need reasons to be-*

lieve in this world [*nous avons besoin de raisons de croire en ce monde*]. It is a whole transformation of belief [*toute une conversion de la croyance*].⁶⁵

The 'images' and 'constellations' that, according to Benjamin, create the world anew in and as something truly different and purely 'spiritual' are such products or works of thought. They *bring about* the affirmation of change and actively *generate* the reasons to believe in this world. Benjamin builds his *Passagen-Werk* on the suggestion that modern phenomena such as the arcades and the *flâneur*, the commodity fetish and fashion are the material expression of the ideal of social equality. It would be a mistake to read these 'elements of a classless society' (AP 4, 894, 943) as the mere reactualization or *Nachleben* of a 'pure' past that has spontaneously survived over time. Rather than *counteract* forgetting and recover the collective memory of the nineteenth century, the 'primal history' and 'utopian' ideals of universal equality demonstrate a universal 'ungrounding' and a forgetting that has been rendered complete. The 'primal history' and 'utopian images' of universal equality are so antithetical to the dominant forces in history that they cannot even be properly inscribed into memory, let alone be easily recollected or reactualized. 'Primal history of the nineteenth century—this would be of no interest if it were understood to mean that forms of primal history are to be recovered [*wieder gefunden werden*] among the inventory of the nineteenth century' (AP, 463; GS V, 579). Benjamin conjures the metaphor of 'a triumphal procession in which current rulers step over those who are lying prostrate' to describe how the course of history unceasingly conspires against social justice (SW 4, 391). For this reason, Benjamin carefully differentiates these 'wish-images' from images of 'memory'. Throughout the *Passagen-Werk*, Benjamin never uses the term 'memory' to describe the dream images of social justice. He only takes recourse to this term to describe the moment of *awakening*, which signals that the dream has *come to an end*. 'Awakening is the great exemplar of memory' (AP, 389). The dream itself does not recover anything. What is more, even the 'memory of the dream' entails a 'pass[ing] through . . . what has been [*[das] Gewesenes . . . durchzumachen*]' (AP, 389; GS V, 491). Because the 'primal history' and 'utopian' images of social justice are marked with the precariousness of everything that is chanceless within history, they ceaselessly pass away and need to be produced anew with every new generation.⁶⁶

Rather than 'memory images' these dream images should be termed 'unforgettable' ones. In an important essay on Dostoyevski's *The Idiot*, and in his essay on translation, Benjamin has coined the term 'unforgettable' to describe the product of a forgetting that is complete but transmuted. In *The Idiot* the concept of 'unforgettable' [*unvergeßlich*] refers to a character that is 'utterly modest, even humble' and 'completely unapproachable'. Myshkin's 'life passes aimlessly, even when he is at his best, and in this he resembles nothing so much as an ailing incompetent [*gleich dem eines untüchtigen kränkelnden Menschen*]. He is seen to fail not just in society's terms; even his closest friend—if the novel's rationale did not prevent him from having one—would be unable to discover any idea or purposive goal in his life. On the contrary, he is surrounded in a quite unobtrusive way by an aura of complete isolation' (SW 1, 79; GS II, 238). Like the non-actual and purely 'spiritual' dream universe of the nineteenth century, Myshkin's existence does indeed seem incapable of being preserved or commemorated. It exposes the 'failure' to reconnect a presence in history with whatever type of legitimating ground. '[H]is life emanates an order at whose center we find a solitude that is almost absolute' (SW 1, 79). Benjamin calls such seemingly exposable and chanceless elements 'unforgettable', and even 'immortal [*unsterblich*]' (SW 1, 80), because in his reading these concepts do not any longer have anything to do with qualities that can withstand the passage of time. 'One might speak of an unforgettable life or moment', writes Benjamin in his essay on translation, 'even if all men had forgotten it' (SW 1, 254). What is unforgettable is even antithetical to the concept of 'duration [*Dauer*]' (SW 1, 80). It does not thrive on the survival of a past moment but sets up a radically different 'realm in which [the capacity to withstand forgetting] is fulfilled' (SW 1, 254). The unforgettable raises the expression of transience to a level of self-annihilation and, hence, gives shape to a force of 'persistence'. Benjamin associates such an uncanny force to subsist, not with human memory, but with a 'thought of God' [*ein Gedenken Gottes*] (GS IV, 10). Because the unforgettable inevitably makes visible the distance between our world and ultimate or divine truths, it is a mistake to translate such a 'thought of God' as 'God's remembrance' (SW 1, 254). Benjamin makes very clear that the unforgettable is independent of whatever type of ground.[67] It 'has no monument or memorial, or perhaps even any testimony' but nonetheless reopens the world on completely new terms. 'We observe here a quite remarkable fact', writes Benjamin in his analysis of Prince Myshkin, 'every event, however remote from him it appears to be, seems to gravitate toward him'. Whether it is a deeply incompetent literary character or an age-old ideal of social equality, what is unforgettable may not be able to go against the passage of time, but it does make use of it to replenish our belief in radical change (SW 1, 80).

Benjamin emphasizes that the resurfacing of the ideal of social justice presupposes the neutralizing powers of 'sleep' and not at all the preserving work of memory. 'The nineteenth century [is] a space time [*Zeitraum*] (a dream time [*Zeit-traum*]) in which the individual consciousness more and more secures itself in reflecting, while the collective consciousness sinks into ever deeper sleep' (AP, 389). The conception of sleep that underlies the description of nineteenth-century Paris as a 'dream universe' runs parallel to the analysis of '(de-)sleeping' [*entschlafen*] in the Hölderlin essay. In this early text, sleep had already been framed as both a universalization *and* a neutralization of transience: we '*pass away* into sleep' (Hölderlin), but not without thereby dislodging an experience of irremediable loss. We can thus recall Heraclitus's statement that 'Waking, we indeed see death—but in sleep we see sleep'. In the *Passagen-Werk* as well, sleep is described as the activity that dispels transience by making it all-encompassing. This explains why Benjamin's title for 'Convolute K' connects 'dream city and dream house' with 'anthropological nihilism'. When sleep produces images of a wholly different world, this is not at all because these ideals have had the strength to withstand centuries of social injustice and economic inequality. Sleep gives shape to images of a truly other universe because it is itself an activity of passing away. For that reason alone, sleep does manage to cancel out precisely those forces that are an obstacle to radical change. The goal of the *Passagen-Werk* is not to go against the passage of time but, as Benjamin put it in the theses on 'The Concept of History', to 'have a unique experience *with* the passage of time'. The *Passagen-Werk* manages to transform passage into work. Only the creation of an interval with regard to our surroundings, and no act of mere protection or anticipation, enables us to imagine the present in a wholly different manner. As Benjamin puts it, sleep embodies a 'retreat into its insides' [*in sein Inneres sich vertieft*] (AP, 389; GS V, 492 [translation modified]) that 'translate[s]' the physical world into the stuff of dreams and wishes. '[A]rchitecture, fashion—yes, even the weather—are, in the interior of the collective, what the sensoria of organs, the feeling of sickness or health, are inside the individual' (AP, 389). Rather than affiliated with the preserving capacities of memory, sleep is a form of *Einge-*

denken or an 'extravagantly heightened inner awareness' [*seinen unerhört geschärften innern Sinnen*] that produces the present anew in and as the reality of a future that is wholly other (AP, 389; GS V, 491). Its 'retreat into its insides' negates those forces that negate history but, by that token, it produces images and constellations that affirm the irreducible potential of change. In Benjamin's view, it is in sleep that a genuine future is fashioned, albeit in the form of a 'primal history' and 'utopian ideal' that is forever prevented from entering into the continuum of actual history.

A NOTE ON THEODOR ADORNO

In the very first paragraph of the preface to his magnum opus *Negative Dialectics* (1966), Adorno uses no uncertain terms to differentiate his philosophical project from a 'negation of negation'. '*Negative Dialectics*' is a phrase that flouts tradition. As early as Plato, dialectics meant to achieve something positive by means of negation; the thought figure of a 'negation of negation' later became the succinct term. This book seeks to free dialectics from such affirmative traits without reducing its determinacy. The unfoldment of the paradoxical title is one of its aims'.[68] On 11 November 1965, Adorno devoted an entire lecture to a systematic development of the concept 'negation of negation'. Adorno associates it, first of all, with Hegel's 'positive' dialectics that sublates the opposition between thought and reality. Such an 'objective idealism' overcomes the first moment of negation, that is, the process in which abstract thought retreats into itself, by way of a second negation, that is, the process in which thought's abstraction gives shape to the products of society.[69]

> [T]hat this subjectivity must negate itself, that it must become conscious of its own limitations in order to be able to transcend itself and enter into the positive side of its negation, namely into the institutions of society, the state, the objective and, ultimately, absolute spirit. This, then, is the model of positive negativity: the negation of the negation as a new positive that appears in Hegelian philosophy as a new model.[70]

Adorno takes Hegel to task for ridding the dialectical method of its critical and truly negating powers. Through sublating the opposition between thought and reality, thought is used as a legitimation of the societal status quo instead of making visible the injustices and exclusions that underlie this status quo. In Adorno's view, the institutions of the state are not at all the 'higher factor' that allow abstract thought to become a presence in reality. They are but a 'mechanism of coercion' and use ideology to conjure the dangerous illusion that thought can leave behind all traces of the world in which it is being developed. 'Does not the retreat to this supposedly higher authority signify the regression of the subject, which had earlier won its freedom only with great efforts, with infinite pains?'[71] A second illustration of the 'negation of negation' brings Adorno to his criticism of Nietzsche. In his reading, Nietzsche, as well, is deemed incapable of truly grasping the power of negation. Nietzsche presents but a shallow form of affirmation that says 'yes' to whatever event that occurs, regardless of whether this event does in fact deserve to be affirmed. '[W]hen I speak of "negative dialectics" not the least important reason for doing so is my desire to dissociate myself from this fetishization of the positive. . . . We have to ask *what* has to be or has not to be affirmed, instead of elevating the word "Yes" to a value in itself, as was unfortunately done by Nietzsche with the entire pathos of saying yes to life'.[72] Adorno emphasizes that his own project of a truly negative dialectics 'calls for the very opposite' of the 'negation of negation'.[73] His negative dialectics revolves around a 'disenchantment of the concept' and annuls Hegel's sublating of the opposition between thought and reality. It hinges on an assertion of the 'primacy of the object' and the 'non-conceptual' reality that resides within the heart of all thought.[74] Negative dialectics starts from the claim that thought is inevitably mediated by the societal reality in which it is produced. Adorno, moreover, differentiates this negative dialectics from Nietzsche's 'yea-saying' because he considers it the prime method of coming to terms with a deeply rooted lack of meaning.[75] In contrast to Hegel and Nietzsche's project of affirmation, Adorno's negative dialectics takes seriously those powers that are wholly *opposed* to thought. It revolves around 'the question whether thought can bear the idea that a given reality is meaningless and that mind is unable to orient itself; or whether the intellect has become so enfeebled that it finds itself paralyzed by the idea that all is not well with the world'.[76]

Adorno's rejection of both Hegel's positive dialectics and Nietzsche's ontologized becoming does not at all stand in the way of an affirmation of change. Despite his criticism of Hegel's positive dialectics, Adorno's negative dialectics remains wedded to the dialectical method because it rediscovers the very opposition between thought and reality as the legitimation of our ongoing investment *in* that reality. In Adorno's view, thought is unable to truly enter into the heart of objective reality, but this does not fully close the door on its ability to present truth. It is precisely the ability to express its own incapacities that enables thought to continue to expose the societal forces it runs up against. The confrontation with the rift between thought and reality is exactly what sends thought back to that reality, albeit only to ceaselessly expose the distance to it. The 'ability to keep one's distance as a spectator and to rise above things' brings to the surface 'an inhuman part' because it makes visible the finitude of thought. 'In the final analysis', however, this same ability is 'the human part, the very part resisted by its ideologists'.[77]

Adorno only very rarely agreed with that other intellectual *compagnon de route* of Benjamin's, Gershom Scholem, but, like him, he argues that the requirement to expose the fundamental inadequacy of all human thought is not itself underdetermined.[78] 'If thought is not measured by the extremity that eludes the concept, it is from the outset in the nature of the musical accompaniment with which the SS liked to drown out the screams of its victims'.[79] Because it is rooted in an opposition between thought and reality that he by no means seeks to neutralize, Adorno refuses to negate his own plea for negation. Adorno, as well, uses dialectics to raise negation itself into a power of affirmation. Parallel to Scholem's 'duty' to negate history, Adorno even calls for a 'new categorical imperative' that 'has been imposed by Hitler upon unfree mankind: to arrange their thoughts and actions so that Auschwitz will not repeat itself, so that nothing similar will happen'.[80] Adorno's hypostatization of the opposition between thought and reality explains why not even the utter meaninglessness of Auschwitz invalidates the project of metaphysics and morality. Quite the contrary, 'nothing else, is what compels us to philosophize'.[81] Therefore, when Adorno famously writes that '[a]ll post-Auschwitz culture, including its urgent critique, is garbage [*Müll*]', this should not be confused with the claim that we are left with nothing but ideology.[82] This denunciation itself testifies to the ongoing belief in a type of thought that unceasingly confronts reality, and this precisely because such thought is capable of indicating the ultimate inaccessibility of that reality.

Adorno's negative dialectics differs from Benjamin's dialectics-at-a-standstill in a fundamental manner. Benjamin's project is not built on the rigid opposition between thought and reality but on the *neutralization of this opposition*. As we have seen, it revolves around the creation of 'images of thought' that are simultaneously real *and* merely 'spiritual'. Benjamin refuses to burden thought with lack and discovers it as a power that gives shape to a reality of its own. For Benjamin, as well, thought affirms change, though not for the reason that it can ceaselessly oppose reality as it is, but because it manages to produce it anew in and as something entirely different. This explains why Benjamin's conceptualization of the relation between thought and injustice is wholly different from Adorno's. In Adorno's negative dialectics, the reinvestment of thought in reality is motivated by its obligation to negate that reality. For this reason, the expression of the facticity of social injustice goes hand in hand with its denunciation. 'After Auschwitz, our feelings resist any claim of the positivity of existence as sanctimonious, as wronging the victims'.[83] Adorno's negative dialectics is built on the 'categorical imperative' to make visible that injustice *has not been avoided* even though it *should have been*. Benjamin's philosophy, to the contrary, does not merely consider injustice to be an undeniable reality that needs to be negated by thought. In a letter to Benjamin, Max Horkheimer makes a suggestion that easily fits into Adorno's framework. 'Past injustice has occurred and is completed [*ist geschehen und abgeschlossen*]. The slain are really slain . . . only the injustice, the horror, the sufferings of the past are irreparable [*nur das Unrecht, der Schrecken, die Schmerzen der Vergangenheit irreparabel sind*]'. Benjamin's reply is meant to offer 'a corrective to this line of thinking' since he suggests that thought can make the 'complete (suffering) into something incomplete [*Unabgeschlossenen*]' (AP, 471; GS V, 589). For Benjamin, thought does not simply make visible that a past injustice *should* have been avoided but, first and foremost, that it *could have been*, and this because no event in history is supported by a legitimating ground. Making suffering into 'something incomplete' requires a complete nihilism that negates everything that lays claim to an ultimate determination, including the 'categorical imperative' to negate the injustices of the past. For Benjamin, complete nihilism allows us to move even beyond the negation of past suffering and thereby reopen the possibility of a 'utopian' world that has fully done away with all injustice. 'As long as there is still one beggar around, there will still be myth' (AP, 400). For this reason, Benjamin's philosophy is not rooted in a metaphysical or moral project but in a *political* and *ethical* one. Deleuze frames the difference between morality and ethics as follows:

> [M]orality presents us with a set of constraining rules of a special sort, ones that judge actions and intentions by considering them in relation to transcendent values (this is good, that's bad . . .);

ethics is a set of optional rules that assess what we do, what we say, in relation to the ways of existing involved. We say this, do that; what way of existing does it involve?[84]

Because Adorno's negative dialectics hypostatizes the opposition between thought and reality, it cannot shake off a final remnant of the appeal to transcendent values. His negative dialectics result in the 'categorical imperative' to negate. Benjamin's complete nihilism, on the other hand, is not at all antithetical to an ethics. By deeming thought capable of negating everything that negates the possibility of change, including the opposition between thought and reality, this complete nihilism replenishes the belief in a truly different way of existing.

Thirty years prior to Adorno's claim that 'all post-Auschwitz culture is . . . garbage', Benjamin already stated that it is possible to 'capture an image of history [*Bild der Geschichte festzuhalten*]' in 'the detritus [*Abfällen*] of present existence'.[85] The difference between Adorno's *Müll* and Benjamin's *Abfall* might seem a trivial one but it is fundamental and revelatory.[86] Benjamin's concept of *Abfall* is by no means a metaphor for a 'culture [that] has turned entirely into the ideology it had been potentially'.[87] *Abfall* belongs in the same series of concepts as *Aufgabe*, *Abbild* and 'failure'. It cannot be reduced to ideology, false consciousness or escapism because it is precisely in its *Abfall* that history is made visible as a realm that is lacking in determination. In its *Abfall*, history is exposed as empty and groundless. For Benjamin, this disenchanting engagement with the *Abfall* of history is an extremely important one because it uncovers an openness to-be-determined. Only in this nihilistic manner can the belief in radical change be replenished. The difference between Adorno's *Müll* and Benjamin's *Abfall* illuminates the crux of their dispute about the argument that the dream of social justice is reproduced by way of 'dialectical images'. In Adorno's view, Benjamin's argument is '*undialectical*' because it fails to expose the 'dream collective' as part of the 'garbage' of ideology. In the final analysis, the dream collective is, according to Adorno, but the symptom of the escapist longing for a truly different world, thereby running the risk of turning the current one into an inescapable condition. '[D]ialectical images are generated . . . in alienated bourgeois individuals. . . . The collective consciousness was invented only to divert attention from true objectivity and its correlate, namely, alienated subjectivity'.[88] Adorno is mistaken when he thinks that Benjamin fails to distinguish between the fetishes of ideology on the one hand and the ideals that inspire an authentic fight for social justice on the other. It is in no uncertain terms that Benjamin describes modernity as a 'hell' without any prospect of progress and he is not at all implying that the dream collective is a progressive presence in history.[89] The 'elements of a classless society' that it produces are not the *goals* of our fight for social change. Benjamin considers the images of the dream collective to be of a much more fundamental importance than whatever immediate aims for action one might envision. The dream collective *neutralizes* its presence in history through 'sleep', pushing the ideal of a truly egalitarian society wholly *outside* of history by way of images that are *realities-in-themselves*. In other words, Benjamin's dream collective *does* serve as proof of the alienation of the consumer, but it simultaneously rises above it by producing images that cannot possibly be reconciled with the world in which we live. This neutralization of the sphere of history at large is urgent since our fight for social change is at risk of becoming a despairing one. Centuries of social injustice have not failed to deprive us of the hope that a classless society will one day become a historical reality. Adorno's philosophy of negation leaves no space whatsoever for such images of a truly different universe. In the 'Finale' of his *Minima Moralia* he likens 'redemption' to 'a light that is shed on the world' and discovers it as an example for a 'philosophy that can responsibly be practiced in the face of despair'.[90] Benjamin's own conception of radical change exemplifies no mere 'light on the world' that can continue to inspire our commitment to it, even 'in the face of despair'. His affirmation of true change is nihilistic to the core and it *results from* despair, albeit a despair that has thus managed to carve out a space for hope.

NOTES

1. For more on this issue, see Rainer Nägele, 'Benjamin's Ground', in *Benjamin's Ground: New Readings of Walter Benjamin*, ed. by Rainer Nägele (Detroit, MI: Wayne State University Press, 1986), 19–37.

2. The same interpretation, but less developed, can also be found in Stéphane Symons, 'Wo bist du Nachdenkliches! Sobriety and Poetic Determinability in Hölderlin and Walser', in *Benjamin, Adorno and the Experience of Literature*, ed. by Nathan Ross and Corey McCall (New York and London: Routledge, 2018), 221–34. For an excellent analysis of Benjamin's concept of *Gedichtete*, see for example, Beatrice Hanssen, '"Dichtermut" and "Blödigkeit": Two Poems by Hölderlin Interpreted by Walter Benjamin', in *MLN* 112, no. 5 (1997): 786–816.

3. For the canonical discussion of this issue, see the work of Samuel Weber, for example, his 'Benjamin's "-abilities": Mediality and Concept Formation in Benjamin's Early Writings', in *Benjamin-Studien* 1, ed. by Daniel Weidner and

Sigrid Weigel (München: Wilhelm Fink, 2008), 75–89 and 'Prehistory: Kant, Hölderlin-et cetera', in *Benjamin's -abilities* (Cambridge, MA, and London: Harvard University Press, 2008), 11–19.

4. In the following paragraph, I build upon the argumentation that has been developed by Samuel Weber in his *Benjamin's -abilities*.

5. For an excellent analysis of this issue see Bart Philipsen, '»ein gelobtes Land«. Hölderlins Nüchternheit zu Ende gelesen (mit Benjamin, Adorno, Szondi, Agamben)' in *Gattung und Geschichte. Literatur- und medienwissenschaftliche Ansätze zu einer neuen Gattungstheorie*, ed. by C. Liebrand and O. Kohns (Bielefeld: Transcript Verlag, 2012), 127–50.

6. See also Andrew Benjamin, 'The Absolute as Translatability: Working through Walter Benjamin on Language', in *Walter Benjamin and Romanticism*, ed. by Beatrice Hanssen and Andrew Benjamin (New York: Continuum, 2002), 109–22 and the chapter on 'Language' in Eli Friedlander, *Walter Benjamin: A Philosophical Portrait* (Cambridge, MA: Harvard University Press, 2012).

7. Contrast this to the statement that 'Benjamin allow[s] us to think . . . that all names keep a certain memory of the name, of the gift, because they are singular only in so far as they keep such a memory, a memory which keeps nothing, nothing but the given name which does not let itself be kept, which withdraws and is forgotten the moment it is given. . . . The "logic" of the gift is an impossible "logic": a gift which did not include forgetting would not be a gift'. In Alexander García Düttmann, *The Gift of Language: Memory and Promise in Adorno, Benjamin, Heidegger and Rosenzweig*, transl. by Arline Lyons (London: The Athlone Press, 2000), 80.

8. The essay on mechanical reproduction, moreover, makes clear that the concept of *Aufgabe* belongs in the same group as the word *Abbild*. In a famous sentence, Benjamin claims that '[e]very day the urge grows stronger to get hold of an object at close range in an image [*Bild*], or better, in an *Abbild*, a reproduction' (SW 4, 255). Like *Aufgabe*, *Abbild* consists of the combination of a prefix that indicates a move away [*Ab-/Auf-*] and a main root that suggests the possibility of a fully fledged truth revelation (the auratic *Bild* or Image/the divine *Gabe* or Gift). In line with his use of the word *Aufgabe*, Benjamin takes recourse to the term *Abbild* to describe the *distance* from supposedly eternal and absolute truths and the concomitant openness to a world that can be altered. Benjamin's philosophy of reproduction highlights that original works can be released from the pseudo-religious context that ties them to a 'cult value'. Instead of triggering a merely contemplative and absorptive response that thrives on the mistaken belief in absolute truths, the mechanical production and reproduction of art open our surroundings anew as a 'space-for-play' that can always be acted upon (see chapter 3). Only in this manner can art 'tackle the most difficult and most important tasks' and 'mobilize the masses' (SW 4, 268–69).

9. For a handful of references, see for example, his notion of 'mere life' in his essay on violence (SW 1, 251), the 'saturnine vision [that] piles up fragments ceaselessly' (O, 179), a 'conception of history that considers only shallow, causal forms' (GS I, 935) and his analysis of Paul Klee's *Angelus Novus* (SW 4, 392). For a discussion of this theme see Sigrid Weigel, *Walter Benjamin: Images, the Creaturely and the Holy*, transl. by Chadwick Smith (Stanford: Stanford University Press, 2013) and the chapter on 'Myth' in Eli Friedlander, *Walter Benjamin*. For an analysis of Benjamin's interpretation of the eternal return, see Stéphane Mosès, 'Benjamin, Nietzsche et l'idée de l'éternal retour', *Europe, revue littéraire mensuelle* 74 (804) (1996): 140–58.

10. For more on the relation between Benjamin and *Lebensphilosophie*, see my *More than Life* (2017) and Nitzan Lebovic, *The Philosophy of Life and Death: Ludwig Klages and the Rise of a Nazi Biopolitics* (New York: Palgrave MacMillan, 2013).

11. Benjamin's interpretation of Hölderlin's concept of *Denken* and spirit is the mirror-image of Heidegger's. Heidegger connects Hölderlin's concept of *Andenken* to the recovery of a formative ground that, in spite of having been forgotten, has never fully ceased to give itself. For this reason, *Andenken* ['Remembrance'] is paired with the concept of *Gedächtnis* [memory] since it is only by way of a specific type of memory that this ultimate foundation of truth can be taken up (see Martin Heidegger, 'Remembrance', in *Elucidations of Hölderlin's Poetry*, transl. by Keith Hoeller [New York: Humanity Books, 2000], 101–74). In Benjamin's account, to the contrary, Hölderlin's concept of *Denken* is disconnected from memory and indicative of an affirmation of *change*. For more on the relation between Benjamin and Heidegger's reading of Hölderlin, see Joanna Hodge, 'Sobriety, Intoxication, Hyperbology: Benjamin and Heidegger Reading Hölderlin', in *Sparks Will Fly: Benjamin and Heidegger*, ed. by Andrew Benjamin and Dimitris Vardoulakis (Albany: SUNY Press, 2015), 189–215.

12. For interesting readings of the 'Theological-Political Fragment', singling out the issue of the universality of transience, see for example, the essays by Annika Thiem ('Benjamin's Messianic Metaphysics of Transience'), Peter Fenves ('Completion Instead of Revelation: Toward the "Theological-Political Fragment"') and Judith Butler ('One Time Traverses Another: Benjamin's "Theological-Political Fragment"'), all included in *Walter Benjamin and Theology*, ed. by Colby Dickinson and Stéphane Symons (New York: Fordham University Press, 2016).

13. Gilles Deleuze, *Nietzsche and Philosophy*, transl. by Hugh Tomlinson (New York: Columbia University Press, 2006), 54.
14. Ibid., 61.
15. Ibid., 64–65.
16. Ibid., 54.
17. Ibid., 66.
18. Ibid., 68.
19. Ibid., 69.
20. Ibid.
21. Ibid.
22. Nietzsche, quoted on ibid., 70. The original passages can be found in Gilles Deleuze, *Nietzsche et la philosophie* (Paris: Presses Universitaires de France, 1983), 79.
23. Gilles Deleuze, *Nietzsche and Philosophy*, 71.
24. Ibid., 70.
25. Ibid.
26. Ibid.
27. Ibid., 71. The original passages can be found in Gilles Deleuze, *Nietzsche et la philosophie*, 81.
28. On the issue of Benjamin's nihilism, see for example, Mauro Ponzi's *Nietzsche's Nihilism in Walter Benjamin* (Cham: Palgrave MacMillan, 2017), esp. chapter 2 and Irving Wohlfahrt, 'Nihilismus kontra Nihilismus. Walter Benjamin's "Weltpolitik" aus heutiger Sicht', in *Theologie und Politik. Walter Benjamin, ein Paradigma der Moderne*, ed. Bernd Witte and Mauro Ponzi (Berlin: Erich Schmidt Verlag, 2005), 107–36. Neither of these authors conceptualizes the 'complete' nihilism that my reading focuses on, nor do they thematize the issue of forgetting from this perspective. Ponzi, however, does come close to the topic of a *transmuted*, creative nihilism in his discussion of the connection between

Benjamin and Löwith (pp. 83–85). In his extensive analysis of Nietzsche's influence on Benjamin, James McFarland, as well, draws attention to the parallels between Benjamin's nihilism and Löwith's concept of a 'willed destruction', while simultaneously noting that 'the true value of Löwith's book for Benjamin lies less in its interpretation than in the extensive quotations from Nietzsche's own work that it contains', in James McFarland, *Constellation. Friedrich Nietzsche and Walter Benjamin in the Now-Time of History* (New York: Fordham University Press, 2013), 236.

29. See Irving Wohlfarth, 'No-Man's Land: On Walter Benjamin's "Destructive Character"', *Diacritics* 8 (2) (1978), 47–65.

30. In his *Notebooks for an Ethics*, Jean-Paul Sartre takes issue with the type of all-encompassing destruction that Benjamin describes as a productive force. For Sartre, too, violence is characterized by a propensity to become all-consuming. The violent man 'wants to be pure, universal and destructive freedom, that is, the ruin of the world, the disappearance of being' (p. 176). In such forms of violence, 'I am at the origin of the nothingness of the world, I am the Anticreator, I dream of a continuous destruction. . . . It is to be a pure nihilating power, pure freedom. Violence is unconditioned affirmation of freedom' (p. 175). Like Benjamin, Sartre emphasizes that such forms of violence can no longer be described with phenomenological categories, since they seek to annul the intentionality of consciousness and being-in-the-world. 'The universe is no longer a means but the dense and inessential obstacle between the violent man and the object of his desire. . . . Indeed, violence, being destructive, cannot *produce* an object. It can only remove the obstacles that conceal it' (p. 174). In contrast to Benjamin, Sartre *opposes* this destructive desire to be 'purely free' to genuine freedom. The relentless longing to be free that marks extreme violence is for Sartre but a token of a *lack* of freedom and creativity. For Sartre, it is a sign of 'bad faith' because it bespeaks an inability to come to terms with the facticity of human existence (p. 175). In Jean-Paul Sartre, *Notebooks for an Ethics*, transl. by David Pellauer (Chicago: The University of Chicago Press, 1992).

31. In the *Passagen-Werk*, for instance, Benjamin associates the eternal return with a hellish repetition-without-differentiation and a mythic totality that makes historical novelty impossible. 'On eternal recurrence: "The great thought as a Medusa head: all features of the world become motionless, a frozen death throe"' (AP, 115).

32. Gershom Scholem, 'Toward an Understanding of the Messianic Idea', in *The Messianic Idea in Judaism and Other Essays on Jewish Spirituality* (New York: Schocken Books, 1995), 14.

33. Ibid., 11.

34. Scholem, 'Redemption Through Sin', in *The Messianic Idea in Judaism and Other Essays on Jewish Spirituality*, 130. For the relation between Scholem and Benjamin, see Eric Jacobson, *Metaphysics of the Profane: The Political Theology of Walter Benjamin and Gershom Scholem* (New York: Columbia University Press, 2003) and Stéphane Mosès, *The Angel of History: Rosenzweig, Benjamin, Scholem*, transl. by Barbara Harshav (Stanford, CA: Stanford University Press, 2009). While both emphasize the paradoxical nature of Benjamin and Scholem's messianism (as a force of affirmation), neither Jacobson nor Mosès opposes Benjamin and Scholem's views in the manner presented here (cf. infra).

35. Scholem, 'Redemption Through Sin', 110.

36. Ibidem., 78 and 94.

37. Ibidem., 110.

38. The reference to Scholem's 'dialectics' comes from Benjamin Lazier (who does not, however, oppose this stance to Benjamin's), in Benjamin Lazier, *God*

Interrupted: Heresy and the European Imagination between the World Wars (Princeton, NJ: Princeton University Press, 2008), 160.

39. The reference to 'return to immanence' comes from Willem Styfhals; see his *No Spiritual Investment in the World: Gnosticism and Postwar German Philosophy* (Ithaca, NY: Cornell University Press, 2019). I thank Willem Styfhals for his suggestions, ideas and feedback on Scholem and the relation between Scholem and Benjamin.

40. Scholem in a letter to Benjamin on 1 August 1931, quoted in Scholem, *Walter Benjamin: The Story of a Friendship*, transl. by Harry Zohn (New York: Schocken Books, 1981), 171. For more on Scholem's reading of Kafka, see Stéphane Mosès, 'Gershom Scholem's Reading of Kafka: Literary Criticism and Kabbalah', *New German Critique* 77 (1999): 149–67 and chapter 8 of his *The Angel of History: Rosenzweig, Benjamin, Scholem*. For more on the comparison between Scholem and Benjamin's interpretation of Kafka, see Robert Alter, *Necessary Angels: Tradition and Modernity in Kafka, Benjamin, and Scholem* (Cambridge, MA: Harvard University Press, 1991). None of the texts I have found develop the opposition that I focus on.

41. Scholem in a letter to Benjamin on 20 September 1934, quoted in *The Correspondence of Walter Benjamin and Gershom Scholem 1932–1940*, ed. by Gershom Scholem, transl. by Gary Smith and Andre Lefevere (New York: Schocken Books, 1989), 142.

42. Scholem, *Walter Benjamin*, 170–71.

43. This concept of a messianic intervention that, in the words of Werner Hamacher, 'changes the relations of space and of time . . . the relation called "coming"' has become a topos in post-war, continental thought. It belongs to the most important themes in the works of Jacques Derrida, Jean-Luc Nancy and Giorgio Agamben. For an interesting discussion of this theme, see the collection of essays in *Messianic Thought Outside Theology*, ed. by Anna Glazova and Paul North (New York: Fordham University Press, 2014). The quotation comes from an essay by Werner Hamacher that has been published in this volume, 'Messianic Not', 221.

44. Gilles Deleuze, *Difference and Repetition*, transl. by Paul Patton (London and New York: Continuum, 1997), 82. The original formulation can be found in Gilles Deleuze, *Différence et Répétition* (Paris: Presses Universitaires de France, 2011), 111. For more on Bergson and Deleuze's concept of a 'pure past' and the link with memory see for example, Alia Al-Saji, 'The memory of another past: Bergson, Deleuze and a new theory of time', in *Continental Philosophy Review* 37 (2) (2004): 203–39. For an analysis and overview of Deleuze's 'syntheses of time' see David Lapoujade, *Aberrant Movements: The Philosophy of Gilles Deleuze*, transl. by Joshua David Jordan (South Pasadena, CA: Semiotext(e), 2017), especially chapter 3 and Henry Somers-Hall, *Deleuze's Difference and Repetition* (Edinburgh: Edinburgh University Press, 2013), especially chapter 2.

45. Gilles Deleuze, *Difference and Repetition*, 85.

46. See also the following statement in ibidem., 102: 'The passing present which bears itself away has never been better opposed to the pure past which perpetually differs from itself and whose universal mobility and universal ubiquity cause the present to pass'. For more on Bergson's concept of a 'pure past', see chapter 2.

47. Ibidem., 84.

48. For more on Deleuze's concept of thought, see Jonathan Sholl, 'Thought and Repetition in Bergson and Deleuze', in *Deleuze Studies* 6 (4) (2012): 544–63. The relation between Deleuze's analyses of memory and thought, and the concomitant opposition between a Bergsonian and a Nietzschean framework is

developed in Nathan Widder, 'Deleuze on Bergsonian Duration and Nietzsche's "Eternal Return"', in *Time and History in Deleuze and Serres*, ed. by Bernd Herzogenrath (London and New York: Continuum, 2012), 127–46. For more on Deleuze's concept of event, see François Zourabichvili, *Deleuze: A Philosophy of the Event*, ed. by Gregg Lambert and Daniel W. Smith, transl. by Kieran Aarons (Edinburgh: Edinburgh University Press, 2012), 33–135.

49. Gilles Deleuze, *Difference and Repetition*, 88.
50. Ibid., 67.
51. Ibid., 111.
52. Ibid., 91.
53. Ibid., 90. The original phrasing can be found in Gilles Deleuze, *Différence et Répétition*, 122.
54. Gilles Deleuze, *Cinema 2. The Time-Image*, transl. by Hugh Tomlinson and Robert Galeta (London: The Athlone Press, 1989), 165.
55. Ibid., 167–68. The original passages can be found in Gilles Deleuze, *Cinéma 2. L'image-temps* (Paris: Les Éditions de Minuit, 1985), 218.
56. Gilles Deleuze, *Cinema 2*, 167.
57. Ibid., 167 (French: p. 218).
58. Ibid., 168 (translation modified; French: p. 219).
59. Ibid.
60. Ibid., 170.
61. Ibid., 171 (French: p. 223).
62. For the references to *effondrement* in the original text, see pp. 216 and 218.
63. Gilles Deleuze, *Cinema 2*, 171.
64. Ibid., 171.
65. Ibid., 172 (French: pp. 222–23).
66. It should be noted, however, that on at least one occasion Benjamin *does* associate the possibility that the 'past is seized [*die Vergangenheit festzuhalten*]' with an 'appropriati[on] of [a] memory [*sich einer Erinnerung bemächtigen*]' (SW 4, 390–1; GS I, 695). In the secondary literature, this has led to an emphasis on memory that, in my reading, contradicts Benjamin's recurrent claims about the universality and inevitability of transience. See, for example, Susan Buck-Morss's claim that 'collective imagination mobilizes its powers for a revolutionary break from the recent past by evoking a cultural memory reservoir of myths and utopian symbols from a more distant ur-past' in *Dialectics of Seeing: Walter Benjamin and the Arcades Project* (Cambridge, MA, and London: The MIT Press, 1989), 116. Buck-Morss does mitigate this reference to the importance of memory by insisting that 'Benjamin is not maintaining that the contents of past myths provide a blueprint for the future. . . . Nowhere in his writings do the ur-images have a status other than that of dream symbol' (ibidem., 116). For the same argument, see her 'The Flâneur, the Sandwichman and the Whore: The Politics of Loitering', in *Walter Benjamin and The Arcades Project*, ed. by Beatrice Hanssen (London and New York: Continuum, 2006), for example, p. 61. Similarly, the contributions of Barbara Johnson, Max Pensky, Esther Leslie and Elissa Marder in *Walter Benjamin and The Arcades Project* connect Benjamin's wish images to the faculty of memory.

67. In his book on *The Unforgettable and the Unhoped For*, Jean-Louis Chrétien, as well, refuses to simply oppose the unforgettable to forgetting, since the unforgettable does not contradict but expresses the 'loss' that is characteristic to forgetting. Like Benjamin, Chrétien uses the unforgettable to conceptualize the possibility of a future that lies 'beyond [the] possibilities [of life]' (p. 96) and a hope that 'transcends all our expectations' (p. 105). However, unlike Benjamin, Chrétien makes the unforgettable and the unhoped for dependent on a

'ground', a 'gift' and an 'encounter' with an 'excessive' and 'inaccessible' presence (pp. 74–75, 32–38, 112, 105). For this reason, Chrétien's unforgettable is one with the 'immemorial' (pp. 1–40). In a revelatory discussion of Augustine, Chrétien states that the unforgettable 'is what can neither be totally lost nor totally abandoned, in our flight and in our refusal' (p. 89). For Benjamin, however, the loss that results from forgetting is so complete that it cannot in any way be said to 'serve memory and permit it to fulfill itself' (Chrétien on p. 92). The unforgettable is not at all 'what does not cease to grasp us and from which we cannot withdraw' (Chrétien on p. 90). The unforgettable serves Benjamin to conceptualize a forgetting that is so complete that it overcomes itself, without thereby bespeaking a 'ground', 'gift', 'encounter' or 'immemorial' presence. Benjamin's concept of the unforgettable revolves around the capacity to *suspend* the relation with the surrounding world and *neutralize* the belief in foundational truths and immemorial forces (see chapter 2). The quotations are from Jean-Louis Chrétien, *The Unforgettable and the Unhoped For*, transl. by Jeffrey Bloechl (New York: Fordham University Press, 2002).

68. Theodor W. Adorno, *Negative Dialectics*, transl. by E. B. Ashton (London and New York: Continuum, 2007), xix.

69. Theodor W. Adorno, *Lectures on Negative Dialectics: Fragments of a Lecture Course 1965/1966*, ed. by Rolf Tiedemann, transl. by Rodney Livingstone (Cambridge: Polity Press, 2008), 14.

70. Ibid., 15.
71. Ibid., 16.
72. Ibid., 18.
73. Ibid., 20.

74. For an illuminating overview of the concepts 'primacy of the object' and 'disenchantment of the concept' see chapter 4 on *Negative Dialectics* in Peter E. Gordon, *Adorno and Existence* (Cambridge, MA, and London: Harvard University Press, 2016).

75. Theodor W. Adorno, *Lectures on Negative Dialectics*, 18.
76. Ibid., 20.
77. Theodor W. Adorno, *Negative Dialectics*, 363.

78. For a clearly-written and revealing overview of the relation between Scholem and Adorno, see Peter E. Gordon, 'The Odd Couple', *The Nation*, 9 June 2016.

79. Theodor W. Adorno, *Negative Dialectics*, 365.
80. Ibid., 365.
81. Ibid., 364.
82. Ibid., 367.
83. Ibid., 361.

84. Gilles Deleuze, *Negotiations 1972–1990*, transl. by Martin Joughin (New York: Columbia University Press, 1997), 100.

85. Benjamin in a letter to Gershom Scholem on 9 August 1935 in Walter Benjamin, *Gesammelte Briefe. Band V. 1935–1937*, ed. by Christoph Gödde and Henri Lonitz (Frankfurt am Main: Suhrkamp, 1999), 138.

86. See also my 'In Praise of Shadows. Commemorative Images and the Atomic Bomb', in *Image and Narrative* 14 (1) (2013): 19–34.

87. Theodor W. Adorno, *Negative Dialectics*, 367.

88. Theodor W. Adorno in a letter to Benjamin on 2 August 1935 in *The Correspondence of Walter Benjamin 1910–1940*, ed. by Gershom Scholem and Theodor W. Adorno, transl. by Manfred R. Jacobson and Evelyn M. Jacobson (Chicago and London: The University of Chicago Press, 1994), 495–97. See also the important chapters 9–11 in Susan Buck-Morss, *The Origin of Negative Dialec-*

tics. Theodor W. Adorno, Walter Benjamin, and The Frankfurt Institute (New York: The Free Press, 1977).

89. For more on this issue of 'hell', see Esther Leslie and Max Pensky's contributions to the collection of essays *Walter Benjamin and The Arcades Project* and Susan Buck-Morss, *Dialectics of Seeing*, pp. 96–108 and 186–87.

90. Theodor Adorno, *Minima Moralia: Reflections on a Damaged Life*, transl. by E. F. N. Jephcott (London and New York: Verso, 2005), 247. See also Giorgio Agamben's analysis of this passage as an instance of 'as-if' thinking, in Giorgio Agamben, *The Time that Remains: A Commentary on the Letter to the Romans*, transl. by Patricia Dailey (Stanford, CA: Stanford University Press, 2005), 35–43.

TWO

What Is the Immemorial? And How Can We Make It Go Away?

'There will no longer be any more reason to say that the past effaces itself as soon as perceived than there is to suppose that material objects cease to exist when we cease to perceive them', writes Bergson in a key passage in *Matter and Memory* (1896), a book that Benjamin called 'monumental' (SW 4, 314).[1] In Bergson's view, remembering a previous occurrence requires that we 'truly mov[e] in the past' and thereby enter a realm that is ontologically distinct from the present.[2] The past is believed to live on as 'pure memory' and, in this 'virtual' state, to differ essentially from any present moment.[3] Unlike perception and consciousness, pure memory does not meet the outside world as a stimulus for possible activity since it is of no immediate use in preparing the body's response to the surrounding world.[4]

Because the pure or virtual past has never itself been summoned by the present, various authors, including Merleau-Ponty, Levinas and Deleuze, have called it 'immemorial'.[5] Therefore, the past around which this chapter revolves refers to a moment that has always already been forgotten and not to an empirical moment that has ever been 'lived'. As we have seen in the previous chapter, Bergson, for instance, believes a dimension of past-ness to always already accompany each present moment as 'the shadow [that] falls beside the body' or the 'image reflected in the mirror'.[6] '[T]he formation of the memory', he claims, 'is never posterior to the formation of perception: it is contemporaneous with it'.[7] The immemorial past cannot indeed be considered an object of conscious recollection or representation and even deserves to be termed 'impossible'.[8] Such a past is not a mere copy or *after*image of the present and, instead of merely replacing a fleeting present, it is marked by spontaneous survival, change and endurance.[9]

Though it is clear that Benjamin's reading of Bergson is tendentious and incomplete, he takes him to task for projecting the preserving capacities of memory outside of the human being's realm of control. Benjamin sharply condemns the idea that conservation is inscribed within the very nature of time. However strange it may sound, Benjamin criticises Bergson's concept of continuous change and variation (duration) for being too much wedded to the belief that there is an *unchanging* and *eternal* principle that streamlines the universe at large. In Benjamin's view, in treating the very principle of change as an unchanging entity (the *élan vital* as an ontological given), Bergson has jumped over history pure and proper and entered the murky ground of metaphysical essences and eternal presences. 'Bergson in his conception of durée has become ... estranged from history' (SW 4, 336). In spite of Bergson's focus on irreducible alteration and renewal, Benjamin criticizes his inability to consider transience as the most fundamental characteristic of life. Quoting from Horkheimer's essay on Bergson and time (most likely Benjamin's main source in dealing with Bergson's ideas), Benjamin states that 'Bergson the metaphysician suppresses death' and thereby suggests that he is incapable of coming to terms with a simple fact that is nevertheless of crucial importance to Benjamin's own philosophy: that the principle of life cannot be understood without taking into account an equally fundamental principle of obliteration. '[T]he durée from which death has been eliminated has the bad infinity of an ornament' (SW 4, 336).

The basic notion of an enduring past that is irreducible to any lived present is not only found in the vitalism of Bergson but also in the writings of some of the most influential authors of the first part of the twentieth century. In the first part of this chapter we turn to Sigmund Freud and Martin Heidegger who inserted the concept of an immemorial past into philosophical systems that were very different from Bergson's vitalism. Their essays were written around the time when Benjamin was thinking through his philosophy of history. Still, in all its various forms, be it inspired by vitalism, psychoanalysis or ontology, the emphasis on the past's duration is in conflict with Benjamin's focus on transience and productive forgetting. A philosophy of time that builds on the concept of survival is at odds with the experience of a 'total' and 'eternal' 'passing-away' that is nonetheless potentially creative.

The difference between Bergson, Freud and Heidegger's focus on duration and Benjamin's philosophy of transience is therefore the one that Nietzsche already highlighted in his rendition of a conversation between a human being and an animal.[10] The turn to duration appeals to the specifically human capacity to remember that one forgets but it cannot come to terms with the ability to forget forgetting itself. Consequently, philosophies of duration run the risk of reducing forgetting to a phenomenon that is of secondary importance. Their focus on the survival of the past presupposes that forgetting is a process that is but serviceable to the powers of memory. '[W]e no longer have to explain the preservation of the past', Bergson already noted, 'but rather its apparent abolition. We shall no longer have to account for remembering, but for forgetting'.[11] Rather than opposing memory and forgetting, the emphasis on duration takes the faculty of memory for granted and understands forgetting as the paradoxical *condition* of memory. It is precisely because the faculty of memory does not allow *all* past experiences to resurface that Bergson introduced the idea that the past is an immemorial horizon that makes the present intelligible.[12] Only in such 'forgotten' form can the past retain the potential to assist our practical needs without determining us, unlike the present which does require an immediate response on our part.

Bergson denies the existence of an unconsciousness that truly *acts*, but the concept of a forgotten past that endures rather than disappears can also be uncovered in Freud's 'psychopathology of everyday life'. Freud, as well, makes an important distinction between the phenomenon of forgetting and a process of mere disappearance. In his view, forgetting is indicative of a repression that enables the past to move beyond the conscious registration of a lived present. The 'mechanism of forgetting' refers first and foremost to a 'mechanism of names escaping the memory, of being *temporarily* forgotten' and this on account of 'the interference with the intended reproduction of the name by an alien train of thought which is not at the time conscious'.[13] When we think we have forgotten a name, word or sets of words, this most often involves the presence of mental obstacles that unconsciously prevent the work of recollection to perform its task. In other words, Freud, as well, separates the analysis of forgetting from the issue of transience and associates it instead with an intricate work of unconscious preservation and retention. In my analysis of Freud's writings, I will consider how this prioritization of the powers of memory over forgetting rests on assumptions about the presence of an immemorial past in the deeper strata of our psyche. On account of this emphasis on endurance and repetition rather than impermanence and transience, Freud is neither interested in nor capable of understanding how this persistent afterlife of an immemorial past can be *overcome*. Even his much-debated concept of the death-drive is, as we will see, not at all to be confused with Benjamin's conception of a complete and productive nihilism that 'strive[s] for . . . an eternal and total passing away'.

In Heidegger's view an ontological memory, the immemorial ground of Being as such, will always remain more foundational than whatever type of forgetfulness, including the 'forgottenness of Being' that plays such an important role in his writings. For Heidegger, Being is marked by an ontological survival that resists our conscious efforts at recollection and representation. Here, as well, a specific type of forgetting conditions the very work of memory: the fundamental concealedness of truth (λήθη) belongs to the heart of truth itself (truth as unconcealedness or ἀλήθεια). Heidegger's prioritization of memory over forgetting results in a similar inability to understand what nihilism truly is. Incapable of conceptualizing a nihilism that is *complete*, Heidegger, as well, shrinks back at the possibility that the affirmation of transience and impermanence can result in a productive stance.

'This question has today been forgotten' are the famous opening words of *Being and Time* (1927), Heidegger's study of the nature of Being and the existence of man that went on to become a foundational text for twentieth-century metaphysics.[14] The question that in Heidegger's view has been forgotten is, as is well-known, the very question of Being as such from which all his other concerns inevitably take their cue. Our assumption in the first part of this chapter, however, will be that what has been largely forgotten by thinkers such as Bergson, Freud and Heidegger himself, is the very issue of forgetting. In the second part of this chapter we will therefore turn to Benjamin's interpretation of Baudelaire and Proust. On first view, these readings are indebted to the concept of a 'deep' or 'true' experience [*Erfahrung*] that preserves an immemorial past. Still, I will argue that Benjamin's claim that the human faculties of memory always bear the stamp of history and society introduces an important shift in the philosophical explorations of the so-called pure past. Ultimately of more importance than his concept of 'deep' or 'true' experience, the 'about-turn' that is fashioned by allegory motivates Benjamin to take the literary expression of transience and forgetting seriously as a productive phenomenon.

FREUD CONTRA TRANSIENCE

'We hold the wax under our perceptions and thoughts and take a stamp from them', Plato wrote in explanation of the human faculty of memory.[15] Aristotle added: 'The process of movement [sensory stimulation] involved in the act of perception stamps in, as it were, a sort of impression of the percept, just as persons do who make an impression with a seal'.[16] Almost twenty-five hundred years after both Plato and Aristotle made use of the image of a wax block and a seal to understand the work of recollection and memory, it is picked up by Freud in a discussion of the so-called mystic writing pad (1925). In Freud's reading, this small device, which consists of a covering sheet made out of celluloid and an underlying wax slab that is inserted directly underneath it, illustrates the interaction between the two main dimensions of the human psyche, consciousness and the unconscious. At first sight, Freud's example of the mystic writing pad does not differ all that much from Plato and Aristotle's wax block and seal: an experience is inscribed on a surface and thereby leaves a mark that (unconsciously) survives after the experience itself has disappeared. However, Freud's analysis of the mystic writing pad introduces ideas on memory and forgetting that cannot at all be identified with the classical view of Plato and Aristotle. In contrast to Plato's wax block and Aristotle's seal, there is no direct contact between the initial experience received by the covering sheet and the final mark left behind on the wax slab, the stylus never even directly touching the pad's bottom layer. As a consequence, Freud is most of all fascinated with the mystic writing pad's combination of two capacities that are usually believed to be mutually exclusive: the celluloid sheet is a 'receptive surface that can be used over and over again' (like a slate) while the wax slab preserves the 'permanent traces of what has been written' (like an ordinary paper pad).[17] Freud underscores that the receptive surface and the preserving material of the mystic writing pad operate independently. The mystic writing pad combines the capacities for receiving and preserving *'by dividing them between two separate but interrelated component parts or systems.* But this is precisely the way in which . . . our mental apparatus performs its perceptual function'.[18] Freud therefore understands consciousness as a faculty of mere reception, incapable of preserving anything and the unconscious, by contrast, as a faculty of mere preservation, incapable of directly receiving whatever type of external stimulation. Consciousness is described as a 'protective shield against stimuli' because it cannot retain the impressions it receives and thereby prevents them from having an effect on the deeper strata of our psyche. The unconscious, on the other hand, is deemed too fragile to be directly exposed to the outside world. As a mere reservoir of preservation, it requires 'a protective sheath . . . to keep off injurious effects from without'.[19]

That the faculties of reception and preservation work independently from each other has an important consequence: the memories that are retained in the unconscious need to be considered as more than sheer 'traces' of the experiences that are consciously received. Because the mind's receiving and preserving faculties work independently from each other, memories can take on meanings that were not at all part of the initial experience. Memories are not merely informed by the experiences in which they originated but also by the unconscious interaction with other memories that are seemingly unrelated to them. This insight that memories continue to be operated upon after their moment of imprint, is, of course, of key importance to the psychoanalytic investigation of how people can recollect things that do not correspond to a past event. In his account of the 'Rat Man' case, for instance, Freud notes 'that people's "childhood memories" are only consolidated at a later period, usually at the age of puberty, and that this involves a complicated process of remodeling, analogous in every way to the process by which a nation constructs legends about its early history'.[20] Similar instances of false memories are considered in Freud's essay on screen-memories, in his analysis of the case of Emma in 'Project for a Scientific Psychology'; in the relation between screen-memories and dreams in 'Remembering, Repeating and Working-Through'; in the comparison between screen-memories and the fetish in the 1920 version of 'Three Essays on the Theory of Sexuality'; and in 'Leonardo da Vinci and a Memory of his Childhood', where memory serves to cover up a fantasy of the mother with a penis. These false memories make palpable that our past can never be reduced to the present it once was. While living on in our unconscious, memories gain an extraordinary capacity of endurance. Retained in an unconscious and 'immemorial' reservoir that always also includes the memories of so many other experiences and events, our memories are not merely the outcome of the initial experience but, like the mystic writing pad's wax slab, they are ceaselessly overwritten.

Freud's insight that our mind's receiving and preserving faculties work independently results in the view that forgetting should not at all be considered a process that runs counter to memory. On account of the protective function of consciousness, an excitation that is wholly absorbed by our conscious faculties is incapable of reaching the deeper layers of memory: '[T]he excitatory process becomes conscious in the system Cs. but leaves no permanent trace behind there . . . [C]onsciousness *arises instead of a memory-trace*'.[21] The reason why an experience can continue to live on after the moment of its initial taking place is therefore none other than that it has at least partly bypassed the grasp of consciousness: it is only *because* an experience partially eludes consciousness that it can be retained. The very existence of a memory-mark in the unconscious, as a consequence, indicates that an experience has first undergone a process of forgetting. Freud's update of Plato's and Aristotle's metaphor of wax blocks and seals thus includes a crucial modification of their views. Both Plato and Aristotle underscore that all memory involves loss, since the presence of a memory-trace simultaneously signals that the initial experience is no longer there. Memory, writes Aristotle, is entwined with 'a time elapsed' and 'the consciousness of formerly'.[22] On a more fundamental level, however, forgetting is reduced to no more than the antithesis of memory. 'Whatever is impressed upon the wax we remember and know so long as the image remains in the wax', Plato has Socrates say, 'whatever is obliterated or cannot be impressed, we forget and do not know'.[23] In this classical interpretation of forgetting, even the memory trace of the absent past is believed to have disappeared, thereby resulting in what can be called a *double* absence. Freud's alternative view of forgetting, to the contrary, does not testify to such a twofold loss (the loss of the trace of a lost experience) but to the possibility of an unsuspected *presence*. In Freud's view, the unconscious knows no time and no negation, only 'contents, cathected with greater or lesser strength'.[24] As Ricoeur puts it, a sharp distinction should be made between a 'forgetting through the erasing of traces' (the classical view) and a 'backup forgetting, a sort of forgetting kept in reserve (*oubli de réserve*)'.[25] This latter type of forgetting evidences the very 'persistence of traces'.[26] Rather than epitomizing transience, the forgetting that in Freud's view rules over the unconscious is believed to have the capacity to grant an initial experience an unsuspected afterlife. Such an alternative type of forgetting is not at all a powerless negation of memory but it becomes its very condition. In Freud's paradigm, forgetting is not so much a sign of lack as an indication of a 'surplus' of experience that survives beyond the conscious registration of a present moment.

In spite of these differences with Plato and Aristotle's views on memory and forgetting, Freud's alternative view reinstalls the age-old primacy of duration and repetition over transience. For Freud, an experience that manages to bypass consciousness and thus reach the deeper strata of memory is, by that very token, forgotten but it is not at all immune to the faculty of recollection. This is the exact place where, in Freud's view, the metaphor of the mystic writing pad reaches its limit since 'once the writing has been erased, the Mystic Pad cannot "reproduce" it from within [while] our memory could accomplish that'.[27] Psychoanalytic therapy does indeed rest on the belief that the forgotten contents of memory can nonetheless be brought back to our consciousness by way of a mechanism such as free association or transference. While Freud at times argues that these very therapeutic practices do ultimately aim for a type of forgetting, by the time he developed his ideas on the mystic writing pad an important transition in his thought had set in. In one of his most well-known texts, 'Beyond the Pleasure Principle' (1920), which was written five years before the essay on the mystic writing pad, Freud describes how difficult it is for a therapist to make use of the patient's powers of recollection as an instrument to loosen up the connection with the past.[28] These difficulties to achieve a therapeutic forgetting can partly be explained by the fact that the process of repression can grant memories an almost ineradicable life in our unconscious. What is repressed triggers an unconscious compulsion to repetition.[29] Most important to Freud, however, is that this obstacle against the forgetting of certain experiences cannot only be accounted for by the *external* counterforce of repression since it suggests the presence of something that endures *within* the drive itself. Freud expresses his astonishment about certain phases in the therapeutic process when patients behave like 'children' and do not tire to repeat the same stories of their youth in a manner that has no beneficial impact whatsoever.[30] Observations such as these necessitate Freud to reconsider his earlier views on the nature of the drive in an important manner. Freud's earlier concept of the drive revolved around the idea that it triggers certain actions that discharge the unpleasant tension that is built up by excitation. In early texts, such as his 'Project for a Scientific Psychology' (1895), *The Interpretation of Dreams* or 'The Two Principles of Mental Functioning' (1911),

Freud discovered the pleasure principle (or, in *The Interpretation of Dreams*, the 'unpleasure principle') as the most important dynamic that animates the drive: '[U]nder the dominance of the pleasure principle, motor discharge [serves] as a means of unburdening the mental apparatus of accretions of stimuli'.[31] This led to the view that the nature of the drive is flexible and plastic, assisting the organism in making both internal and external excitation go away as fast as possible. Drives can seek out the most different aims and objects, the sole criterion being that these activities and objects are of use in unburdening the organism.[32] However, '[i]n the case of a person in analysis . . . the compulsion to repeat the events of his childhood in the transference evidently disregards the pleasure principle in every way. . . . This same compulsion to repeat frequently meets us as an obstacle to our treatment when at the end of an analysis we try to induce the patient to detach himself completely from his physician'.[33] The concept of a repetition that does not in any way serve the pleasure principle to discharge unpleasant tension 'strikes [Freud] as strange because [he] [had] become used to see in [drives] a factor impelling towards change and development'.[34] In 'Beyond the Pleasure Principle', Freud therefore develops a new theory of the drive that replaces this focus on the drive's propensity to change with an emphasis on its *inability* to transform itself: '[W]e are now asked to recognize in [drives] the precise contrary—an expression of the *conservative* nature of living substance'.[35] Drives, in other words, are not characterized by flexibility and plasticity but by endurance and a *resistance* to change.

In 'Beyond the Pleasure Principle' this exploration of the drive's inherent refusal to change leads to the shift from an understanding of the drive as a Bergsonian *élan vital* to the concept of a death drive. In the final lines of the essay, Freud even goes as far to suggest that '[t]he pleasure principle seems actually to serve the death drives'.[36] It would be a mistake to consider this shift towards the death drive as evidence for an increased interest in the phenomenon of transience. It does not entail a rejection of the emphasis on endurance and memory since the death drive is not at all an expression of the longing for impermanence, let alone of the type of 'total' and 'eternal transience' that was focused on in the previous chapter. In spite of the confusing term, the death drive does not actively seek annihilation. The death drive describes the 'daemonic' presence of something that does not really want to live, but not a striving towards death (Moyaert).[37] It is marked by a tendency 'to restore an earlier state of things which the living entity has been obliged to abandon under the pressure of external forces; it is . . . the expression of the inertia inherent in organic life'.[38] The death drive is the foremost expression of what Freud in the very *in*aptly titled essay 'On Transience', has called the drive's 'cling[ing] to its objects'.[39] Rather than aiming for a complete detachment or passing-away, the death drive stubbornly *counters* the transience that is nonetheless built into the temporal realm. The death drive indicates a deceleration that is at work within all drives and, instead of moving along with the passage of time, or even trying to speed it up, it goes *against* temporal succession. 'The elementary living entity would from its very beginning have had no wish to change; if conditions remained the same, it would do no more than constantly repeat the same course of life'.[40] Freud dismisses the view that death is external to life and that it would only occur after it: the death drive exposes death as an immemorial presence within life, pre-existing the generation of life. As an irreducible 'inertia' that continues to weigh down any supposed power of life, the death drive is an obstacle for any genuine transformation.

Since Freud's concept of the death drive signals the 'conservative nature of living substance' and 'an inertia inherent in organic life', it is at odds with the complete nihilism that I focused on in the previous chapter. Not surprisingly, in spite of the large number of pages that Freud devotes to issues like the death drive, aggression, violence, war, melancholy and mourning, only one reference to the concept of nihilism can be found in the entirety of his writings.[41] Freud's lack of interest in the issue of nihilism can be explained by the fact that his concept of death drive indicates a refusal to disappear rather than a will to annihilate. In fact, Freud's prioritisation of forces of endurance and repetition over the rhythm of transience and impermanence has such far-reaching consequences that the concept of the death drive even serves him as an antidote *against* the destructive and disintegrating dynamic of complete nihilism. Deleuze highlights that Freud's concept of the death drive falls short in illuminating the principle of genuine change and transformation that, though inseparable of life, deserves to be called Thanatos. In Freud's view of the death drive, repetition is not understood as such a universal dynamic of differentiation since it is tamed into the 'bare and brute power *behind* the disguises, the latter affecting it only *secondarily*, like so many variations'.[42] Deleuze's own view, to the contrary, is much closer to Benjamin's since death embodies in the view of both thinkers a force of transformation that is relentless and capable of uprooting everything that is. Both Deleuze and Benjamin associate death with a repetition that is not merely a 'variation' of something that remains the same. 'Death', writes Deleuze, 'does not appear in the objective model of an indifferent inanimate matter to which the living would "return"'.[43] Rather than being marked by 'conservation' or 'inertia', Deleuze's own concept of death exposes a force of repetition that 'is woven from disguise and displacement, without any existence apart from these constitutive elements'.[44] As we have seen in the previous chapter, such a principle of universal transience and groundlessness is inseparable from an empty and merely formal time. Deleuze takes recourse to the same vocabulary when he states that 'death ... is not a material state; on the contrary, having renounced all matter, it corresponds to a pure form—the empty form of time'.[45] Freud's emphasis on 'inertia' and 'conservation' results in an unwillingness to truly affirm such an empty and merely formal time. This prevents him from taking the possibility of a complete and productive nihilism seriously and brings him instead to 'reduce death to negation'.[46]

The Belgian philosopher Paul Moyaert helps us to further understand why Freud's concept of the death drive is indeed deployed as a defense against the threat of nihilism and not as its expression. By injecting an immemorial lifelessness within the heart of the drive itself, Moyaert argues, Freud stresses that the capacities of individuals to perfect themselves and construct pliable and harmonious identities are limited: the mental life of human beings cannot ever be fully released from elements that are unproductive, closing them off from a dynamic interaction with the outside world and other people. For Freud, however, these inert and inflexible elements are not forces of fragmentation since they make genuine individuation *possible*. 'It is certain that much of the ego is itself unconscious, and notably what we may describe as its nucleus'.[47] In Freud's view, only the stubborn and timeless resistance of something that does not evolve along with the individual organism can set him apart from any overarching unity, thereby providing the distance that is required to fashion a true self. Moyaert observes that this surprising, individuating effect of the death drive sheds light on the patient's deep attachment to his symptoms and his resistance against the therapeutic process. In his early discussion of paranoia, Freud already made the observation that '[i]n every instance the *delusional idea* is maintained with the same energy with which another, intolerably distressing, idea is fended off from the ego. Thus they love *their delusions as they love themselves*. That is the secret'.[48] This attachment to one's symptoms and the resistance to therapeutic treatment illustrate that the 'clinging' that is attested to by the death drive can have the unexpected effect of *protecting* the ego's unity. The conservative function of the death drive can thus be beneficial for the cohesion of an organism. The death drive's refusal to be wholly swept up by change is not a merely damaging, let alone nihilistic, feat. It *runs counter to* the dynamic of self-annihilation or total 'passing away' that characterizes complete nihilism. The decelerating function of the death drive, instead, can result in a type of necessary isolation that shields the 'nucleus' of the individual from the potentially harmful impact of external and internal elements.

HEIDEGGER'S GROUND

While motivated by the wish to understand the workings of the human psyche, Freud's considerations about the unconscious afterlife of an immemorial past and the conservative nature of the death drive go beyond such psychoanalytic and anthropological concerns. Because his later conception of the drive opens to ideas about the essence of life, death and time, the research that is undertaken in 'Beyond the Pleasure Principle' is inseparable from a metaphysics. Though his self-image as a hardcore scientist prevented him from presenting his work in this manner, Freud's writings do raise the most fundamental problems concerning the core of time and being. In fact, in underscoring that it is always but the *conditio humana* which sheds light on overarching and metaphysical issues, his later explorations of the nature of the drive can even be read as a precursor to a book that would come out seven years after 'Beyond the Pleasure Principle'—a book that addresses ontological questions in a more straightforward manner but is no less reluctant to separate them from an analysis of human existence. There is no evidence that Freud read Heidegger's *Being and Time* during the final twelve years of his life and the name Heidegger is not even mentioned once in the thousands of pages that he has authored. Moreover, since the publication of the transcription of the Zollikon seminars, we know that Heidegger, for his part, was wholly unwilling to grant Freud's philosophical project any relevance for ontology, at some point even going as far as to imply that he was a 'physicist' instead of a philosopher:[49]

> Freud's basic approach [genetic-causal explanation] is far from [providing] a phenomenological direction. It specifically neglects to determine the human being's character of being [*Seinscharakt-*

er], [the character] of the human being, who radically articulates his being human with language. Were there even a trace of a phenomenological-ontological determination present in Freud's basic approach, then it would have prevented him from the aberration of his 'theory'.[50]

However, despite this palpable opposition between a thinker whose interest in the human psyche led him to metaphysical questions and a thinker whose ontological pre-occupations resulted in a *Daseinsanalyse*, it is worthwhile to retrace how Heidegger, like Freud, develops a notion of the immemorial that indicates a prioritization of the power of memory, repetition and duration over forgetting, impermanence and transience. The philosophical affinities between Freud and Heidegger stretch out beyond the obvious parallel between their conception of the distinction between (object-less) anxiety and (object-connected) fear. Like Freud, Heidegger underscores the past's endurance and refuses to meet the destruction of what is deemed immemorial as a potentially liberating event. No more than Freud does Heidegger properly address the possibility of a complete nihilism that enables a 'forgetting of forgetting' and embraces, rather than counters, the passage of time.

The concept of forgetting figures most prominently in Heidegger's thesis on the 'forgottenness of Being' [*Seinsvergessenheit*]. This claim is as clear-cut as it is far-reaching: while it concerns, in truth, the 'most basic and at the same time most concrete question', the question of Being is, instead, confused with the analysis of something 'universal', 'indefinable' and 'self-evident'.[51] In Heidegger's account, the reasons behind this forgetting are, likewise, at once simple and wide-ranging: while Parmenides and Heraclitus did not shrink back from the endeavor to comprehend the overarching dynamic of Being, the history of Western metaphysics, from Plato and Aristotle onwards, restricted itself to an exploration of thing-like entities, that is, to the question of beings and not of Being. However, 'the Being of beings "is" itself not a being', since Being as such is, in Heidegger's view, indicative of a revelatory movement that cannot simply be defined and categorized by human thought. Unlike the beings that surround us, the foundational ground of Being *offers itself* to man. The post-Socratic quest to comprehend the supposed essence of all existing things, including the essence of the highest existing being, God, is thus believed to have pushed out of sight the much more fundamental concern with the self-expressive movement of a Truth that *gives itself* and always, to a certain extent, resists the active grasp of human reason.

In his *Contributions to Philosophy* (1936–1938), compiled about ten years after *Being and Time*, Heidegger casts the concept 'abandonment by Being' [*Seinsverlassenheit*] as the 'ground' of this ontological forgetting: '[E]ven the forgottenness of being . . . is not the most original destiny of the first beginning; rather, that is the abandonment by being'.[52] The concept of 'abandonment by being' allows Heidegger to describe how it came to be that the things that surround us are given 'the appearance that they themselves, without needing anything else, are now there to be grasped and used'.[53] Targeting the era of 'machination', and addressing issues such as 'speed', 'calculation' and the 'absence of plight', Heidegger denounces the human propensity to reduce the universe to 'what "is made" and "can be made", if only the "will" to it is summoned up'.[54] Ontological forgetting cannot be separated from the underlying experience that everything that is needs to be considered first and foremost as having been created by something else. Though this idea is inherited from Christianity, its roots can be retraced to the attempt of ancient philosophy to identify the essence of a phenomenon (εἶδος) with the 'first cause' (αἴτιος) that brought it into existence. In Heidegger's view, this age-old philosophical obsession with creation and first causes has led to a worldview in which man considers himself the master of all other beings.[55] The outcomes of this process are detrimental to the way human beings understand themselves, their surroundings and the question of Being at large.

This inextricable connection between the 'forgottenness of being' and the 'abandonment by being', however, brings to the fore that the former does not in Heidegger's view denote a clear-cut loss or absence. 'The abandonment by being', writes Heidegger in *Contributions*, 'determines a unique era in the history of the truth of beyng'.[56] For Heidegger, it is not the case that Being has withdrawn itself because it has been forgotten, but, vice versa. Being has been forgotten because it has withdrawn itself. As a consequence, it cannot be believed to *have altogether disappeared*: in order to perform this movement of abandoning, Being needs to have preserved itself in some way and needs to have retained at least *some* form of existence. While the concept '*Sein*' [Being] is a *genitivus objectivus* in the formula *Seinsvergessenheit* [forgottenness of being] (Being is not what forgets but what *is* forgotten), its 'ground' remains at all times a movement of *Seinsverlassenheit* [abandonment by being] in which the concept '*Sein*' is a *genitivus subjectivus* (Being is not what *is* abandoned but what abandons). The 'abandonment by beyng' denotes that its 'essence is distorted' but also that it is still able to 'bring itself into truth'.[57] Ontological forgetting does suspend the *intimate relation* between Being and man, but it does not at all obliterate or suspend the dynamic through which Being gives itself to man.

In his lectures on Parmenides, taught during the dark years of the Second World War, Heidegger expands on a suggestion that he had already briefly introduced five years earlier. 'The *forgottenness of being*', it is stated in the *Contributions*, 'does not know anything of itself'.[58] In *Parmenides* (1942–1943), Heidegger builds on Pindar's description of a 'signless cloud' of concealment, to indicate the 'essence' and the 'uncanny character of forgetting'.[59] For what seems most specific to ontological forgetting is the fact that we are not even aware of our having forgotten the question of Being. 'The forgetter not only forgets the forgotten, but along with that he forgets himself as the one for whom the forgotten has disappeared'.[60] 'Forgetting itself already occurs in an oblivion'.[61] This conception of a 'forgetting of forgetting' should not at all be confused with the *creative* and *productive* 'forgetting of forgetting' that, as we have seen, underlies Nietzsche's essay on history and Benjamin's philosophy of history. Heidegger does not at all introduce the formula 'forgetting of forgetting' to indicate an unexpected and redemptive 'turning of time'. On the contrary, when even the forgetting of Being is being forgotten, this installs a distance between truth and man that can only be overcome by a recollective process. Though his interests are of foremost ontological nature, Heidegger follows the lead of Bergson and Freud in shrinking back to the possibility that the affirmation of the transience and impermanence of the world can have a positive outcome. For Heidegger, as well, the only counterpower to the forgetting of Being is an external one since it is but a deeply rooted *memory* that is capable of restoring the deep experience of truth.

The crux of Heidegger's argument about ontological forgetting in *Parmenides* therefore revolves around a close reading of the concluding myth in Plato's *Politeia*. Memory is at the heart of this close reading. Heidegger starts from Plato's sentence that '[i]t is necessary for everyone to drink a certain amount of th[e] water' of forgetfulness.[62] Of most crucial importance to Heidegger, however, is Plato's suggestion that human beings are characterised by a faculty that is more fundamental than forgetting and that, for this reason, can help to rein in its powers. It is this faculty that Heidegger connects to 'insight', 'philosophy', 'rescue', and, ultimately, to 'memory' and 'recollection'. For, crossing the Lethe and drinking the water of forgetfulness comes together with the risk of drinking 'more than the measure' and thereby losing all grasp of one's surroundings and all consciousness of a self. 'Complete, measureless oblivion, i.e., concealment, would exclude the least ground of the essence of man, because such oblivion would allow no disclosure and would deny unconcealedness its essential foundation'.[63] In Heidegger's account, only philosophical insight by way of memory, or, in other words, a type of anamnesis, allows man to determine the right measure of forgetting and to thus avoid the danger of utter obliteration. With his idea that philosophical insight is inseparable from a distinct type of memory, Heidegger formulates an important warning against the threat of a forgetting that has forgotten *itself* and is therefore most aptly called oblivion. Heidegger introduces what can best be termed an 'ontological memory' as a force that runs counter to this excess of forgetting. Such type of memory allows for the preservation of the connection to Being and it allows man to retain an openness to truth despite an inevitable work of forgetting. As a counterforce to oblivion, such memory does not just refer to anything 'psychological' or an empirical experience of 'something "forgotten" welling up in man once again' but to a connection with something that did not ever really go away. 'The conserving is grounded in a perpetual saving and preserving'.[64] For Heidegger the faculty of memory makes up the core of philosophy because it makes palpable that, even though man is perpetually at risk of suspending the intimate relation with truth, it belongs to the very nature of truth that it offers itself to man and cannot altogether be obliterated. 'Philosophy means to be addressed by Being itself' and it 'is first of all the care for Being'.[65] For Heidegger, it is not the case that Being forever retains a form of existence because we are always capable of remembering it but, vice versa, we can always remember Being (and thereby re-establish a connection with truth) because it has never ceased to give itself in some way or another.

Moreover, like Bergson and Freud, Heidegger's concept of memory is not a mere antithesis of the process of forgetting. Heidegger, as well, emphasizes the paradox that the conservation of what endures *involves* a process of initial forgetting. For Heidegger, Being is constitutive of an immemorial and enduring process of 'presencing' since the truth that it grounds cannot be considered an empirical object that was ever fully lived. Being cannot simply be brought back at our own will and it is only experienced when it simultaneously expresses this structural incapacity on the part of man. This notion of an inaccessibility that pertains to the very essence of Being is one of the most fundamental concerns of Heidegger's overall philosophy. The movement through which Being reveals itself is believed to constitute an 'event' [*Ereignis*] that is marked by a dynamic of simultaneous self-revelation *and* withdrawal. This element of withdrawal precludes the objectification of Being by human thought and installs the so-called ontological difference between Being and beings. While thought to offer itself through beings, Being is also believed to pull back from them in such a manner that its overarching dynamic cannot itself be considered as a thing-like entity. 'In th[e] opening of appropriation, the event offers itself as a gift [*ver-schenkt*] in the manner of refusal (it never emerges to the fore as something representable in a possible objectification)'.[66] Heidegger's thoughts on the issue of the simultaneous self-revelation and withdrawal of Being revolve around his well-known interpretation of the Greek concept of ἀλήθεια (truth as unconcealedness) in which he further develops this issue of an inseparable 'distortion', 'withdrawal', 'concealment', or, indeed, 'forgetting'. Because Being is forever bound to surpass conscious reasoning and voluntary memory, it is only made accessible through a form of remembrance that takes common course with forgetting.[67]

In Heidegger's view, the philosophical insight that can reach man by way of anamnesis wards off oblivion but it does not overcome the forgetting that belongs to the heart of Being.[68] For this reason he describes the positive moment when man establishes a connection with truth as the movement in which Being is 'unforgotten' and not as the recollection of an empirical moment.[69] Heidegger's concept of the 'unforgotten' serves as the exact mirror-image of Benjamin's notion of the 'unforgettable' that was laid out in the previous chapter. It refers to the immemorial and enduring nature of Being, while Benjamin's notion of the 'unforgettable' is the expression of a precarious and transient life that does not even have any 'monument or memorial, or perhaps even any testimony' (SW 1, 80). Heidegger's notion of the unforgotten underscores the presence of a stabilizing, ontological ground and it is not at all meant to argue for the possibility of genuine change and innovation. Benjamin's concept of the unforgettable indicates that the groundlessness of an empty time can be embraced by pure thought and that forgetting can thus be interrupted from *within*. Benjamin makes the concept of the unforgettable dependent on the capacity to think in the very absence of anything that offers itself to *be* thought. Heidegger's notion of the unforgotten, to the contrary, harks back to a memory that recovers a process of truth-revelation and a deeper 'call' of Being.

This opposition between Benjamin's philosophy of transience and forgetting and Heidegger's considerations about an ontological memory and ground allows us to understand why Benjamin criticizes Heidegger for a view of time that is fundamentally flawed. 'Heidegger', writes Benjamin in the *Passagen-Werk*, 'seeks in vain to rescue history for phenomenology abstractly through "historicity"' (AP, 462). In spite of Heidegger's philosophical explorations of time, Benjamin criticizes him for giving insufficient weight to the irrevocable impermanence of everything that takes place in history. Heidegger's philosophy cannot, in Benjamin's view, be separated from a belief in an a-historical presence that surpasses man and preserves itself over time. This assumption of an eternal ground of Being testifies, according to Benjamin, to a 'secularization' (AP, 472) and even needs to be qualified as 'reactionary' because it clings to a determining principle that cannot be affected by way of human intervention (AP, 545).[70]

In clear opposition to Benjamin's concept of *Auf-gabe* [to give up], Heidegger does indeed consider it the 'task' [*Aufgabe*] of philosophy to *not* give up the belief in a foundational dynamic that offers itself to man.[71] In texts such as *The End of Philosophy and the Task of Thinking* [*Das Ende der Philosophie und die Aufgabe des Denkens*] (1964), Heidegger makes this unshakeable faith in a grounding movement of Being very explicit by insisting that '[w]hether or not what is present is experienced, comprehended or presented, presence as lingering in openness always remains dependent upon the prevalent opening. What is absent, too, cannot be as such unless it presences in the *free space of the opening*'.[72] In the essay 'Time and Being' (1962), as well, Heidegger makes clear that Being always offers itself to man as a gift. Playing on the German formula 'there is/it gives' [*es gibt*] he states that '[w]e say of beings: they are. With regard to the matter "Being" and with regard to the matter "time", we remain cautious. We do not say: Being is, time is, but rather: there is [*es gibt*] Being and there is [*es gibt*] time'.[73] Consequently, throughout the lecture on Parmenides, forgetting is described as the 'counteressence' of truth but only in order to highlight that 'λήθη pertains to the essence of ἀλήθεια' and that 'un-concealedness itself cannot be the mere *elimination* of concealedness. The ἀ in ἀ-λήθεια in no way means simply an undetermined universal "un-" and "not"'.[74] Fully in line with the ideas laid out in *Contributions*, Heidegger reaffirms that even the suspension of the intimate relation between man and Being is initiated by the Gift of Being itself. Being continues to offer itself and retains a form of existence, at the very same moment that it pulls back from man and his surroundings.

Unlike Freud, Heidegger did study Nietzsche's work in a detailed manner, devoting many pages to his analysis of nihilism.[75] Nihilism can even be considered one of the main tropes in Heidegger's writings. Heidegger makes the issue of nihilism inseparable from the forgetting of Being that reduces beings to objects of human domination. In his lectures on Nietzsche delivered between 1936 and 1940, and repeated and summarized in 1943, he casts Nietzsche's concept 'will to power' as a nihilistic 'will to will' to indicate an 'empowering of power' that continuously strives to go beyond itself.[76] In Heidegger's view, Nietzsche's philosophy of will and power legitimizes the technological era in which man encounters the surrounding world as no more than an instrument that should serve his needs. Nietzsche's Overman, for instance, is considered capable of taming the universe into a moldable and makeable object.[77] Heidegger reads Nietzsche's philosophy not as the overcoming of nihilism but as its 'consummation' because his worldview degrades Being to a value.[78] Rather than encountering Being as a dynamic of simultaneous self-revelation and withdrawal that cannot ever become an object of domination, the will to power only affirms what can be transformed by man.[79] Yet, in an argumentative move that is symptomatic of Heidegger's overall ontology, he emphasizes that Nietzsche's nihilistic framework, while 'overturning' metaphysics, does not at all *cancel it out*. 'Despite all his overturnings and revaluings of metaphysics, Nietzsche remains in the unbroken line of the metaphysical tradition when he calls that which is established and made fast in the will to power for its own preservation purely and simply Being, or what is in being, or truth'.[80] Nietzsche's philosophy is believed to stand fully in the philosophical tradition since its ambition to revalue all values is still crafted in ontological terms. Therefore, even the confrontation with Nietzsche's consummation of nihilism does not shake Heidegger's belief in the ground of Being. Nihilism indicates for Heidegger a specific mode of Being's self-revelation and not at all its annihilation or disappearance: '[N]ihilism would be in its essence a history that runs its course along with Being itself. It would lie in Being's own essence, then, that Being remain unthought because it withdraws. Being itself withdraws into its truth. It harbors itself safely within its truth and conceals itself in such harboring'.[81]

Because of this idea that the ground of Being cannot ever be fully abolished, Heidegger's concept of nihilism is as antithetical to Benjamin's 'strive for . . . a passing away' as was Freud's concept of the death drive.[82] With the consideration that even nihilism confirms rather than contradicts the existence of truth, the possibility of truly doing away with the immemorial ground of Being becomes unthinkable. Heidegger's inability to address a nihilism that is rooted in an affirmation of transience and forgetting rather than persistence and memory becomes most palpable in his discussion of the fragment 'On Redemption' in Nietzsche's *Thus Spoke Zarathustra*.

Nietzsche's fragment 'On Redemption' revolves around the transformation of transience into a creative force. Nietzsche describes how the inability to overcome the passage of time only leads to revulsion, wrath and annoyance. Confronted with the irreversibility of time, human beings are likely to turn to otherworldly spirits and values that are supposed to mitigate their frustration. This incapacity of affirming transience as a productive force is the cause of what Nietzsche calls the 'spirit of revenge' and reactive nihilism (Deleuze's first type of nihilism). '"It was": thus is called the will's gnashing of teeth and loneliest misery. Impotent against that which has been—it is an angry spectator of everything past. The will cannot will backward; that it cannot break time and time's greed—that is the will's loneliest misery'.[83] Zarathustra's productive, strong and complete nihilism (Deleuze's third type of nihilism) overthrows this reactive attitude and fosters the will to embrace the contingencies and the finitude of his own existence. Such active nihilism is rooted in the adage that transience cannot be counteracted by the recovery of a stable and enduring ground. 'The will is a creator'. All 'it was' is a fragment, a riddle, a grisly accident—until the creating will says to it: "But I will it thus! I shall will it thus!"'[84] This complete nihilism introduces the notion of an eternal return that manages to transmute the 'it was' into a 'so be it'. Nietzsche's concept of an eternal return should not be reduced to a return of the *same* since it abolishes precisely the belief in exact repetition and the power to survive over time. Nietzsche makes active or complete nihilism inseparable from an outbreak of 'madness' because it lets go of any belief in permanency and harmony, associating it instead, as we have seen in the previous chapter, with an ability to negate negation. A *willed* return makes transience productive by taking it as an object and thereby enabling it to ultimately interrupt *itself*. Only the full assertion of the irrevocability of transience manages to dislodge it from within, giving shape to the possibility that even the passage of time might conceivably pass away. 'Everything passes away, therefore everything deserves to pass away! And this itself is justice, this law of time that it must devour its own children'.[85]

In his lectures on Nietzsche, Heidegger zooms in on precisely this passage from *Thus Spoke Zarathustra*. Heidegger reads Zarathustra's definition of 'revenge' as 'the will's ill will toward time and its "It was"' alongside Nietzsche's description of the will to power as that which 'stamp[s] Becoming with the character of Being'.[86] In sharp opposition to Deleuze's interpretation of Nietzsche, Heidegger is not at all convinced by Nietzsche's suggestion that only a complete affirmation of the passage of time is capable of overcoming the frustration that it triggers.[87] Heidegger rejects the belief that the negating 'spirit of revenge' can itself be negated into a complete but productive nihilism. In his view, affirming the universality of transience only serves to make it even more irrevocable, adding to the frustration rather than lifting it. 'What is left for us to say, if not this: Zarathustra's doctrine does not bring redemption from revenge? We do say it'.[88] Heidegger's conviction that even nihilism testifies to an ontological ground runs counter to Deleuze's belief in the possibility of an internal dislocation of transience. Wedded to the trust in an unshakeable ground, Heidegger cannot conceive of the affirmation of transience as a willed annihilation of all sense of stability and permanence. Instead, he associates Nietzsche's nihilistic assertion of transience and becoming with an 'ill-will' that transforms the very distance of truth into a stable and permanent presence. 'The supreme will to power, that is, what is most vital in all life, comes to pass when transiency is represented as perpetual Becoming in the eternal recurrence of the same, in this way being made stable and permanent'.[89] From Heidegger's perspective Nietzsche's eternal return is not a dynamic of productive transformation and transmutation but a recurrence of the same, depleting transience from any redemptive qualities. Incapable of conceiving the possibility that the passage of time can be interrupted from within, Heidegger reads Nietzsche's complete affirmation of the passage of time as the epitome of a withdrawal of truth. This withdrawal is a stable and enduring movement because it originates in Being itself. The affirmation of transience '*stamps* the character of Being on beings. [It] takes Becoming, to which perpetual collision and suffering belong, into its protection and custody. Does such thinking overcome prior reflection, overcome the spirit of revenge? Or does there not lie concealed in this very *stamping*—which takes all Becoming into the protection of eternal recurrence of the same—a form of ill will *against* sheer transiency and thereby a highly spiritualized spirit of revenge?'[90]

A NOTE ON ERNST JÜNGER

In the essay 'Across the Line' (1950), originally written as a contribution to a *Festschrift* for Heidegger's sixtieth birthday, Ernst Jünger, as well, considers the question of whether the nothingness and emptiness of historical time can be transmuted into productive forces. This leads to what he calls 'diagnostic remarks' about nihilism.[91] Like Nietzsche, Jünger refuses to consider nihilism as a merely negative event, stressing that nihilism can be 'as much the sign of the weakness as of the strength'.[92] For Jünger, nihilism has nothing to do with disease ('[O]ne will find that physical health is connected with [nihilism]—above all where it is vigorously at work'),[93] evil ('There are proven remedies against evil. More disturbing is the fusion, indeed the total confusion of good and evil, which often eludes the sharpest eye')[94] or chaos ('[N]ihilism can in fact harmonize with vast worlds of order, and . . . it even needs them in order to become active on a large scale').[95] In line with Heidegger, however, Jünger connects the phenomenon of nihilism with the modern age of automation and mechanicity. For him, as well, increased specialization precludes a lived experience of absolute values. In Jünger's view, humanity has crossed a line that makes impossible the return to an era with stable values and an intimate feel for transcendence. For this reason, man no longer has the freedom to decide between a nihilistic world and a world with an undamaged moral sensibility. Jünger connects nihilism to the 'inevitability of destruction'.[96] Replete with references to the First and Second World War and written during the Cold War, he draws attention to a degree of violence that is potentially all-consuming. 'There is no doubt that our situation as a whole is crossing over the critical line. With this, danger and security change. One can no longer think how to remove one house, one single property, from the path of the firestorm. Here no ruse, no flight can help'.[97] Since this cosmological expansion of nihilism has been completed, the only alternative that can be taken seriously is the one between a 'pessimistic' nihilism that stands in the way of genuine innovation (it 'corresponds to the impossibility of bringing forth higher types, or even conceiving of them, and flows into pessimism')[98] and an 'optimistic' one that expresses 'the uselessness of the other world, not however of the world and of existence in general'.[99]

In his response to Jünger's text, initially entitled 'Concerning "The Line"' (1955) but then, revealingly retitled 'On the Question of Being', Heidegger agrees with Jünger's perspective that nihilism has become a global phenomenon for which there remains no direct alternative, let alone the possibility of a return to a previous era with supposedly intact moral values. However, Heidegger dismisses Jünger's suggestion that nihilism is first and foremost a process that was initiated by man. His criticism singles out Jünger's statement that '[t]he moment in which the line is passed brings a new turning approach of Being, and with this, what is actual begins to shine forth'.[100] Heidegger's ontological presuppositions bring him to reverse Jünger's argument, resulting in the reiteration of the above-mentioned claim that even nihilism is a mode of Being.

> Above all, I would wish to ask whether, conversely, it is not a new turning of being that would first bring the moment for crossing the line.... Presumably the turning itself, albeit in a way that is as yet veiled, is That which, in a quite perplexed and indeterminate manner, we name 'being'. Yet does not such turning also, and a strange way, occur under the domination of nihilism, namely, in such a way that 'being' turns away and withdraws into absence?[101]

Heidegger's philosophy is thereby once more revealed as founded on the belief in a possible 'call' of truth and the Gift of Being. This ontological ground installs a memory through which man can retrieve the disclosure of Being. In *Contributions* Heidegger had already mentioned that a sense of 'plight' can be recovered by way of a 'resonating of beyng' which 'seeks to bring back beyng in its full essential occurrence as event'.[102] It is such a 'plight' that, rather than fully overcoming forgetting, discovers it as a quintessential element of the most important type of memory. Such memory remains aware of the structural presence of forgetting and is capable of somehow making it serviceable for memory.[103]

In spite of these references to an ontological ground that cannot be eradicated, it would be a mistake to consider Heidegger's philosophy as merely *anti*-nihilistic. Because Being is an immemorial ground that resists voluntary recollection, it is inseparable from a dimension of nothingness. Because forgetting and withdrawal are *internal* to the revelatory moment with which Being gives itself to man, Heidegger even goes as far as to suggest that metaphysics as such, including his own ontological framework, is nihilistic. 'The essence of nihilism is nothing nihilistic, and that nothing is detracted from the ancient worthiness of metaphysics by the fact that its own essence shelters nihilism within it'.[104] In his view, the nihilistic line that was mentioned by Jünger is indicative of a 'zone' that cannot be exited. Still, this 'zone' is cast as an eternal clearing or opening that does not altogether block the revelatory movement of Being. Because he injects nothingness within the heart of Being itself, Heidegger fails to develop a theory of nihilism that is properly speaking *complete*. Heidegger's concept of nothingness is unrelated to whatever type of groundlessness. To indicate this inseparability of, rather than opposition between, Being and nothingness, Heidegger crosses out the word ~~Being~~.[105] This crossing out makes visible the immemorial and inaccessible nature of the ground of Being and not at all a lack of ontological foundation. Since its becoming visible is not constitutive of an empirical moment that can be voluntarily recollected, the very Gift of Being encompasses a dimension of nothingness that should not be confused with a process of disappearance. The concept of ~~Being~~ does not run counter to the revelatory movement of Being but it makes palpable that this process always entails a moment of withdrawal. Heidegger's ontological framework is therefore incapable of coming to terms with a genuinely annihilating movement in which groundlessness and a truly empty form of time hollow out the supposed offer of truth.

BENJAMIN AND EXPERIENCE

On first view, the paradox that, in various ways, underlies Bergson's, Freud's and Heidegger's work can be retrieved in the writings of Benjamin as well. From the late twenties onwards, Benjamin develops the idea that there is an 'immemorial' past that is situated beyond the grasp of conscious recollection and that forgetting does indeed constitute the condition rather than the antithesis of true memory.

In his interpretation of literary modernism Benjamin develops a duality between recollection [*Erinnerung*] and memory [*Gedächtnis*] that he explicitly borrows from Bergson's *Matter and Memory* and Freud's 'Beyond the Pleasure Principle'. Benjamin uses the distinction between, on the one hand, the faculty that allows a past moment to be brought back to the present (recollection) and, on the other, the deep strata where our past is being preserved (memory) to back up the second distinction between conscious, lived or isolated experience (all are synonyms for the German word *Erlebnis*) and unconscious, long, deep or true experience (all synonyms for *Erfahrung*). Benjamin adopts Freud's formula that consciousness is 'a protective shield' that allows a human being to truly 'live' a given stimulation, thereby absorbing and warding off the shock that such stimulation may generate. Lived or isolated experience, hence, is stopped in its tracks by consciousness before it can reach the deeper layers of our psyche. '[T]he more efficiently [consciousness screens stimuli], the less impressions enter long experience and the more they correspond to the concept of isolated experience' (SW 4, 319). Bergson and Freud also allow Benjamin to comprehend the nature of long, deep or true experience that preserves an immemorial past. Much closer related to the common use of the term 'experience', true experience is indicative of a psychical event that unconsciously endures over time and thus even enables a process of learning or wisdom. It is associated with 'accumulated and frequently unconscious contents [*Daten*] that flow together' (SW 4, 314 [translation modified]). True experience, as was suggested by both Bergson and Freud, can be conserved by memory because it entails a surplus (Bergson's 'virtual past', Freud's 'permanent traces') that cannot be fully absorbed by an individual's conscious response. For this reason, true experience surpasses, in Benjamin's view, both the initial moment when a human being reacts to a given stimulus and the merely *individual* nature of such a reaction. 'Where there is experience in the strict sense of the word, certain contents of the individual past combine in the memory with material from the collective past'. True experience instills an intimate feeling of belonging and a deep attachment to a shared frame of reference, be it cultural, religious or socioeconomic. An important part of Benjamin's late writings expands on the concept of true, immemorial experience under the guise of an analysis of concepts such as 'tradition', 'ritual', 'contemplation', 'cult', 'aura' and 'story'.

In Benjamin's view, Bergson and Freud's opposition between a lived or isolated experience and a true, long, deep or immemorial experience requires a crucial update. Both thinkers are insufficiently aware of the 'historical determination of memory' and overlook the fact that an analysis of the human apparatus of perception cannot do without an analysis of society. Bergson's work is 'oriented towards biology' (SW 4, 314) and Freud's hypotheses can only be tested 'in situations far removed from the one he had in mind when he wrote' (SW 4, 317). Benjamin will aspire to an alternative analysis of the human mind and body that does take into account the historical, social and economic context of our lives.[106] In Benjamin's view, the Enlightenment has done away with all forms of *spiritual* authority and cannot shake off a 'lower and inferior nature of experience'. The unconscious preservation of the immemorial, collective past is therefore threatened by a societal evolution of relatively recent date, that is, by the overemphasis of rationality and factual verifiability. This, for its part, has resulted in a 'religious and historical blindness' that 'pertain[s] to the entire modern era' (SW 1, 101). Motivated by an interest in wide-ranging phenomena such as industrialization, technical reproduction, the modern hunger for facts and information, the demise of a metaphysical account of experience and the perplexing feeling that the horror of the Great War could not even be communicated by way of the age-old activity of storytelling, Benjamin diagnoses a modern 'poverty of experience' that seems irrevocable.

Because both Baudelaire and Proust are chroniclers of the decline of 'true' experience in a society that is increasingly dominated by consciousness and rationality, it is their work that in Benjamin's view contains the most interesting descriptions of the loss of the 'immemorial'. Drawing attention to the word 'lost' [*perdu*] in both Baudelaire's line 'and even Spring has lost its sweet allure' [*Le Printemps adorable a perdu son odeur!*] and the title of Proust's magnum opus, *In Search of Lost Time* [*À la recherche du temps perdu*], Benjamin first and foremost explores the work of the two authors as a literary monument to the disappearance of true experience and memory.[107] Both Baudelaire's concept of *correspondances* and Proust's famous *mémoire involontaire* are made visible as the final signposts of true experiences that have managed to bypass consciousness to endure over time. 'The important thing is that *correspondances* encompass a concept of experience which includes ritual elements. Only by appropriating these elements was Baudelaire able to fathom the full meaning of the breakdown which he, as a modern man, was witnessing' (SW 4, 333). The term *correspondances* refers to the title of the fourth poem in *Les Fleurs du mal* wherein Baudelaire famously likens nature to 'forests of symbols' that call out to man with a voice that is at once deeply intimate and irretrievably distant.[108] For Benjamin, *correspondances* embody a type of beauty, now lost, that thrives on 'ritual' value. *Correspondances* signal the ambiguous blurring of beauty and cult, aesthetics and religion that will later be termed 'aura'.

The word 'lost', however, has a double meaning in Baudelaire's work. It not only indicates that the capacity to have and share true experiences has been lost to modern man, but also that such true experiences refer, like all things immemorial, to a past that *had in fact always already been lost*. *Correspondances* allow for a puzzling recovery of a past that was never even a part of the present to begin with. They are indicative of a history that was preserved in time for the very reason that it was not ever consciously lived. 'What is past murmurs in the *correspondances*, and the canonical experience of them has its place in a previous life'. Baudelaire, consequently, does not only raise true experience to the level of an *ideal* in order to highlight that it is endangered by the speed of life, the anonymity and downright ugliness of the modern metropolis (all expressed with the term 'spleen') but also to underscore that it should not be confused with an *actual* event in time. 'True' experiences can be described as a *virtual* past that cannot be reduced to the present it once was. Because, of all human senses, the sense of smell is least capable of firmly anchoring a given experience within our conscious minds, true experience is associated with scent that 'deeply anesthetizes the sense of time' (SW 4, 335). True experience thus testifies to the presence of 'heterogeneous, conspicuous fragments' that are granted an unconscious afterlife within the normal, chronological succession of time.

A second important reference to an immemorial past is Proust's famous *mémoire involontaire*. Benjamin's analysis of Proust mirrors the earlier interpretation of Baudelaire in that the *souvenir involontaire* is considered an example of the 'true' (deep or long) experience. In Benjamin's view, the *mémoire involontaire* testifies to a form of unconscious memory [*Gedächtnis*] that allows for a sense of selfhood: the *mémoire involontaire* makes it possible that 'an individual forms an image of himself' (SW 4, 315). While the *mémoire involontaire* corresponds to what Benjamin calls a 'calendar' constitutive for the remembrance of meaningful moments of the past, the *mémoire volontaire*, to the contrary, only gives 'information ... about the past' but 'retains no trace of that past' (SW 4, 315). The *mémoire volontaire*, therefore, is 'in the service of the intellect' (SW 4, 315) and exemplifies the lived (or isolated) experience in which differences and variations are smoothed over. While Freud and Bergson analyze the human mind independently of societal issues, Proust is of more interest to Benjamin because he, like Baudelaire, does include the 'historical determination' of human experience. Two important characteristics of Proust's *souvenir involontaire* confirm its precarious status in modern society: it presents itself at random and it cannot be shared with others. 'According to Proust, it is a manner of chance whether an individual . . . can take hold of his experience' (SW 4, 315). This ephemerality and unrepeatability of Proust's reminiscences confront us with the fact that even our most intimate sentiments of selfhood cannot be fully appropriated. Because the *souvenir involontaire* does not allow for a full recovery of the former self that it fleetingly brings back, it evidences that even our deep self somehow remains ungraspable. In Benjamin's view, this alienating fact that we are dependent on sheer chance when we strive to access our intimate, psychical lives can only be explained by the excessive importance of rationality in modern societies. We are no longer capable of retrieving a firmly rooted identity and stable sense of belonging by way of contemplation because we have been taught to take hold of our surroundings with the help of rational intellect alone. While the *souvenir involontaire* indicates a 'restorative will' (SW 4, 334) it thus inevitably also confirms the individual's insulated position. The *souvenir involontaire*, however enlivening as it may seem, confirms that we can no longer root our individual lives within a broader whole. Addicted to facts and information delivered by newspapers and photographs, modern society is dominated by the urge to 'isolate events from the realm in which they could affect the experience of the reader' (SW 4, 315–16). Proust's rendition of the *souvenir involontaire* 'bears the traces of the situation that engendered it; it is part of the inventory of the individual who is isolated in various ways' (SW 4, 316). In this regard, it is hardly surprising that 'rituals, with their ceremonies and their festivals [are] probably nowhere recalled in Proust's work' (SW 4, 316).

Benjamin's interpretation of Proust also mirrors his ideas on Baudelaire for a second reason. The unrepeatability and isolating features of the *souvenir involontaire* are not only evidence of the decline of 'true' experience in a modern society but also underscore that the moment that is thus brought back has never fully been possessed by the individual's consciousness. As an individualized version of Baudelaire's *correspondances*, Proust's *mémoire involontaire* is read as a reservoir of experiences that have, indeed, always already been forgotten. The *mémoire involontaire* is, according to Benjamin, 'much closer to forgetting than [to] what is usually called memory' because remembrance and forgetting have become as inseparable as, respectively, the 'woof' and 'warp' in a piece of woven cloth (SW 2, 238). '[O]nly what has not been experienced explicitly and consciously, what has not happened to the subject as an isolated experience, can become a component of *mémoire involontaire*' (SW 4, 317). The *mémoire involontaire* is capable of retaining traces of the past for the very reason that they are situated beyond the grasp of consciousness, registering only those impressions that have escaped the intellect's 'protective shield'. Because in *mémoire involontaire* forgetting and memory *work together* to preserve the past, it is to be considered, in Benjamin's view as well, 'immemorial' (SW 2, 240) and should therefore not be pitted against forgetting but against consciousness and rationality. It is precisely 'our purposeful activity, and even more, our purposive remembering' which is to be held accountable for 'unravel[ing] the web, the ornaments of forgetting' (SW 2, 238). In Benjamin's view, Proust's *mémoire involontaire* contains 'not a life as it actually was but a life as it was remembered by the one who had lived it' (SW 2, 237–38). Of central importance is not only the fact that it has managed to retain an imprint of 'the great passions, vices, insights that called on us' but also that 'we, the masters, were not home' (SW 2, 244–45). Only because it was thus left unattended to by our consciousness, was the past capable of growing beyond the present it once was. In the *souvenir involontaire*, a scent or taste that was not in fact all that remarkable to begin with *has become* strangely remarkable and this for the sole reason that it could somehow be retrieved so many years later. The deep strata of our memory thus grant an unexpected afterlife to a moment that did not even seem worthy of it. In Benjamin's view, Proust shows us that 'an experienced event is finite [and] confined to one sphere of experience', whereas 'a remembered event is infinite [and] a key to everything that happened before it and after it' (SW 2, 238). Never even having been a lived 'present' pure and proper, the most banal moments of our past can nonetheless be picked up again, not by the conscious will that streamlines voluntary recollection and only delivers an empty repetition of the same, but by the contingency that dominates our faculty of remembrance and animates these forgotten moments with a significance that does not seem quite fitting.

TO HAVE DONE WITH THE IMMEMORIAL

Benjamin's own consideration of the inseparability of forgetting and remembrance in the *oeuvre* of Baudelaire and Proust undeniably bears the traces of a nostalgic longing for 'deep' experiences that allow for a shared sense of belonging and a stable image of the self.

Indeed, a large part of Benjamin's exploration of the importance of an immemorial past, auratic images, stories and the power of tradition is mournful about the decline of the human faculty of remembrance. It is clear that, for him, the concomitant, bleak view that history is no more than an indifferent passage of time is harmful to the human being's confidence in both himself and the world. However, it is important to note that a recovery of 'deep' experience is for Benjamin ultimately neither possible nor desirable. In opposition to Heidegger's concept of a revelatory process of truth that survives even the modern era of machination and quantifiability, Benjamin's own take on the 'lower and inferior nature of experience' in modernity kills off all hope that the immemorial might in some way have preserved itself. For him, the shallow worldview of modern man has led to an *irrevocable* discontinuity between past and present. Moreover, the modern inability to retrieve the immemorial strata where forgotten and shared memory-contents are conserved, is not only an irrevocable fact; it even indicates an evolution that Benjamin, in crucial places of his *oeuvre*, heralds with great gusto. In some of his sharpest passages, Benjamin warns that the human longing for 'deep', unconscious experiences and an intimate sense of immemorial unity can easily be exploited for political means. His famous analysis of the fascist 'aestheticization of politics' contains an urgent alert for and, in hindsight, an uncanny foreknowledge of the horror that inevitably results from an ideological appeal to the 'pre-historical' past that supposedly unifies a *Volk* (SW 3, 121).[109] In Benjamin's view, the concept of a stable, ontological ground testifies to deeply 'mythic' convictions. The notion of a foundational Being is tantamount to the illusionary belief that life is a continuous and interrupted force, chaining man to a Destiny that cannot be overthrown. For this reason, Benjamin celebrates the arrival of a 'new kind of barbarism' and 'destructive character' that counters this 'aestheticization of politics'.[110] These new barbarians and destructive characters personify Benjamin's 'task of world politics, whose method must be called nihilism'. It is at this precise point that the opposition between Benjamin's philosophy on the one hand and the writings of Bergson, Freud and, especially, Heidegger, becomes most clear. Benjamin's new barbarians and destructive characters let go of the priority of memory over forgetting and they, instead, 'strive for . . . a passing away' that transmutes the transience of history into a productive force. '[W]hat does poverty of experience do for the barbarian?' Benjamin asks himself. 'It forces him to start from scratch; to make a new start; to make a little go a long way; to begin with a little and build up further, looking neither left nor right. Among the great creative spirits, there have always been the inexorable ones who begin by clearing a tabula rasa' (SW 2, 732). Benjamin's new barbarians and destructive characters are therefore in no way inspired by Heidegger's 'plight' to recover any supposed 'gift' of Being since they, instead, actively seek the dissolution of any belief in a supposed ontological ground. 'Poverty of experience. This should not be understood to mean that people are yearning for new experience. No, they long to free themselves from experience; they long for a world in which they can make such pure and decided use of their poverty—their outer poverty, and ultimately also their inner poverty—that it will lead to something respectable' (SW 2, 734). In Benjamin's view, the seemingly negating stance that emphasizes the irrecoverability of absolute truths and values can itself be negated, the outcome of such a negation of negation being a deeply affirmative attitude vis-à-vis *this* world. The 'new barbarians' and 'destructive characters' embody the *complete* nihilism that could not be accommodated by any author that prioritizes memory over forgetting, and endurance over transience. Having done away with any belief in the supposed self-preservation of truth, Benjamin insists that modern man clear the path for the discovery of his immediate surroundings as a room-for-play [*Spielraum*].[111] For Benjamin, the world we live in cannot be reconnected to any supposed ontological underpinnings but, by this token precisely, it is reopened as a space that can be *transformed*. Benjamin's nihilistic celebration of a generation of 'new barbarians' and 'destructive characters' is therefore of much more fundamental concern to him than the seemingly wistful observations about the decline of 'deep' experience. That the human apparatus of experience is historically determined entails that our psychical and bodily set-up has drastically changed over time, thereby making it de facto impossible for modern man to re-establish an intimate connection with the immemorial 'prehistory' that firmly anchors the identity of an individual. Benjamin's concepts of 'distraction' [*Zerstreuung*] and 'innervation', for instance, are steeped in the awareness that an analysis of modern society requires a renewed view on the faculties of human apperception. Sociological observations going hand in hand with anthropological concerns, Benjamin invites us to rethink the workings of the human body and mind in an era that is no longer heedful of the slowness and duration that 'deep' experience requires.

The reconstruction of Benjamin's celebration of the complete, affirmative nihilism of 'new barbarians' and 'destructive characters' sends us back to his readings of Baudelaire and Proust. Beyond his interest in Baudelaire and Proust's mournful descriptions of the 'loss' of deep experience, Benjamin retrieves in their work an active quest to have done with the supposed endurance of the immemorial past. In the *Passagen-Werk* and 'Central Park', Benjamin identifies a duality that runs throughout Baudelaire's work, dividing it in two parts that interact but cannot be reconciled. Alongside Baudelaire's seemingly nostalgic interest in the *correspondances*, his writings include marked descriptions of the distinctly modern poverty of experience that are not all regretful or backward-looking. There is, writes Benjamin, a 'tension [between] the doctrine of *correspondances* and ... the principle of allegory. Baudelaire never made the slightest attempt to establish any sort of relations between these two forms of speculation, both of the greatest concern to him. His poetry springs from the interaction of the two tendencies, which are rooted in his temperament' (SW 4, 177; AP, 272, 329). The category of allegory is one of the most important in Benjamin's entire oeuvre, having been introduced in his groundbreaking work on the baroque mourning play or *Trauerspiel*. Here Benjamin differentiates the *Trauerspiel* authors from the Renaissance authors in that they reduce nature to 'the over-ripeness and decay of her creations. In nature, they saw eternal transience [*ewige Vergängnis*]'. This 'saturnine vision' that 'piles up fragments ceaselessly' is the 'polar opposite to the idea of transfigured nature [*der verklärten Natur*]' (O, 179–81; GS I, 355–56). In Benjamin's view, allegory is the literary mode deployed by the baroque authors to indicate a view of time that is wholly dominated by impermanence. 'The word "history" stands written on the countenance of nature in the characters of transience' (O, 177; see also AP 348: 'The experience of allegory, which holds fast to ruins, is properly the experience of eternal transience'). Depicting nature and history alike as realms that are emptied from within, allegory is used by the baroque authors to exemplify the fact that nothing can endure in a meaningful way. With this *topos* of universal annihilation, the baroque authors evacuate nature and history of all signification.

> This is the heart of the allegorical way of seeing, of the baroque, secular explanation of history as the Passion of the world [*weltlichen Exposition der Geschichte als Leidensgeschichte der Welt*]; its importance resides solely in the stations of its decline [*Stationen*

ihres Verfalls]. The greater the significance, the greater the subjection to death, because death digs most deeply the jagged line of demarcation between physical nature and significance. (O, 166; GS I, 343)[112]

In Benjamin's view, Baudelaire's poetry is deeply allegorical because it similarly clings to an experience of universal decay and insignificance. Like the baroque authors, Baudelaire was fixated on the idea that history can be made visible as an irredeemable succession of annihilation, antithetical to whatever type of meaningful conservation. Though Baudelaire turns his attention towards a specific *society* rather than history and nature at large, Benjamin considers the well-known topic of 'spleen' in Baudelaire's work as heavily indebted to the baroque experience of 'eternal transience'. Moving away from the baroque interest in pre-romantic thought-figures such as ruins and nature's power to overtake history, Baudelaire treats the distinctly social-economic process of commodification as an equally destructive force. Baudelaire thus encounters loss and forgetting wherever he turns his gaze. 'The specific devaluation of the world of things, as manifested in the commodity, is the foundation of Baudelaire's allegorical intention. . . . This devaluation of the human environment by the commodity economy penetrates deeply into the poet's historical experience. What results is the "ever-self-same". Spleen is nothing other than the quintessence of historical experience' (SW 4, 96; see also AP, 22). For both the baroque authors and Baudelaire, the soulless body, for instance, is an important image of this entropic view on the world at large. For Baudelaire, moreover, it is not just the cadaver that epitomizes the irrevocability of decay but also the body of the prostitute. In this manner, Baudelaire introduces the idea that even our deepest desires and our mental universe have been commodified (AP, 335). In Benjamin's view, hence, Baudelaire follows the example of the baroque authors in deploying the literary mode of allegory as an '*apparat de destruction*', but he shifts his attention from the outside world to the psyche of the human being (SW 4, 96). The irrevocable transience of the world is thus captured in an emotional fixation on the past-ness of mental experiences and the propensity to encounter all that is, as somehow already lost. 'The souvenir is the complement to "isolated experience". In it is precipitated the increasing self-estrangement of human beings, whose past is inventoried as dead effects. In the nineteenth century, allegory withdrew from the world around us to settle in the inner world' (SW 4, 183).

Both the baroque authors and Baudelaire are so unyielding in emphasizing the indifference and impermanence of this world that they bar the belief that these features can be interrupted by an external principle: there is, to be sure, no exception to the universal law of decay and fragmentation. The universe of both the baroque *Trauerspiel*-authors and Baudelaire is expressive of an *ontological* forgetting, blocking the way to any supposed redemptive intervention by memory, let alone an ontological memory along the lines of Heidegger's ontology. Why, then, does Baudelaire's use of the mode of allegory exemplify the *creativity* of forgetting and, hence, a *positive* account of the modern 'poverty of experience' if it is a strategy of affirming relentless commodification and overall loss? The awareness that there is no *external* counterpower to ontological forgetting does not mean that the 'eternal transience' that is expressed by the baroque authors and Baudelaire cannot be interrupted from *within*. In the final chapter of the *Trauerspiel*-book Benjamin introduces the puzzling 'about-turn' that exposes the very transience of the world as a condition that can be overcome.[113] The possibility of such a disruption, however, does not rest on a principle of conservation that runs against this all-encompassing movement of decay. This possibility is conditioned by the idea that the baroque *Trauerspiel* reworks the transience that dominates over history into a unity with specifically *artistic* features. Benjamin's interpretation of the baroque *Trauerspiel* ultimately hinges on the idea that an artwork can enable transience to, so to speak, take itself as object. 'Ultimately in the death-signs of the baroque the direction of allegorical reflection is reversed; on the second part of its wide arc it returns, to redeem'. It is in this manner that the baroque authors could display 'transitoriness . . . as . . . the allegory of resurrection' (O, 232) while nonetheless dismissing the concept of eternal life. Though expressive of fragmentation and lack of unity, the literary construct of the *Trauerspiel* is itself not a mere fragment but an added, non-actual reality and a unity in its own right. As an artwork, the baroque *Trauerspiel* retains an autonomy vis-à-vis the deeply insignificant world that it nonetheless ceaselessly makes visible. As we have also seen in the previous chapter, transience is transmuted into a productive feature when it serves to build up a work of art that has a coherence and consistency *of its own*. Consequently, in Benjamin's view, the allegorical expression of impermanence does not counteract the impermanence of the world at large but it *completes* it. The *Trauerspiel* transforms mourning [*Trauer*] into play [*Spiel*], allowing transience to become infinite in a creative manner: such artworks make visible that the eternal rhythm of impermanence might *itself* be of an impermanent nature.[114] When produced anew in and as a unified, literary text, the very experience of decay can become a rejuvenating event: in the *Trauerspiel*, nothing but the artistic rendering of fragmentation as an inescapable feature of history at large (rather than the characteristic of specific, historical phenomena or events) installs the hope that this same fragmentation can somehow be *overcome*.

In Benjamin's view, Baudelaire's work contains similar instantiations of such 'hope against all hope'. Though Baudelaire's use of allegory clearly betrays a 'destructive impulse' it is 'nowhere concerned with the abolition of what falls prey to it' and it 'at once shatter[s] and preserve[s]' (SW 4, 169). Though annihilation is turned into a lawfulness that cannot be acted upon from without, Baudelaire's bleak view does at times hollow itself out. For when introduced into the sphere of art, the 'spleen' of history can shed its destructive features and become a productive dynamic. In Baudelaire's work, it is precisely the relentless, poetic exposure of universal transience that carves out a space in which this universal law of destructiveness might conceivably pass away.

This 'about-turn' can be illustrated with one of Baudelaire's poems. According to Benjamin, the poem 'Une Martyre' 'holds a central place in Baudelaire's work' (SW 4, 96).[115] One reason for this assessment could be that it does indeed modify the allegorical depiction of annihilation into a potentially redemptive force. The poem revolves around the decapitated body of a murdered prostitute and makes ample use of descriptions of lifelessness and fragmentation, zooming in on a scene devoid of intimacy and individuality.

> where lilies sorrowing in crystal urns / exhale their final sigh / and where, as if the room were under glass, / the air is pestilent, / a headless corpse emits a stream of blood / the sopping pillows shed / onto thirsty sheets which drink it up / as greedily as sand.[116]

Throughout the poem, Baudelaire's allegorical use of the trope of death is drawn out with unrelenting systematicity. However, the incessant description of death's ability to bring everything to a stop, epitomized by the prostitute's stiffened body, results in the literary image of its opposite: the uncanny possibility of resurrection. Bringing together the words 'constant' and 'death' in a single line allows Baudelaire to rework the prostitute's cadaver into an aesthetic expression of both death *and* deathlessness at once. The image of the cadaver is used to back up the startling intuition that the very irrevocability of death can be made visible as an 'immortal form': 'your bridegroom roves, and your immortal form / keeps vigil when he sleeps; / like you, no doubt, he will be constant too, / and faithful unto death'.[117] It is for this reason that Baudelaire's work exemplifies that allegory's unstoppable depiction of decay does not necessarily succumb *to* it: 'Allegory *holds fast* to the ruins [and] offers the image of petrified unrest' (SW 4, 169 [emphasis added]). Wholly antithetical to the concept of an eternal life and, instead, wedded to the transmutation of 'eternal transience' into a literary work, Baudelaire's poem retrieves an eerie potential to endure within the absolute stillness of the prostitute's corpse itself.

Benjamin's reading of Proust revolves around a like-minded concept of universal transience and an analysis of commodification and loss. Closing in on the same nineteenth century that motivated Baudelaire's work, Proust's novel nonetheless takes in a point of view from above rather than below. *Ex negativo*, Proust's salons bear the stamp of the process of modernization that also uprooted Baudelaire's universe. Proust's novel may be peopled by 'snobs' whose foremost aim in life is to conceal 'everything that has a part in production' (SW 2, 243), their false consciousness nonetheless paints a picture of the world that is no less disenchanted and hollowed out than Baudelaire's. For, while Baudelaire's protagonists are victimized by their indifferent surroundings and worn out by the cruelty of a modernization-gone-wild, the aristocrats in Proust's novel evidence a spiritual void that epitomizes a 'satiated society' (SW 2, 241). Benjamin, as a consequence, agrees with Proust's self-assessment that he is a 'disillusioned, merciless deglamorizer of the ego, of love, of mortals' and adds to this the remark that Proust 'turns his whole limitless art into a veil for this one most vital mystery of his class: the economic aspect' (SW 2, 243). Proust shows no pity in disclosing the 'physiology of chatter' and even draws a specific type of 'comedy' from the activity of emptying out the words and gestures of the bourgeoisie: '[H]is laughter does not toss the world up but flings it down—at the risk that it will be smashed to pieces, which will then make him burst into tears' (SW 2, 241).

A return to the earlier-mentioned concept of the *souvenir involontaire* is required to fully understand why Proust's work, like Baudelaire's, revolves around the issue of an 'eternal passing away'. In crucial pages of his essay on Proust, Benjamin seems to contradict his own statement, quoted above, that the *souvenir involontaire* allows 'an individual [to] form an image of himself' (SW 4, 315). At times, Benjamin suggests an altogether different interpretation of the *souvenir involontaire*. Benjamin identifies an 'elegiac' undertone in Proust's writings that rests on an experience of 'eternal repetition' in which 'everything that happens appears not in identical but in similar guise, opaquely similar to itself' (SW 2, 239). This life-draining awareness, for its part, explains why 'Proust transforms existence into a preserve of memory' as if even his dealings with the present had always already been occluded by a more fundamental impression of past-ness (SW 2, 239). Rather than exemplifying the 'deep' experience or unconscious type of memory that establishes a stable identity, the *souvenir involontaire* is here associated with the suggestion that Proust, like Baudelaire, encounters loss all around. The importance of the theme of memory for Proust, it is suggested, does not ultimately lie in an interest in the capacity of unconscious preservation. Benjamin is much more interested in the idea that human beings might altogether *lack* this capacity. Indeed, the *souvenir involontaire* enables neither the recovery of a virtual or pure past nor an immemorial and continuous Self. The *souvenir involontaire* is first and foremost a confrontation with the *ir*recoverability of a multiplicity of discontinuous selv*es*. Consequently, Benjamin mentions Proust's unyielding efforts to shrug off the fullness and unity of a deep ego and states that 'Proust could not get his fill of emptying the dummy, his self' (SW 2, 240). However important the faculty of remembrance may be to Proust's work, it cannot be understood as a power that *goes against* the overall transitoriness of our experiences. In Proust's writings, it is not so much forgetting which is overcome by the faculty of memory as the faculty of memory which is defenseless against the overall passing-away of things. Benjamin describes this demise of memory by an ontological forgetting as follows: Proust's 'true interest is in the passage of time in its most real—that is, intertwined—form, and this passage nowhere holds sway more openly than in remembrance within and aging without' (SW 2, 244). Proust's *souvenir involontaire* entails the sharpest awareness of the impermanence of our most intimate experiences and it urges us to let go of the hope that our faculty of memory, be it voluntary or involuntary, will ultimately win over the universal law of decay. 'Proust has brought off the monstrous feat of letting the whole world age a lifetime in an instant' (SW 2, 244). Benjamin is adamant that Proust's novel cannot accommodate a concept of eternal life and that he gives up the belief that there is a counterprinciple to the universal law of impermanence. 'Proust's eternity is by no means a platonic or a utopian one' and he 'does not enable an individual to approach "the higher regions which a Plato or Spinoza reached with one beat of the wings"' (SW 2, 244).

Rather than appealing to the counterpowers of memory, Benjamin argues that Proust's work, like the *Trauerspiele* and some of Baudelaire's poems, conjures the hope that this 'eternal transience' can somehow be interrupted from within. Proust is believed to have retrieved an awkward force of 'resurrection' that is internal to the experience of the world's ephemerality. In Benjamin's view, Proust was capable of drawing an unsettling vivacity from the impermanence that lies at the heart of the *souvenir involontaire* itself: '[T]h[e] very concentration, in which things that normally just fade and slumber are consumed in a flash, is called rejuvenation' (SW 2, 244). Proust replaces the belief in an eternal life with the awareness of an infinity of 'rapturous' time: 'The eternity which Proust opens to view is intertwined time, not boundless time' (SW 2, 244). Proust, in other words, is believed to have rescued the possibility to escape from the world's transience, not by referring to the capacity to overcome this transience from without, but by underscoring the uncanny ability to accelerate it in such a manner that it can be *worked through to the end*. The possibility that the world's impermanence can be thus exhausted is described as a chance for 'happiness' [*Glück*]. Benjamin connects Proust's earlier mentioned concept of 'eternal repetition' with an 'eternal restoration of the original, first happiness' and an 'elegiac idea of happiness' (SW 2, 239). As we have seen in the previous chapter, the same, 'indissolubl[e]' connection between the affirmation of 'transience', an unexpected hope of 'redemption' and the 'idea of happiness' is made explicit in Benjamin's 'On the Concept of History',[118] in the 'Theological Political Fragment' and in a letter to Max Horkheimer that is included in the *Passagen-Werk*: 'To the spiritual *restitutio in integrum*, which introduces immortality, corresponds a worldly restitution that leads to the eternity of downfall, and the rhythm of this eternally transient worldly existence . . . is happiness' (SW 3, 306). In Benjamin's view, a specific 'spiritual presence' can indeed modify 'happiness' from something 'incomplete' into something 'complete' (AP, 471). Rather than 'determining' or eternalizing the moments of joy and bliss, this process of completion indicates that these moments have been fully surrendered to the passage of time. Making 'happiness' complete or infinite indicates that it can fully *run its course*. Such an intervention does not work *against* transience but *with* it, holding back the quest for preservation and conservation. Consequently, in his essay on

Proust, Benjamin rejects the commonly held idea that the 'rejuvenating' force of the *souvenir involontaire* is derived from the happiness and innocence of the forgotten moment that this *souvenir involontaire* brings back. Because the *souvenir involontaire* inevitably signals that such moments are *lost*, the *souvenir involontaire* cannot be expected to truly *recover* the initial feeling of bliss.

Near the end of his essay, Benjamin suggests that we can only gauge the significance of this 'rejuvenating' and 'restorative' impulse if we do not merely focus on specific scenes or experiences that are recounted in Proust's novel. In his novel, transience and restoration, forgetting and memory are much more than literary themes or subject matter. Benjamin remarks that what matters most in Proust's cycle is not the 'author or plot' of the novel but its 'structure' and the 'syntax of boundless sentences'. He mentions an intimate connection between the structure of Proust's novel and his literary style on the one hand and his severe breathing problems on the other: 'Proust's syntax rhythmically, step by step, *enacts* his fear of suffocating. . . . On a larger scale, however, the threatening, suffocating crisis was death, which he was constantly aware of, most of all while he was writing' (SW 2, 246 [emphasis added]). In Benjamin's view '[a]sthma became a part of [Proust's] art—if indeed his art did not create it' [*wenn nicht seine Kunst es geschaffen hat*] (SW 2, 246; GS II, 323). Because the structure and style of the book *takes over* the discontinuous pattern of his breathing, Benjamin argues that reading Proust's novel is tantamount to a sustained confrontation with the possibility of cessation. However, the rhythmic quality of Proust's 'boundless sentences' also conditions the reiterated *postponement* of this moment of cessation. Proust's novel triggers at once the experience that each sentence could very well be the last *and* the puzzling observation, repeated time and again, that it nevertheless was not. Because the book's final end is thus continually delayed, the experience of a constant passing away is allowed to fully run its course, giving way to an unsuspected experience of continuity. Like the *Trauerspiele* and Baudelaire's work, Proust's novel contains both a relentless exploration of impermanence *and* a startling interruption of it: it marks both an unyielding announcement *and* an ongoing deferral of the moment of death.

With this parallel between the rhythmic quality of Proust's sentences and the pattern of his breathing, Benjamin does not suggest that Proust's work can only be understood with the help of biographical elements. Both Benjamin and Proust explicitly reject the very duality between work and life and emphasize, instead, that both are inseparable. In the first pages of his doctoral thesis on the German Romantics, Benjamin rejects theories of art that turn to 'artistic consciousness and . . . artistic creation', or 'questions of the psychology of art' (SW 1, 117–18). In the final volume of his novel, Proust elaborates on the same issue of the inseparability of life and art. In the scene that takes place in the library of Prince de Guermantes, Proust remarks that 'real life, life at last laid bare and illuminated—the only life in consequence which can be said to be really lived—is literature, and life thus defined is in a sense all the time immanent in ordinary men no less than in the artist'.[119] Proust makes a human being's life visible as a singular view on the world, and even as a unique world in its own right. However, these unique viewpoints or worlds do not *give* or *reveal* themselves to others and are bound to remain hidden in ordinary life. They can only become accessible when they are transfigured into the added, and created, reality of an *artwork*. Style 'is the revelation, which by direct and conscious methods would be impossible, of the qualitative difference, the uniqueness of the fashion in which the world appears to each one of us, a difference which, if there were no art, would remain for ever the secret of every individual'.[120] Benjamin's description of Proust's novel as a 'life-work' [*Lebenswerk*] should therefore be taken literally: his life and work having become inseparable from each other, Proust's novel is nothing less than an artistic reworking of all the different and discontinuous selves that he has lived through. While none of these selves can be truly recovered in life, Proust's genius consists of introducing them into the sphere of art.

This translation of the writer's life into a work of art transmutes the passage of time and the irrevocable forgetting that belongs to it into creative powers. The puzzling unity of the artistic construct enables the writer to produce his life anew, thereby at once expressing *and* suspending the fragmented state of his existence. For this reason, Proust's novel does not, in Benjamin's view, 'determine' or eternalize moments from the past but it allows the passing away that is inscribed within the life of an individual to enter into the sphere of art. By that token, temporal succession is both made infinite *and* interrupted. From Benjamin's perspective, the completion of the passage of time in and as an artwork *is* the interruption of the passage of time.[121] It is no exaggeration to state that this inseparability between Proust's singular existence and his literary production does indeed indicate the crux of Proust's novel. Near the end of his cycle, Proust puts it as follows: 'And I understood that all these materials for a work of literature were simply my past life; I understood that they had come to me, in frivolous pleasures, in indolence, in tenderness, in unhappiness, and that I had stored them up without divining the purpose for which they were destined or even their continued existence any more than a seed does when it forms within itself a reserve of all the nutritious substances from which it will feed a plant'.[122] Proust highlights that the very unity of his novel entails a reproduction and completion of the contingency of his life. Only the artwork itself can open the space where a confrontation with transience can nonetheless give way to a puzzling type of 'happiness'. Nowhere but in the coherence of the novel itself can the repetition, and even acceleration, of experiences of loss bring about the unexpected 'about-turn into salvation and redemption' (O, 232).

Since the *souvenir involontaire* always signals the concomitant loss of the past, Proust's rejuvenating and restorative impulse needs to come from elsewhere than the faculty of memory. For Benjamin, only the structural and syntactic qualities of the literary *construct* can explain its redemptive potential. In his view, Proust does not so much *describe* moments of rejuvenation and restoration as *write them into being*. This argument that the impermanence of an individual's life can only be interrupted by way of a *work*, marks the sharpest opposition between Proust's view of time on the one hand, and the belief in the *spontaneous* survival of an immemorial past on the other. In contrast to Bergson, Freud and Heidegger, Proust did not just describe the 'deep' memory that requires the help of forgetting, but he created a work of art in which forgetting interrupts transience by taking itself as an object. This suggestion that an artwork can enable a Nietzschean 'forgetting of forgetting' can also be retrieved in Deleuze's interpretation of Proust. In Deleuze's view, the similarities between Proust's and Bergson's view of time are, in the final analysis, superficial. Proust is ultimately not all that interested in conceptions of time and memory since he shifts the focus to the issue, and the creation, of art. Deleuze argues that

> [w]e must not regard art as a more profound means of exploring involuntary memory. We must regard involuntary memory as a stage, which is not even the most important stage, in the apprenticeship to art. It is certain that this memory sets us on the path of essences. Further, reminiscence already possesses essence, has been able to capture it. But it grants us essence in a slackened, secondary state and so obscurely that we are incapable of understanding the gift we are given and the joy we experience.[123]

Both Benjamin and Deleuze identify a dimension in Proust's writing that goes beyond the analysis of the *virtual* or *pure* past that is believed to spontaneously live on. Both associate Proust's work with a type of complete nihilism that could not be accommodated by any of the authors who focus on the supposed survival of an immemorial past and the preserving capacity of memory, regardless of whether these concepts are understood in vitalist, psychoanalytical or ontological terms. As Deleuze puts it in a 'Note on the Proustian Experience' that is included in *Difference and Repetition*, what matters most to Proust is a 'death instinct that finds its glorious issue in the work of art, over and above the erotic experiences of the involuntary memory'.[124] Proust is not in search of an immemorial time that restores the confidence in a 'deep' or intimate Self (Bergson's *moi profond*, Freud's unconscious 'nucleus' of the ego, Heidegger's 'authenticity') but in search of a lost time that can be transfigured into the specific unity of a work of art. Both Benjamin and Deleuze's analysis of Proust revolves around the possibility that art can complete, rather than prevent, the collapse of a continuous Self and a stable identity. Such a form of artistic production enables a lived sense of impermanence and fragmentation to be reworked into 'the autonomy of the product, the independence of the work'.[125] As Deleuze suggests, Proust's formula 'a little time in its pure state' [*un peu de temps à l'état pur*] ultimately lets go of the belief in a pure or virtual past that has continued to live on and replaces it with a truly empty and merely formal time. 'The Proustian formula "a little time in its pure state" refers first to the pure past, the in-itself of the past or the erotic synthesis of time, but more profoundly to the pure and empty form of time, the ultimate synthesis, that of the death instinct which leads to the eternity of the return in time'.[126] Affirming this 'purity' of time requires that it is transmuted into the specific and non-actual unity of an artwork. This, for its part, involves a forgetting that is both complete *and* made productive.

A NOTE ON MARCEL, ALBERTINE AND GILBERTE

The penultimate volume of Proust's cycle illustrates what Benjamin and Deleuze might have had in mind with such a completion of the passage of time into art. 'Grieving and Forgetting', the first chapter of *The Fugitive* [*Albertine Disparue*] begins with the exclamation 'Miss Albertine has left!' and thereby starts off a lengthy description of recurring experiences of loss.[127] A large part of the book revolves around Marcel's confused response to the news that his former lover did not just leave him but was subsequently killed when she was thrown off a horse. Most remarkable in Proust's rendition of Marcel's grief is that it is not depicted as a gradual process but as a series of distinct stages that do not dissolve into each other but abruptly fall away one by one. For Marcel's sadness does not slowly give way to a renewed interest in life. The development through which he overcomes his initial sorrow, rather, is described as the succession of a series of multiple and discontinuous selves that cannot coexist. As Marcel exclaims about the death of his lover, 'Only a real death of my self, . . . (were it not impossible), would be capable of consoling me for her death'.[128] The different selves that are described one by one in *Albertine Disparue* therefore inevitably replace each other: despite his interest in the possibility that various selves resonate with each other over time (as is the case in the *souvenir involontaire*) Proust lays bare that they do not survive. With the unexpected news that Albertine has left, for instance, Marcel's earlier indifference towards her vanishes without a trace, as if the earlier self that had wanted to end his relationship with her has now become wholly inaccessible. At odds with Marcel's awareness that he was no longer happy with their relationship, the truly new self that is called forth by Albertine's disappearance introduces a passion that is more intense than ever before. A similar temporal succession of multiple selves arises after Marcel finds out about Albertine's death, each new self being marked by the incapacity of retrieving the previous one. At first, of course, this unceasing passing away of selves only increases Marcel's despair since it confronts him with the irrevocable disappearance of his lover.

> [N]ot being able to link simultaneously what I was then and what I would become, I thought in despair of this whole integument of kisses, caresses and friendly slumber, which I would soon have to shed for ever. The wave of such tender memories, coming to break over the idea that Albertine was dead, overwhelmed me with the clash of such contrary tides that I could not lay still.[129]

Initially overcome by this inability to recapture his lost past, however, Marcel ends up with yet another self, albeit with one that has now become wholly indifferent to his previous lover: not even a telegram that mistakenly announces that Albertine is alive and well after all, now manages to reanimate his feelings. 'I was tending to move into an entirely new character. It is not because others have died that our affection for them weakens, it is because we ourselves are dying'.[130]

The different selves that are thus depicted one by one in *Albertine Disparue* cannot be considered as constitutive of a deep, underlying Self. One of the prime effects of the recurring pattern with which those different selves fall away is that Proust's novel gives up the attempt to conjure the intimate unity and continuity of an actual human being that can be empathized or identified with by the reader. The alterations in Marcel's mental state occur in such an abrupt and unexpected manner that the foundation and stability of an underlying self is exploded by the multiplicity of mutually exclusive selves. '[M]y life appeared to me to be something . . . lacking the support of an individual, identical and permanent self, . . . something . . . easy for death to terminate here or there without any kind of conclusion'.[131] Cut off from the reference to the identity and selfhood of an actual person, it therefore becomes palpable that *Albertine Disparue* derives its unity from nothing else than the very series of discontinuous selves. Steeped in an expansive confrontation with transience, the succession of selves in *Albertine Disparue* is organized in such a manner that the novel itself is not at all lacking in unity, however impermanent these selves may be. This constant movement of falling-away, to the contrary, is described in such a rhythmical manner that it sets up a puzzling continuity. It is on account of this paradoxical unity, internal to the novel itself and co-constituted by the mind of the reader, that Proust ultimately conjures the surprising possibility that this law of transience can be reversed. For, as suggested by Benjamin, Proust does indeed end his novel by explicitly referring to 'an operation which made me relatively happy' [*opération qui me rendit assez heureux*].[132] In the final scene of *Albertine Disparue*, Marcel visits Gilberte Swann-Forcheville who, many years before, had been the object of an unreturned passion on the part of Marcel. Now married to his friend Robert de St. Loup, Gilberte reflects on the times she spent together with Marcel and shares with him a piece of information that he had never expected to receive: the very gesture that Marcel, so many years ago, had interpreted as a sign of rejection had in fact been a positive response to his advances. In other words, Gilberte had not been disinclined to return Marcel's feelings at all. One would expect that Marcel's sudden awareness that he has suffered for no reason would trigger an intense feeling of frustration and regret on his part. The reason why it nonetheless conjures 'happiness' is that this realization confirms, so many years later, that his youthful self and the sufferings that were concomitant with it have expired completely. 'And indeed, does death not come between us and women whom we no longer love but meet again years later, just as if they were no longer of this world, since the fact that our love no longer exists makes of the women that they used to be, or the men that we were, dead people?'[133] In line with Benjamin's suggestions, Proust does not indeed link the topic of happiness with the recovery of a past or the discovery of a *counter*-principle *against* transience. Happiness, to the contrary, has here become the prime token of the ephemerality of an individual's life itself, and, as a consequence, of the certainty that one's sufferings will at some point vanish without a trace. Carefully positioned at the end of a novel that revolves around sadness and loss, Proust's final scene includes an unsuspected 'about-turn': the nearly endless descriptions of life's impermanence, it now turns out, have prepared the reader's mind for the puzzling feeling that even this very impermanence and the sadness that it triggers might at some point give way. Proust puts it as follows: 'For in this world where everything wears out, where everything perishes, there is one thing that collapses and is more completely destroyed than anything else, and leaves fewer traces than beauty itself: and that is grief'.[134] The 'happy' turn towards the past with which Proust ends the novel that directly precedes *Time Regained* is therefore not at all meant to indicate that a blissful and forgotten past can be retrieved. What is at stake in the final scene of *Albertine Disparue* is not at all an *overcoming* of transience but an *acceleration* of it. With the puzzling awareness that even the sadness about the world's passing away might at some point pass away, Marcel amplifies the experience that our lives lack an ultimate ground. However, he thereby rids himself of any attachment to his past and, instead, carves out a space for a novel reality that cannot in any way be made accessible by our thoughts and feelings. Rather than triggering a feeling of regret, the knowledge that he had been completely unaware of the possibility to satisfy his desires, restores Marcel's belief in a life that is radically different from the one we live. 'I was pleased, as I realized that the happiness which I had striven with all my might to achieve in those days, and which nothing could ever now restore, had existed elsewhere than in my thoughts, and indeed so near to me. . . . And I had no idea!'[135] For this reason, what matters here is not so much an experience of a regained *past* or a lived *present* as a perception about a truly different *future*. Like Kafka's exclamation that there is '[a]n *infinite amount of hope, but not for us'*, Marcel replaces the longing for new possibilities in *this* life with an affirmation of *change* that is much more radical. Rather than seeking to anticipate or predict what is still to come, Marcel uses the awareness that his own existence is lacking in determination to replenish his hope for a life that is truly other.

NOTES

1. Henri Bergson, *Matter and Memory*, transl. by Nancy Margaret, Paul and William Scott Palmer (New York: Zone Books, 1991), 142.

2. Ibid., 151. In this context, Deleuze even speaks about a 'Platonic inspiration' because '[t]he reminiscence also affirms a pure being of the past, a being in itself of the past, an ontological Memory that is capable of serving as the foundation for the unfolding of time'. In Gilles Deleuze, *Bergsonism*, transl. by Hugh Tomlinson and Barbara Habberjam (New York: Zone Books, 1991), 59.

3. See Bergson, *Matter and Memory*, 149–50: 'But how can the past, which, by hypothesis, has ceased to be, preserve itself? Have we not here a real contradiction? We reply that the question is just whether the past has ceased to exist or whether it has simply ceased to be useful. You define the present in an arbitrary manner as *that which is*, whereas the present is simply *what is being made*'.

4. The virtual past can at most *become* useful to the body's dealings with the present. However, this resurfacing of the past requires that it is summoned by perception and consciousness and thereby sheds its purity or virtuality. '[I]t is from the present that the appeal to which memory responds comes, and it is from the sensori-motor elements of present action that a memory borrows the warmth which gives it life'. In ibid., 153. 'Virtual, [pure] memory can only become actual by means of the perception which attracts it. Powerless, it borrows life and strength from the present sensation in which it is materialized'. In ibid., 127.

5. For a discussion of the concept of immemorial in Merleau-Ponty, see Alia Al-Saji, 'The Temporality of Life: Merleau-Ponty, Bergson, and the Immemorial Past', in *The Southern Journal of Philosophy* 45 (2) (2007): 177–206. For the reference to the concept of immemorial in Levinas's work, see for example, *Otherwise than Being. Or, Beyond Essence*, transl. by Alphonso Lingis (Boston: Kluwer, 1978), 11. For the reference in Deleuze's work, see for example, *Bergsonism*, 57 and *Difference and Repetition*, 85, 88, 140, 144, 273.

6. Henri Bergson, 'Memory of the Present and False Recognition', in *Mind Energy*, in *Key Writings*, ed. by Keith Ansell Pearson and John Mullarkey, transl. by Melissa McMahon (London and New York: Continuum, 2002), 144 and 147.

7. Ibid., 144.

8. See for instance Maurice Merleau-Ponty, *The Visible and the Invisible*, ed. by Claude Lefort, transl. by Alphonso Lingis (Evanston: Northwestern University Press, 1968), 123. See also Alia Al-Saji, 'The Temporality of Life: Merleau-Ponty, Bergson, and the Immemorial Past', 184.

9. The past, in Bergson's words, 'is preserved by itself, automatically'. In Henri Bergson, *Creative Evolution*, transl. by Arthur Mitchell (New York: The Modern Library, 1944), 7. Because the immemorial past has never been an empirical present, the emphasis on duration can very well inspire a belief in ongoing transformation. The indivisible stream of becoming that Bergson terms 'élan vital' consists of nothing else than the entirety of the past contracted in its pure

or virtual form. Consequently, the hypothesis of an enduring, immemorial past that was always already forgotten serves Bergson to deploy a philosophical framework that revolves around change and movement. '[I]t might be said of life, as of consciousness, that at every moment it is creating something'. Ibid., 34.

10. Nietzsche, 'On the Uses and Disadvantages of History for Life', 60–61. See Introduction.

11. Bergson, *Matter and Memory*, 263. According to Bergson, amnesia, for instance, is not to be associated with an overall destruction of memories but with the difficulty of retrieving memories that have in truth not altogether disappeared.

12. 'The brain', Bergson claims, 'contributes to the recall of the useful recollection, but still more to the provisional banishment of all the others'. Ibid., 177.

13. Sigmund Freud, 'The Psychopathology of Everyday Life', in *The Standard Edition of the Complete Psychological Works of Sigmund Freud. Volume VI*, ed. and transl. by James Strachey, in collaboration with Anna Freud, assisted by Alix Strachey and Alan Tyson (London: The Hogarth Press, 1956–1974), 40. See also Sigmund Freud, 'The Psychical Mechanism of Forgetfulness', in *Standard Edition. Volume III*, 289–97.

14. Martin Heidegger, *Being and Time*, transl. by Joan Stambaugh (New York: State University of New York Press, 1996), 2.

15. Plato, *Theaetetus*, 325 (191d).

16. Aristotle, 'De Memoria et Reminiscentia (On Memory and Reminiscence)', 607 (450b).

17. Sigmund Freud, 'A Note Upon the "Mystic Writing-Pad"', in *Standard Edition. Volume XIX*, 230.

18. Ibid., 230.

19. Ibid.

20. Sigmund Freud, 'Notes Upon a Case of Obsessional Neurosis', in *Standard Edition. Volume X*, 206.

21. Sigmund Freud, 'Beyond the Pleasure Principle', in *Standard Edition. Volume XVIII*, 25.

22. Aristotle, 'De Memoria et Reminiscentia (On Memory and Reminiscence)', 607 (449b).

23. Plato, *Theaetetus*, 325 (191d-e).

24. Sigmund Freud, 'The Unconscious', in *Standard Edition. Volume XIV*, 186.

25. Paul Ricoeur, *Memory, History, Forgetting*, transl. by Kathleen Blamey and David Pellauer (Chicago and London: The University of Chicago Press, 2004), 414.

26. Ibid., 427.

27. Sigmund Freud, 'A Note Upon the "Mystic Writing-Pad"', 230.

28. In what follows, I lean strongly on Paul Moyaert's excellent analysis of the concept of the death drive, in Paul Moyaert, *Opboksen tegen het inerte. De doodsdrift bij Freud* (Nijmegen: Vantilt, 2014).

29. Sigmund Freud, 'Beyond the Pleasure Principle', 19–20.

30. Ibid., 35.

31. Sigmund Freud, 'Two Principles of Mental Functioning', in *Standard Edition. Volume XII*, 221.

32. See, for example, Sigmund Freud, 'Three Essays on Sexuality' in *Standard Edition. Volume VII*, 168: 'By a drive is provisionally to be understood the psychical representative of an endosomatic, continuously flowing source of stimulation. . . . The simplest and likeliest assumption as to the nature of drives would seem to be that in itself a drive is without quality, and, so far as mental life is

concerned, is only to be regarded as a measure of the demand made upon the mind for work' (translation modified).

33. Sigmund Freud, 'Beyond the Pleasure Principle', 35.
34. Ibid., 36 (translation modified).
35. Ibid. (translation modified).
36. Ibid., 63 (translation modified).
37. In the words of Paul Moyaert, 'the death drive is not a force that strives towards death, but a force that leads to death if it is not inhibited'. In Paul Moyaert, *Opboksen tegen het inerte. De doodsdrift bij Freud*, 26.
38. Sigmund Freud, 'Beyond the Pleasure Principle', 36.
39. Sigmund Freud, 'On Transience', in *Standard Edition. Volume XIV*, 306.
40. Sigmund Freud, 'Beyond the Pleasure Principle', 38.
41. Moreover, this sole reference is not even a very relevant one since Freud uses the term nihilism to describe what should in fact be called relativism. 'There have certainly been intellectual nihilists of this kind in the past, but just now the relativity theory of modern physics seems to have gone to their head. They start out from science, indeed, but they contrive to force it into self-abrogation, into suicide; they set it the task of getting itself out of the way by refuting its own claims. One often has an impression in this connection that this nihilism is only a temporary attitude which is to be retained until this task has been performed'. In Sigmund Freud, 'New Introductory Lectures on Psychoanalysis. Lecture XXXV. The Question of a Weltanschauung', in *Standard Edition. Volume XXII*, 212.
42. Gilles Deleuze, *Difference and Repetition*, 112 (emphasis added). See also Deleuze's discussion of the 'death instinct' (*sic*) in his essay on masochism. Deleuze emphasizes that Freud considers the death instinct as the 'foundation' of the pleasure principle and not at all as its 'contradiction' or 'exception'. The power of repetition that is embodied by the death instinct is believed to enable the pleasure principle to perform its discharging task. The death instinct repeats the 'abyss of the groundless' and the 'indifference of the inexcitable' or 'inanimate' to make such a process of tension-reduction possible. For this reason, Freud's concern is termed a 'transcendental' one and the death instinct is believed to be 'inseparable' from the binding process that is performed by the pleasure principle. In Gilles Deleuze, 'Coldness and Cruelty', in *Masochism*, transl. by Jean McNeill (New York: Zone Books, 1991), 111–21.
43. Gilles Deleuze, *Difference and Repetition*, 112.
44. Ibid.
45. Ibid.
46. Ibid.
47. Sigmund Freud, 'Beyond the Pleasure Principle', 19. See Paul Moyaert, *Opboksen tegen het inerte. De doodsdrift bij Freud*, 52–54. Compare, however, with the footnote at the beginning of Chapter III of 'The Ego and the Id', where Freud confesses to have changed his mind. In 'The Ego and the Id', in *Standard Edition. Volume XIX*, 28.
48. Sigmund Freud, 'Draft H – Paranoia', in *Standard Edition. Volume I*, 210–12. See also Paul Moyaert, *Opboksen tegen het inerte. De doodsdrift bij Freud*, 52.
49. Martin Heidegger, *Zollikon Seminars. Protocols-Conversations-Letters*, ed. by Medard Boss, transl. by Franz Mayr and Richard Askay (Evanston: Northwestern University Press, 2001), 20.
50. Ibid., 224. For an elaborate discussion of Heidegger's criticism of Freud, see Fred Dallmayr, 'Heidegger and Freud', *Political Psychology* 14 (2) (1993), 235–53. For an attempt to bring Heidegger's views closer to Freud's views (read

through Lacan), see William J. Richardson, 'Heidegger and Psychoanalysis', in *Natureza humana* 5 (1) (2003), 9–38.

51. Martin Heidegger, *Being and Time*, 8, 2–3. Much has been made of Heidegger's *Kehre*, that is, the process through which his 'fundamental metaphysics', which approached the question of Being by way of an analysis of human existence, was replaced with an ontological project that puts the question of Being first. The *Kehre* marks a shift in Heidegger's theory of ontological forgetting. While in the first phase of Heidegger's philosophy, the forgetting of Being was primarily due to *Dasein*'s self-forgetting when he is absorbed in activity, in the latter phase of his thinking, the forgetting of Being is linked with the movement through which Being simultaneously shows and withdraws itself (cf. infra). For an excellent summary of *Being and Time*, with references to the issue of forgetting, see Mark A. Wrathall and Max Murphey, 'An Overview of *Being and Time*', in *The Cambridge Companion to Heidegger's Being and Time*, ed. Mark A. Wrathall (New York: Cambridge University Press, 2013), 1–54 and, for an in-depth overview, Theodor Kisiel, *The Genesis of Heidegger's Being and Time* (Berkeley, Los Angeles, London: University of California Press, 1993), esp. 309–451. For an overview of the topic of ontological forgetting in Heidegger's writings in general, see Alexandre Schild, 'Oubli de l'être', in *Le Dictionnaire Martin Heidegger*, ed. by Philippe Arjakovsky, François Fédier and Hadrien France-Lanord (Paris: Les Éditions du Cerf, 2013), 937–43. The topic is a key concern to Heidegger's philosophy at large. See also for instance the first chapter of his *Introduction to Metaphysics*, revised and expanded, transl. by Gregory Fried and Richard Polt (New Haven, CT, and London: Yale University Press, 2000), 1–56. For a good introduction to these concerns see Thomas Sheehan, '*Kehre* and *Ereignis*: A Prolegomenon to *Introduction to Metaphysics*', in *A Companion to Heidegger's Introduction to Metaphysics*, ed. by Richard Polt and Gregory Fried (New Haven and London: Yale University Press, 2001), 3–16.

52. Martin Heidegger, *Contributions to Philosophy (Of the Event)*, transl. by Richard Rojcewicz and Daniella Vallega-Neu (Bloomington and Indianapolis: Indiana University Press, 2012), 91.

53. Ibid.

54. Ibid., 86. For more information of Heidegger and technology, see Michael E. Zimmerman, *Heidegger's Confrontation with Modernity: Technology, Politics and Art* (Bloomington: Indiana University Press, 1990).

55. See also the following statement: 'The supreme being, as cause of all beings, took over the essence of beyng. These beings, formerly made by a creator God, then became the *dominion* of humanity, inasmuch as beings are now taken only in their objectivity and come under human domination'. In Heidegger, *Contributions*, 88.

56. Ibid., 95.

57. Ibid., 91.

58. Ibid., 90–91.

59. Martin Heidegger, *Parmenides*, transl. by André Schuwer and Richard Rojcewicz (Bloomington and Indianapolis: Indiana University Press, 1992), 82.

60. Ibid., 71.

61. Ibid., 82. See also the statement that 'λήθη conceals while it withdraws', in ibid., 83 and that 'the very concealment . . . withdraws itself', in ibid., 84.

62. Ibid., 120. Heidegger goes on to describe that '[b]y this drink, taken in measure, the man returning to earth carries an essential belongingness to the domain of the essence of concealment. All dwell to a certain degree within the essential region of concealment', in ibid., 120.

63. Ibid., 123.

64. Ibid., 124. The sentence continues as follows: 'This preserving of the unconcealed comes to pass in its pure essence when man strives freely for the unconcealed and does so incessantly throughout his mortal course on earth. To strive for something freely and to think only of it is in Greek μνάομαι; the 'perpetual' endurance on a path and a course is in Greek ἀνά-; the incessant thinking of something, the pure saving into unconcealedness of what is thought, is thus ἀνάμνησις'.

65. Ibid., 120–21.

66. Martin Heidegger, *The History of Beyng*, transl. by Jeffrey Powell and William McNeill (Bloomington and Indianapolis: Indiana University Press, 2015), 105 (translation modified). The German text can be found in Martin Heidegger, *Gesamtausgabe. Band 69. Die Geschichte des Seyns* (Frankfurt am Main: Vittorio Klostermann, 1998), 123.

67. In his lectures on Parmenides, Heidegger starts from the observation that, for all the references to the concepts of ἀλήθεια (truth) and λήθη (forgetfulness, the linguistic root of the Greek word for truth) in Greek culture (Heidegger singles out, amongst other authors, Hesiod, Pindar, Homer and Plato), ancient literature does not explicitly and systematically reflect on the inseparability of truth's self-revelation and withdrawal. This seeming neglect, however, is to be considered a token of the very importance of the concepts of ἀλήθεια and λήθη since Greek culture revolves around myths and stories that are believed to enable an *experience* of the inevitable forgetting that pertains to truth-revelation. 'The Greeks think and poetize and 'deal' *within* the essence of ἀλήθεια and of λήθη, but they do not think and poetize *about* this essence and they do not 'deal' with it', in ibid., 87. For a good overview of the topic of 'unconcealedness' or 'unconcealment', see Mark A. Wrathall, 'Unconcealment', in *A Companion to Heidegger*, ed. by Hubert L. Dreyfus and Mark A. Wrathall (Oxford and Cambridge: Blackwell Publishing, 2005), 337–57. For an excellent discussion of Heidegger's concern with ontological clearing, see David Farrell Krell, *Intimations of Mortality. Time, Truth, and Finitude in Heidegger's Thinking of Being* (University Park and London: The Pennsylvania State University Press, 1986), 67–94.

68. '[T]he *essence* of man, and not only the individual man in his destiny, is saved only when man, as the being he is, harkens to the legend of concealment', in Heidegger, *Parmenides*, 126.

69. 'Λήθη, the oblivion of withdrawing concealment, is that withdrawal by means of which alone the essence of ἀλήθεια can be preserved and thus be and remain unforgotten. Thoughtless opinion maintains that something is preserved the soonest and is preservable the easiest when it is constantly at hand and graspable. But in truth, and that now means for us truth in the sense of the essence of unconcealedness, it is self-withdrawing concealment that in the highest way disposes human beings to preserving and to faithfulness', in ibid., 127.

70. For an interpretation of Heidegger's work that does consider his concept of historicity and historical meaning of utmost importance, see, for example, Jeffrey Andrew Barash, *Martin Heidegger and the Problem of Historical Meaning* (New York: Fordham University Press, 2003). Barash reconstructs Heidegger's early view of historical meaning by analyzing, amongst other topics, his rejection of the scientific claims that underlie the philosophies of history of authors such as Windelband, Rickert, Dilthey, Troeltsch and Simmel. Barash concedes that Heidegger's concept of history is cast on religious influences (e.g., Lutheranism and Neo-Thomism) and, most important of course, on his philosophy of *Dasein* (in the early phase of his thought) and Being (after the *Kehre*). However, Barash reconciles Heidegger's ontological project with an exploration of *historical* meaning because the former deals in his view with a 'meta-historical leitmo-

tiv' rather than an a-historical ground (cf. e.g., p. 182: '*Seinsvergessenheit*, as the forgetfulness of the finite Being of Dasein in the disclosure of a meaning of Being, serves as a metahistorical leitmotiv linking in a silent unity the motives of a long tradition of reflection stretching back to antiquity'). Anticipating the argument that will be laid out in the following pages, we can already state that the historical evolutions that Benjamin deems responsible for a widespread 'poverty of experience' are, from Heidegger's perspective, of a merely ontic nature and not an ontological one. Vice versa, Heidegger's concept of an ontological ground to history testifies, from Benjamin's perspective, to 'mythic' thinking.

71. For Benjamin's concept of *Aufgabe*, see chapter 1. For a brief but clear discussion of the opposition between Benjamin and Heidegger, see Rolf Tiedemann, *Studien zur Philosophie Walter Benjamins* (Frankfurt am Main: Suhrkamp Verlag, 1973), 90–91. I agree with Tiedemann's argument that Benjamin's consideration of something like a *Seinsvergessenheit* is much more radical than Heidegger's in that it is 'irreconcilable with such [i.e., Heidegger's] flowing back into the originary, [irreconcilable] with the retreat into being, into 'the' event ['*das' Ereignis*]' (p. 90). See also Willem van Reijen, *Der Schwarzwald und Paris. Heidegger und Benjamin* (München: Wilhelm Fink Verlag, 1998), 142–65 and Andrew Benjamin, 'Time and Task: Benjamin and Heidegger Showing the Present', in *Sparks Will Fly*, 145–74.

72. Martin Heidegger, 'The End of Philosophy and the Task of Thinking', in *Basic Writings: From Being and Time (1929) to The Task of Thinking (1964)*, ed. and introduced by David Farrell Krell (San Francisco: Harper Collins, 1977), 386. See also p. 384 where Heidegger describes an 'openness that grants a possible letting-appear' and states that '[o]nly this openness grants to the movement of speculative thinking the passage through what it thinks'.

73. Martin Heidegger, 'Time and Being', in *On Time and Being*, transl. by Joan Stambaugh (New York and London: Harper Torchbooks, 1972), 4–5.

74. Ibid., 124. The sentence continues as follows: 'Rather, the saving and conserving of the un-concealed is necessarily in relation to concealment, understood as the withdrawal of what appears in its appearing'.

75. Compare with Freud's confession that he has never properly read Nietzsche's works in his 'On the History of the Psycho-Analytic Movement', in *Standard Edition. Volume XIV*, 15–16 and 'An Autobiographical Study', in *Standard Edition, Volume XX*, 60.

76. See, for example, Martin Heidegger, 'The Word of Nietzsche: "God is Dead"', in *The Question Concerning Technology and Other Essays*, transl. and introduced by William Lovitt (New York and London: Garland Publishing, 1977), 78. For the full text of Heidegger's writings on Nietzsche, see Martin Heidegger, *Nietzsche. Volumes One and Two*, transl. by David Farrell Krell (San Francisco: Harper Collins, 1991) and *Nietzsche. Volumes Three and Four*, transl. by Joan Stambaugh, David Farrell Krell and Frank A. Capuzzi (San Francisco: Harper Collins, 1991). For a good summary (and defense) of Heidegger's reading of Nietzsche, see chapters 5 and 6 in Louis P. Blond, *Heidegger and Nietzsche. Overcoming Metaphysics* (London and New York: Continuum, 2010), Hans Sluga, 'Heidegger's Nietzsche', in *A Companion to Heidegger*, ed. by Hubert L. Dreyfus and Mark A. Wrathall (Oxford: Blackwell Publishing, 2010), 102–20 and David Farrell Krell, *Intimations of Mortality*, 126–37.

77. See Heidegger, 'The Word of Nietzsche: "God is Dead"', 96: 'The name "overman" designates the essence of humanity, which, as modern humanity, is beginning to enter into the consummation belonging to the essence of its age.

"Overman" is man who is man from out of the reality determined through the will to power, and for that reality'.

78. Ibid., 104.

79. 'When the Being of whatever is, is stamped as a value and its essence is thereby sealed off, then within this metaphysics and that means continually within the truth of what is as such during this age every way to the experiencing of Being itself is obliterated', in ibid., 103.

80. Ibid., 84.

81. Ibid., 110.

82. For an analysis of the inseparability of Being and time in Heidegger's writings, and the argument that this temporality is a *grounding* dynamic, rather than a process that involves *impermanence* and *annihilation*, see Françoise Dastur, *Heidegger and the Question of Time*, transl. by François Raffoul and David Pettigrew (New York: Humanity Books, 1999). See also Barash's argument that, in Heidegger, historicity should be considered as a force of 'coherence' in his *Martin Heidegger and the Problem of Historical Meaning*. See also, of course, Derrida's critique of Heidegger's philosophy of time as a metaphysics of 'presence' in, for example, '*Ousia* and *Gramme*: Note on a Note from *Being and Time*', in *Margins of Philosophy*, transl. by Alan Bass (Sussex: The Harvester Press, 1982), 29–68. For an extensive discussion of Derrida's critique, and the quest for a concept of time that is released from the metaphysics of presence, see David Wood, *The Deconstruction of Time* (Evanston: Northwestern University Press, 2001), esp. parts 3 and 4.

83. Friedrich Nietzsche, *Thus Spoke Zarathustra*, transl. by Adrian del Caro (New York: Cambridge University Press, 2006), 111.

84. Ibid., 112.

85. Ibid., 111.

86. Nietzsche, quoted in Heidegger, *Nietzsche. Volumes One and Two*, 224. David Farrell Krell's translation of Zarathustra's definition of revenge differs from that of Del Caro and Pippin, who render it as 'the will's unwillingness toward time and time's "it was"' (p. 111). For a discussion of Heidegger's analysis of this passage, see also David Farrell Krell, *Intimations of Mortality*, 132–35.

87. See Gilles Deleuze, *Nietzsche and Philosophy*, 48–49 and the chapter on *The Tragic*.

88. Heidegger, *Nietzsche. Volumes One and Two*, 229.

89. Ibid., 228.

90. Ibid.

91. Ernst Jünger, 'Across the Line', in Martin Heidegger and Ernst Jünger, *Correspondence 1949–1975*, transl. by Timothy Sean Quinn (New York and London: Rowman and Littlefield International, 2016), 74. For more background of the discussion between Heidegger and Jünger, see Wolf Kittler, 'From Gestalt to Ge-Stell: Martin Heidegger Reads Ernst Jünger', in *Cultural Critique* 69 (2008): 79–97 and the unpublished MA thesis of Nicholas Johnston, 'Total Mobilization and Standing Reserve. Ernst Jünger and Martin Heidegger on Technology and History' (Institute of Philosophy, KU Leuven, 2017).

92. Jünger, 'Across the Line', 75.

93. Ibid., 79.

94. Ibid., 83.

95. Ibid., 78.

96. Ibid., 89.

97. Ibid., 90.

98. Ibid., 74.

99. Ibid., 75.

100. Ibid., 91.
101. Martin Heidegger, 'On the Question of Being', in *Pathmarks*, ed. and transl. by William McNeill (Cambridge: Cambridge University Press, 2010), 307.
102. Heidegger, *Contributions*, 92. For a reference to nihilism in *Contributions* see, for example, 90–91 and 95 where the 'abandonment by Being' is described as 'beyng ha[ving] withdrawn from beings', entailing nothing less than the 'breakdown of truth', the 'essential decay of beyng' and even 'the ground . . . and more original determination of the essence of . . . nihilism'.
103. See also ibid., 90. 'To make appear by way of recollection the concealed power of this forgottenness as forgottenness and to bring forth therein the resonating of beyng. The recognition of the plight'.
104. Heidegger, 'On the Question of Being', 313.
105. See, for example, ibid., 311. 'As . . . that being which is in essence brought into the need of B̶e̶i̶n̶g̶, the human being is part of the zone of B̶e̶i̶n̶g̶, i.e., at the same time of the nothing. The human being not only stands *within* the critical zone of the line. He himself—but not taken independently, and especially not through himself alone—is this zone and thus the line'.
106. For a very compelling and convincing discussion of the relation between Benjamin and Freud that also highlights the difference between Benjamin's philosophical framework and the psychoanalytical one, see Ilit Ferber, *Philosophy and Melancholy: Benjamin's Early Reflections on Theater and Language* (Stanford: Stanford University Press, 2013), chapter 1.
107. This line is taken from the aptly entitled poem 'Craving for Oblivion' [*Le gout du néant*] in *The Flowers of Evil*. See Charles Baudelaire, *Les Fleurs du Mal*, transl. Richard Howard (Boston: David R. Godine, 1982) , 77–255.
108. Ibid., 15.
109. See also the concept of 'compact mass', as developed in a footnote to the *Artwork* essay (SW 3, 129) and texts such as 'A Different Utopian Will' and 'Theories of German Fascism'.
110. For an excellent analysis of these issues, see Irving Wohlfarth, 'No-Man's-Land: On Walter Benjamin's "Destructive Character"'. See chapter 1. See also Susan Buck-Morss, 'Aesthetics and Anaesthetics: Walter Benjamin's Artwork Essay Reconsidered', *October* 62 (1992): 3–41; Howard Eiland, 'Reception in Distraction', *boundary 2* 30 (1) (2003): 51–66; Gertrud Koch, 'Cosmos in Film: On the Concept of Space in Walter Benjamin's "Work of Art" Essay', in *Walter Benjamin's Philosophy: Destruction and Experience*, ed. by Andrew Benjamin and Peter Osborne (London: Routledge, 1994), 205–15; Miriam Bratu Hansen, 'Benjamin, Cinema and Experience: "The Blue Flower in the Land of Technology"', *New German Critique* 40 (1987): 179–224. See also Sigrid Weigel, *Body and Image-Space: Re-Reading Walter Benjamin*, transl. by Georgina Paul, with Rachel McNicholl and Jeremy Gaines (London: Routledge, 1996).
111. For more on the concept of room-for-play, see the work of Miriam Bratu Hansen, esp. 'Play-Form of Second Nature', in *Cinema and Experience: Siegfried Kracauer, Walter Benjamin, and Theodor W. Adorno* (Berkeley: University of California Press, 2012), 183–204; and 'Room-for-Play: Benjamin's Gamble with Cinema', in *October* 109 (2004), 3–45. See also chapter 3.
112. For more on the issue of allegory, see, for example, Samuel Weber, 'Storming the Work: Allegory and Theatricality in Benjamin's *Origin of the German Mourning Play*', in *Theatricality as Medium* (New York: Fordham University Press, 2004), 160–80; and idem., 'Genealogy of Modernity: History, Myth, and Allegory in Benjamin's *Origin of the German Mourning Play*', in *Benjamin's -abilities*, 131–63. See also Andrew Benjamin, 'Boredom and Distraction: The Moods of Modernity', in *Walter Benjamin and History*, ed. Andrew Benjamin (London

and New York: Continuum, 2005), 156–70; Irving Wohlfarth, 'Et Cetera: The Historian as Chiffonnier', in *New German Critique* 39 (1986): 142–68; and Rebecca Comay, 'The Sickness of Tradition: Between Melancholia and Fetishism', in *Walter Benjamin and History*, 88–101. In her *Philosophy and Melancholy* Ilit Ferber, as well, develops the argument that important elements in Benjamin's philosophy revolve around an 'endless commitment to loss' that is 'productive rather than . . . passive and paralyzing' (p. 13).

113. See O, 232: 'It is to misunderstand the allegorical entirely if we make a distinction between the store of images, in which this about-turn into salvation and redemption takes place, and that grim store which signifies death and damnation. For it is precisely visions of the frenzy of destruction, in which all earthly things collapse into a heap of ruins, which reveal the limit set upon allegorical contemplation, rather than its ideal quality'.

114. Ibid., 232: 'The bleak confusion of Golgotha, which can be recognized as the schema underlying the allegorical figures in hundreds of the engravings and descriptions of the period, is not just a symbol of the desolation of human existence. In it transitoriness is not signified or allegorically represented, so much as, in its own significance, displayed as allegory. As the allegory of resurrection'.

115. For more on Benjamin's interpretation of Baudelaire, and the poem 'Une Martyre', see Debarati Sanyal, *The Violence of Modernity: Baudelaire, Irony, and the Politics of Form* (Baltimore, MD: Johns Hopkins University Press, 2006), 106–12.

116. Charles Baudelaire, 'A Martyr', in *Les Fleurs du Mal*, 121.

117. Ibid., 122.

118. SW 4, 389.

119. Marcel Proust, *Time Regained*, in *In Search of Lost Time. Volume VI*, transl. by Andreas Mayor and Terence Kilmartin, revised by D. J. Enright (New York: The Modern Library, 2003), 298.

120. Ibid., 299.

121. The title of Benjamin's essay on Proust refers to the 'image of Proust' in order to underscore that it is only the realm of art which allows such a reopening of the sphere of life. With this concept of image, Benjamin highlights that experiences of loss can only trigger the hope of a 'restitution' when they are reworked into art. As we have seen, according to Benjamin, 'Proust could not get his fill of emptying the dummy, his self, at one stroke', but this is done 'in order to keep garnering . . . the image which satisfied his curiosity-indeed, assuaged his homesickness'. Such a distinctly non-actual, artistic and imagistic world 'detaches itself from the structure of Proust's sentences' and 'is never isolated, rhetorical, or visionary; carefully heralded and securely supported, it bears a fragile, precious reality' (SW 2, 240).

122. Ibid., 304.

123. Gilles Deleuze, *Proust and Signs*, transl. by Richard Howard (London and New York: Continuum, 2008), 42.

124. Gilles Deleuze, *Difference and Repetition*, 122.

125. Ibid., 90.

126. Ibid., 122.

127. Marcel Proust, *The Fugitive*, in *In Search of Lost Time. Volume V*, transl. and introduced by Peter Collier (London: Penguin, 2003), 387.

128. Ibid., 451.

129. Ibid., 449.

130. Ibid., 560.

131. Ibid., 558.

132. Ibid., 657.

133. Ibid., 656.
134. Ibid.
135. Ibid., 657.

THREE
What Is the Child? Or How Can We Begin Anew?

'Come, my dear father, let's leave! Set the weight of your limbs upon my neck. / *I'll* support *you* on my shoulders. / This labour won't burden me greatly. / Come what may in the fall of events, we'll share every danger. / Safety for one will be safety for both'.[1] Surrounded by the ruins of the city and the dead bodies of his comrades-in-arms, Aeneas has finally managed to convince his father that only an overnight escape from besieged Troy can save them from instant death. Hoisting the old body of Anchises upon his shoulders and taking his infant son by the hand, he sets out for the long flight that is to culminate in the founding of a city grander and greater than any on Earth: Rome. In spite of Aeneas's already having reached adulthood at the moment of the flight from Troy (and having fathered a son of his own), his story can be read as a precursor to a specific view about young age and childhood. For the most diverse philosophers and authors, filmmakers and musicians, ranging from Augustine to Cormac McCarthy and from Roberto Rossellini to the Beach Boys have further explored Virgil's notion that offspring is the harbinger of the truly new. This chapter is devoted to a series of thinkers who introduce the child as a metaphor for the possibility of genuine change. Virgil, Augustine, Nietzsche, Arendt and Benjamin all turn to the child in an attempt to capture the wondrous instant of a new beginning.

To be sure, this notion that the child is endowed with abilities that are lacking in the parent runs counter to the ancient view. Until well after the Middle Ages, the concept of childhood was built on the Aristotelian, teleological assumption that youth is but a preparatory stage for adulthood. In such a view, infants are first and foremost 'young men' who only come into their own through a process of maturation and organic development.² Even William Wordsworth's famous line, 'The Child Is the Father of Man', for instance, does not at all refer to the *difference* between child and father, let alone to the idea that the child is gifted in ways that the parent is not. From the remaining lines of the poem, it becomes clear that Wordsworth's apparent rendition of the primordiality of the child was in fact included to indicate the deep *connection* between the emotional world of the infant and that of the adult he will grow up to become. 'My heart leaps up when I behold / A rainbow in the sky: / So was it when my life began; / So is it now I am a man; / So be it when I shall grow old, / Or let me die!' The figure of the child serves Wordsworth to invoke the continuity of a life that lasts well into the future, and not a capacity to restart.³

My reconstruction of the anti-Aristotelian countertradition that associates youth with a new beginning starts with Nietzsche. In his essays on historiography and *Thus Spoke Zarathustra* (1883–1885), Nietzsche considers the life of the child as the embodiment of a force of renewal and change that is built into the stream of life itself. For Nietzsche, this renewal and change are testified to by a 'creative force' that sets the child apart from the grown-up. Rather than a preparation of old-age, childhood exemplifies the capacity to overthrow the excess weight of history, thereby making possible genuine innovation and replenishment. For this reason, the child is the quintessential figure to understand Nietzsche's concept of a productive 'forgetting of forgetting' and the inherent connection between forgetting on the one hand, and universal becoming on the other.

In Arendt's conception, the life of the child does not share in any supposed power of life. The child embodies no stream of life, but a force that interrupts a more fundamental 'law of mortality'. Arendt moves away from the idea that creativity and continual change are built into life, and builds her philosophy of hope and renewal on the mere 'fact of natality'. In Arendt's view, the interruption of the 'law of mortality' by birth does restore our confidence in the possibility to begin anew. Still, such optimism never takes recourse to an ontological principle of natural regeneration. In her view, the child reinstalls the hope that one can always start anew, but an understanding of such hope requires a highly politicized, humanistic and liberal, but no metaphysical framework.

On the eve of the First World War, Benjamin has already parted with the Nietzschean connection between youth on the one hand, and the supposedly spontaneous process of life's renewal on the other. In the 1910s, youth and childhood are for him prime illustrations of the universalised passing away that, as we have seen in the previous chapters, will grow into a crucial trope of his *oeuvre* at large. Childhood is a force that transmutes annihilation into a productive faculty, thereby dislodging forgetting from within. This impossibility to endure turns childhood into an embodiment of the complete nihilism that will also be put into play in Benjamin's philosophy of history. In the second half of this chapter, therefore, we will analyze Benjamin's ideas about childhood with the help of the concepts *Aufgabe*, *Abfall* and his notion of the *Tagebuch* [diary, book of days].

FROM NIETZSCHE TO ARENDT

The body of Nietzsche's essay on historiography consists of an apology of the type of forgetting that unties an all too stringent connection with the past. As a powerful antidote against the 'excess of history' that weighs down on a culture that, in looking nowhere else but backward, has lost the capacity to renew itself from within, forgetting is deemed to bring 'happiness' and create a 'horizon' for meaningful engagement with the world.[4] 'In the case of the smallest or of the greatest happiness, it is always the same thing that makes happiness happiness: the ability to forget or, expressed in more scholarly fashion, the capacity to feel unhistorically during its duration'.[5] In Nietzsche's view, the child is the quintessential exemplification of such a type of forgetting. Together with the life of animals, the existence of the child can be considered the most important evidence of a truly 'unhistorical' attitude that embraces the present. The child is described as living in 'a state of forgetfulness' and as 'having as yet nothing of the past to shake off, play[ing] in blissful blindness between the hedges of past and future'.[6] In Nietzsche's writings, the connection between the life of the child and the capacity to innovate rests on the concept of *creativity*. In both the essay on historiography and *Thus Spoke Zarathustra*, Nietzsche endows the life of the child with a creativity that is lacking in the adult. In the notorious passage on the three metamorphoses, Nietzsche asks himself 'Why must the preying lion still become a child?' and goes on to describe the child as 'innocence and forgetting, a new beginning, a game, a wheel rolling out of itself, a first movement, a sacred yes-saying. Yes, for the game of creation my brothers a sacred yes-saying is required'.[7] Adults, in Nietzsche's view, are lacking in such creative powers and only *become* productive by virtue of the child they bring forth: 'You should create a higher body, a first movement, a wheel rolling out of itself—a creator you should create. Marriage: that is what I call the will by two for creating the one who is more than those who created it'.[8]

Because of this creativity, Nietzsche's forgetting is not the token of a complete suspension or annihilation of the past. Creative forgetting shares in a 'plastic power' that allows for a selective, productive and critical attitude towards the past.[9] What matters the most to Nietzsche is to learn to determine to what extent the past can be made relevant for the present and to what extent it needs, on the contrary, to be cast aside. Because only forgetting installs the distance vis-à-vis the past that is required to make it useful once again, productive forgetting is to be considered not as a *reactive negation* of the past (a mere rejection) but as an *active renegotiation* of it.[10] The main criterion that ought to be followed in this determination of the right 'degree' of forgetfulness is hinted at in the title of Nietzsche's essay: history is only allowed to become a part of the present when it is made useful for *life*. With this concept of 'life' Nietzsche has in mind a 'higher force that dominates and directs' and 'a dark, driving power that insatiably thirsts for itself'.[11] It is only by virtue of such a *cosmic* principle of spontaneous creativity that forgetting can reinstall a confidence in the capacity to change and be changed. In other words, in his philosophy of forgetting Nietzsche lays the groundwork for that side of his *oeuvre* that Deleuze associated with the second, active type of nihilism.[12] Forgetting is here believed to share in a force that affirms a natural dynamic of rejuvenation. In forgetting, life is released from whatever type of transhistorical ground or ultimate truth and discovered as a process that ceaselessly *gives*. Near the end of his essay, Nietzsche further clarifies why this power of forgetting, animated by the creativity of life as such, is made palpable by what he calls 'the instinct of youth'. Youthfulness is described as the embodiment of 'fire, defiance, unselfishness and love' as endowed with a 'sense of justice . . . [an] honesty and boldness of feeling': '[I]ts fairest privilege [is] its power to implant in itself the belief in a great idea and then let it grow to an even greater one'.[13] Critical of the self-understanding of German culture as a 'nation of heirs' that increasingly evolves into a people of 'dissolute, toothless and tasteless greybeards', Nietzsche puts into place the nihilistic counterforce of youthfulness to highlight an irreducible dimension of productivity on the part of life as such.[14] He turns to youth in order to discover the power to shrug off the restraints of culture, the stifling impact of education and the immobilizing weight of the past. Nietzsche's essay on history is underpinned by the idea that the universal becoming that marks life itself is actualized time and again by the new-born. '[Y]outh still possesses that instinct of nature which remains intact until artificially and forcibly shattered by this education'.[15] Youth is associated with the remarkable ability to 'un-learn' and thereby gain an 'un-culture' that allows for a 'direct observation of life' and an 'ever more intense feeling of life'.[16]

As a consequence of this appeal to the creative powers of life as such, Nietzsche rejects the humanistic presupposition that man is endowed with capacities that are absent in other living beings and set him apart from the world at large. Human beings, to the contrary, are to affirm a dynamic of becoming and transience that can be shared but not wholly *appropriated*. Active forgetting does not refer to an attitude that can be properly called human. If the creativity of forgetting is believed to be 'salutary and fruitful for the future'[17] this is because it is nourished by a principle of creativity that is non-human. This non-human, cosmic dimension of creative forgetting explains why Nietzsche associates youth not only with the 'unhistorical' ('the art and power of forgetting and of enclosing oneself within a bounded horizon') but also with the 'suprahistorical', that is, with the power that 'bestows upon existence the character of the eternal and stable'.[18] This latter notion does not at all conflict with the former one because, rather than pointing towards a realm of supposedly absolute truths and values, the 'suprahistorical' indicates in this context the eternal *absence* of such truths and values, and by that token, the 'stable' presence of nothing but transformation and self-renewal. Nietzsche's view of forgetting does appeal to an ontological principle (life itself), yet refuses to treat this principle as a direct *foundation* for man's thoughts and actions.[19] In Nietzsche's philosophy of forgetting, it is assumed that a lawfulness is at work within the universe at large but, since this lawfulness is one of universal becoming and spontaneous renewal, it cannot ever be considered as an underlying *ground* that gives meaning to the projects and endeavors of man.

On the very last page of her very last, unfinished book, *The Life of the Mind* (1978), Hannah Arendt, as well, draws attention to the importance of true beginnings and the irreducible potential of man to start anew. Like Nietzsche, Arendt introduces the existence of the child as visible proof for this possibility of renewal. 'The very capacity for beginning', Arendt writes, 'is rooted in natality[,] . . . in the fact that human beings, new men, again and again appear in the world by virtue of birth'.[20] The idea that the affirmation of change rests on the fact of natality had already been introduced by Arendt almost twenty years earlier, in the final pages of the section on Action in *The Human Condition* (1958). Again, in seemingly Nietzschean fashion, Arendt emphasizes there that the confidence in the human ability to bring about change is founded on the presence of the child and the moment of birth. 'The miracle that saves the world, the realm of human affairs . . . is ultimately the fact of natality, in which the faculty of action is ontologically rooted. It is, in other words, the birth of new men and the new beginning, the action they are capable of by virtue of being born'.[21] Arendt and Nietzsche, however, part ways when she suggests that there might not in fact exist such a thing as an *ontological* principle of change. What is more, Arendt emphasizes that the capacity to begin anew is rooted 'by no means in creativity' and 'not in a gift'.[22] Arendt's conceptual framework runs counter to Nietzsche's appeal to the inherent creativity of life itself. Rather than discovering life as a 'plastic force' that is marked by spontaneous self-giving and renewal, Arendt emphasizes that the 'law of *mortality* . . . is the most certain and the only reliable law of a life spent between birth and death'.[23] If the fact of natality is indeed a 'miracle that saves the world' it is because this world is, in its 'normal, natural' state, to be understood as a 'ruin'.[24] Life is in Arendt's view not at all a dynamic that ceaselessly *gives* since it is first and foremost characterized by disappearance. The capacity to begin anew is bound to remain at all times a *puzzling* phenomenon that exists *in spite of* a more fundamental force of overall annihilation and falling-away. Therefore, from Arendt's perspective, the capacity to begin anew is always but a *counter*-principle and unexpected *interruption*, going against an otherwise all-determining process of passing-away. 'The life span of man running toward death would inevitably carry everything human to ruin and destruction if it were not for the faculty of interrupting it and beginning something new, a faculty which is inherent in action like an ever-present reminder that men, though they must die, are not born in order to die but in order to begin'.[25]

Arendt's view of politics and history hinges on this possibility that the passage of time can be interrupted. It is framed in opposition with both the ancient and the Christian view. In Greek and Roman culture the commemoration of heroic deeds in the past and the veneration of the authority of ancestors helped man to come to terms with his mortality. Christianity, to the contrary, asserted the irrevocable finitude of everything in nature and history alike, though not without presupposing the *im*mortality of the individual soul. Therefore, both the ancient and the Christian view of history was founded on the connection with a transhistorical ground.[26] The ancient view of politics and history rested on the belief that the powers of remembrance and tradition could justifiably endow historical events with a dimension of permanence while Christianity is either antithetical to politics or gives rise to a politics rooted in absolute truths (Augustine's *Civitas Dei*). The modern conception of politics and history parts with this belief that a transhistorical ground can somehow be recovered from within history. The modern view starts from the experience that 'nothing is meaningful in and by itself'.[27] Along with the past and the future, the present is now discovered to participate in a 'process' that is at odds with absolute truths. '[T]he experience which underlies the modern age's notion of process . . . sprang from the despair of ever experiencing and knowing adequately all that is given to man and not made by him'.[28] Moreover, on account of the deterioration of tradition and the separation of religion and politics (secularization), the present can no longer serve as a natural mediator between past and future. The past and the future now stretch out as two infinite realms that are in conflict both with each other and with the present. In her analysis of Kafka's parable about the antagonism between the present, past and the future, Arendt describes the modern view of history as follows:

> Seen from the viewpoint of man, who always lives in the interval between past and future, time is not a continuum, a flow of uninterrupted succession: it is broken in the middle, at the point where 'he' stands [Arendt refers to the protagonist of Kafka's parable]; and 'his' standpoint is not the present as we usually understand it but rather a gap in time which 'his' constant fighting, 'his' making a stand against past and future, keeps in existence.[29]

The gap between history on the one hand and the realm of absolute truths on the other does not at all drain human action from its capacity to bring about meaningful change. It is precisely the antagonism between present, past and future that can replenish our belief in the possibility of change and thereby make politics possible. Arendt refers to the 'modern emphasis upon time and time-sequence' and claims that '[o]ur notion of historical process . . . bestow[s] upon mere time-sequence an importance and dignity it never had before'.[30] Her famous analysis of human action builds on the awareness that it can truly disrupt the connection between the present, past and future and thereby introduce a series of effects that cannot however be wholly overseen. 'Whoever begins to act must know that he has started something whose end he can never foretell, if only because his own deed has already changed everything and made it even more unpredictable'.[31] Making history and politics dependent on the interruption of the temporal flow, Arendt even goes as far as to introduce a concept of immortality that is purely 'earthly'. In the absence of immortal essences that ground our actions in history, these actions themselves come together with a specific type of endurance. Incapable of releasing himself fully from the laws of temporal succession, yet capable of interrupting its process of passing-away, man is endowed with the potential to inject a principle of change within the world, the outcomes of which are known to no one. While the present is a meeting place for the two antagonistic forces of past and future, it is also a 'definite origin' that 'exerts its force toward an undetermined end as though it could reach out into infinity'.[32]

While Nietzsche's rejection of absolute truths leads him to an active nihilism that embraces a non-human dynamic of change, Arendt's rejection of such ultimate essences results in an apology of an utterly non-nihilistic humanism and liberalism. For Arendt, the capacity to begin that characterizes political action is conditioned by the distinctly human capacity to *not* share in the passage of time, however relentless it may be. In Arendt's view, the passage of time is not at all an 'active' force that should be wholeheartedly embraced by man. To the contrary, 'time is the thinking ego's greatest enemy because [time] . . . inexorably and regularly interrupts the immobile quiet in which the mind is active without doing anything'.[33] Arendt thus pits history and politics against an overall transience and forgetting. She takes recourse to the ability to 'shape the everlasting stream of sheer change into a time continuum' and adds that this meaningful interruption of the passage of time is not owed to 'time itself but to the continuity of our business and our activities in the world, in which *we continue* what we started yesterday and hope to finish tomorrow'.[34] In her view, therefore, man is capable of exploring the 'gap between past and future' as 'a fact of political relevance' and 'the only region perhaps where truth eventually will appear'.[35] Arendt's conception of 'thought' serves as the backbone of her humanism and liberalism. Turning to the question 'where the thinking ego is located in time and whether its relentless activity can be temporally determined', she casts this temporal location of the thinking ego as deeply unstable and inherently ephemeral.[36] 'When I say "now" and point to it, it is already gone'.[37] As a consequence, human thought takes place on a 'battleground' where the present is but an 'in-between' that seeks to carve out a 'rupture'[38] or 'mere gap'[39] between the 'no-longer' of the past and the 'not-yet' of the future. However, what matters the most to Arendt is that human beings can expand this unstable gap between the past and the future into a ground for freedom, deliberation and decision-making. Arendt's conception of history and politics presupposes a specifically human 'non-time space in the very heart of time' from which we can reflect on our situation with the liberty, presence of mind and calmness of spirit that enables true determination.[40] While this 'non-time space' of thought cannot be fully separated from the temporal flux it does remain sufficiently unburdened by it to grant man 'a position from which to judge the forces fighting with each other with an impartial eye'.[41] For Arendt, therefore, the interruption of the passage of time by way of thought is the prime antidote against a 'world-alienation' in which all meaningful experience risks getting lost. Despite being forever disconnected from eternal truths and 'spring[ing], as it were, from the clash of past and future', thought is a specifically human faculty that carves out a 'timelessness', 'nunc stans' and 'immovable present'.[42]

A NOTE ON VIRGIL AND AUGUSTINE

Arendt's reference to the child as a metaphor for the human capacity to begin is inspired by Virgil. In the final chapter of *The Life of the Mind* Arendt introduces Virgil's concept of childhood by way of an analysis of his Fourth and Sixth *Eclogues*, the *Aeneid* and the *Georgics*. Virgil refers to new-born life in order to invoke the beginning of (Augustus's) 'glorious age' and 'a new generation' that 'descends from heaven on high'.[43] He thereby does indeed discover the child as visible proof for the capacity to make a new start. Virgil singles out the child's first smile as the legitimation of the existence of true beginnings, endowing these with a godlike greatness: 'Begin, baby boy, to recognize your mother with a smile: ten months have brought your mother long travail. Begin, baby boy! The child who has not won a smile from his parents, no god ever honoured with his table, no goddess with her bed!'[44] Arendt warns against understanding such passages 'as a prophesy of salvation through a theos soter, a savior god, or . . . as the expression of some pre-Christian religious yearning'. They do not 'predict the arrival of a divine child' but are an 'affirmation of the divinity of birth as such: if one wishes to extract a general meaning from it, this could only be the poet's belief that the world's potential salvation lies in the very fact that the human species regenerates itself constantly and forever'.[45]

Virgil does not merely connect this capacity to begin with an interruption of overall forgetting, but with the faculty of memory, and this on account of his fascination with *foundations*, *tradition* and *authority*. In Arendt's view, Roman culture is characterized by the view of history as 'storehouse of examples' that set up a lived continuity between the present, past and future.[46] In her analysis of Virgil's Fourth *Eclogue* she introduces the important distinction between 'absolute beginnings' and the 're-establishment of a beginning' and argues that Virgil puts into words the significance of 're-starts' and 're-births' rather than 'starts' or 'births' pure and proper. '[C]onstitution and foundation' are here understood 'in terms of the re-establishment of a beginning which, as an absolute beginning, remains perpetually shrouded in mystery'. Arendt stresses that in Virgil's view 'the thread of continuity and tradition, demanded by the very continuum of time and the faculty of memory . . . had never been broken'.[47] In her reading of Virgil's line 'the great cycle of periods is born anew', therefore, Arendt argues that '"this order of the ages" is not *new* but only the return of something antecedent'.[48] For this reason, the child's entrance into the world does not indicate an entirely novel presence but an opportunity to commemorate and renew age-old ideals and communal values. '[A]ll the poet himself says is that every child born into the continuity of Roman history must learn "heroum laudes et facta parentis", "the glories of the heroes and the deeds of the fathers", so as to be able to do what all Roman boys were supposed to do to help "rule the world that his fathers' virtues have set at peace"'.[49] Likewise, the *Aeneid* is in her view to be read as a poem that celebrates the foundation of Rome as a *rebirth* of Troy, 'the first, as it were, of the series of re-nascences that have formed the history of European culture and civilization'.[50] According to Arendt, the Romans knew very well that a genuinely 'new Rome' could not be conceived and that 'the most they could hope for was to repeat the primeval foundation and found "Rome anew"'.[51]

In important places of her work, Arendt follows Virgil's suggestions, going beyond her assertion that the capacity to begin is first and foremost the proof of an interruption of overall forgetting. In those passages, Arendt, as well, emphasizes the importance of memory. 'Remembrance', she writes 'is only one, though one of the most important, modes of thought, [and] helpless outside a pre-established framework of reference [since] the human mind is only on the rarest occasions capable of retaining something which is altogether unconnected'.[52] Still, Virgil's underlying assumptions about memory cannot ultimately be reconciled with Arendt's views because the former takes recourse to a transhistorical foundation to history. Arendt reads Virgil's *Aeneid* alongside his Sixth *Eclogue* and *Georgics*, thereby situating the most fundamental dimension of the Roman myth of origin in *nature* rather than in *history*. Virgil connects the moment of historical rebirth to the resurgence of an absolute beginning that predates history itself. Quoting at length from Virgil's poems in praise of nature, Arendt understands these as descriptions of a 'utopian fairy-tale land outside of history' and as an appeal to inaccessible but everlasting origins. These origins are associated with the 'indestructibility of nature' and, while they are not themselves founded on anything else, they remain present as a permanent source of inspiration and commemoration.[53] In his *Georgics*, for instance, Virgil describes a life lived 'in sacred purity' surrounded by plentiful fauna and flora that nevertheless resists being expressed by man: 'There is no *tale* of the manifold kinds or of the names they bear'.[54] The ultimate ground for the possibility that the past can be renewed through tradition, ritual and recollection thus rests, for Virgil, not just on the human ability to interrupt a principle of transience by way of recollection but in the capacity to *retrieve* a wellspring of *eternity*. It is here that Virgil and Arendt part ways. In Virgil's account, the most fundamental law is not at all one of 'destruction' or 'ruin' but one of cyclical temporality and spontaneous self-regeneration.[55] Such a view on a natural, eternal and indestructible power to renew cannot be reconciled with Arendt's idea of a 'law of mortality' that needs to be interrupted time and again by the actions, thoughts and memory of man.[56]

Moving away from Virgil's reference to the eternal and spontaneous regeneration of nature, Arendt turns to the work of Augustine. Arendt had been studying Augustine's work from a very early age onwards, devoting her doctoral research to his concept of love. On the final page of her final book she returns to Augustine, referring to his *City of God* to conceptualize, once again, the earlier mentioned connection between the existence of the child and the belief in renewal. She mentions Augustine's idea that 'the purpose of the creation of man was to make possible a *beginning*' and quotes the following statement: 'That there be a beginning man was created, before whom nobody was'.[57] In Arendt's view, Augustine's connection between the creation of man and the creation of the possibility to begin revolves around the concept of *individuality*. While the world that pre-exists man was inhabited with creatures that were created 'in numbers', man, on the contrary 'was created in the singular and continued to be "propagated from individuals"'. The beginning of the world, indicated with the word 'principium' is thus a different type of beginning than that of man, indicated with the word 'initium'.[58]

The works of Virgil and Augustine differ in that, as Arendt puts it, Augustine 'first finds it necessary to refute the philosophers' cyclical time concepts, inasmuch as novelty could not occur in cycles'.[59] Augustine assumes that the creation of the world coincides with the creation of time. 'The world', as it is stated in a phrase from *City of God* that Arendt quotes, 'was made *not* in time, but simultaneously with time'.[60] This entails a sharp division between the eternity of God, who exists outside of the temporal realm, and the universe that is God's creation, which cannot be released from temporal succession. Paradoxical as it may sound, it is first and foremost the work of a deeply religious thinker which has inspired Arendt's conception of a 'law of mortality'. In the famous Book Eleven of the *Confessions*, Augustine writes that 'at [God's] nod the moments fly by'.[61] Like Arendt, Augustine makes time inseparable from annihilation and non-being. 'In order to be time at all, the present is so made that it passes into the past' and that 'the cause of its being is that it will cease to be'.[62] It comes as no surprise, therefore, that Arendt quotes Augustine's statement that 'temporal things have no existence before they exist; while they exist, they are passing away; once they have passed away, they will never exist again'[63] and, shifting the focus to the temporal nature of man's life on earth, his famous claim that 'our whole life is nothing but a race toward death'.[64]

Because he discovers transience and annihilation as ineradicable presences within the world Augustine highlights how significant the human capacity to *begin* truly is. Augustine gives up Virgil's suggestion that the faculty of recollection allows for the recovery of the deep, indestructible memory of nature. Instead, he sets up a connection between the faculty of recollection on the one hand and the capacity to interrupt a distinctly *rectilinear* time to the other.[65] Of crucial importance to this conception of the possibility to begin is Augustine's connection between individuality and Will. Arendt considers Augustine's views on birth, beginning, individuality and Will as a philosophical legitimation of human freedom. Augustine discovers the Will as a 'prepar[ation of] the ground on which action can take place'.[66] On account of the interruptive capacity of the human Will, Augustine 'necessitates the primacy of the future in time speculations'.[67] However, Augustine will also help Arendt to come to terms with the significance of the faculty of recollection for political action. When Arendt credits Augustine with having overcome the 'anti-political impulses' of early Christianity, this is not only due to his philosophy of Will, but also on account of his view of memory.[68] At the start of her analysis of Thomas Aquinas's primacy of the intellect, Arendt mentions that, 'in view of Augustine's three mental faculties—Memory, Intellect, and Will—one has been lost, namely, Memory, the most specifically Roman one, binding men back to the past', adding that 'this loss turned out to be final; nowhere in our philosophical tradition does Memory again attain the same rank as Intellect and Will [as with Augustine]'.[69] Arendt deplores the prioritization of Intellect and Will over memory because 'what went out with memory ... was a sense of the thoroughly temporal character of human nature and human existence, manifest in Augustine's homo temporalis'. Moreover, Arendt stresses that this disavowal of memory came together with 'consequences ... for all strictly political philosophy'.[70]

Augustine's many metaphors for the memory of physical objects and experiences, ranging from 'fields and vast palaces' and a 'storehouse' to a 'stomach of the mind', share in presenting recollection as a genuine counter-agent to the overall transience that marks creation.[71] He argues that memory is incapable of retaining the actual physical objects themselves but nevertheless retains the images left behind by perception.

> Memory's huge cavern, with its mysterious, secret, and indescribable nooks and crannies, receives all these perceptions, to be recalled when needed and reconsidered. Every one of them enters into memory, each by its own gate, and is put on deposit there. The objects themselves do not enter, but the images of the perceived objects are available to the thought recalling them.[72]

Augustine's argument is subtler than it might seem. For memory cannot be believed to grant an unexpected duration to the things of the physical world since these, by default, cannot endure: memory, rather *reworks* these physical things into non-physical, mental entities (images), thereby allowing human beings to suspend the 'non-being' that is inevitably at work within creation at large. It is for this reason that Augustine stresses the inherent difference between the actual existence of an object and its memory-image.[73] Because the temporal realm cannot be separated from nothingness, it can only be measured on the condition that it is released from the physical world and transformed into a purely mental entity. 'So it is in you, my mind, that I measure periods of time.... The impression which passing events make upon you abides when they are gone. That present consciousness is what I am measuring, not the stream of past events which have caused it'.[74] Memory grows into a productive faculty that, instead of hopelessly prolonging our *connection* to objects that cannot last anyway, constitutes a meaningful *disconnection* from them and, thereby, retrieves an unsuspected kernel of *presence*. In Augustine's view, memory testifies to the capacity to *detach* oneself from a world that is in a constant state of disappearance, and not to the capacity to remain *attached* to these disappearing objects themselves. This meaningful detachment, for its part, allows man to go against the transience of the created world and counteract its overall ephemerality.[75]

It is from Augustine that Arendt borrows both the concept of unsurpassable transience and the belief in the 'miraculous' capacity to interrupt transience. This does not only become visible in her analysis of action as an 'interruption' of a world that 'in its normal, natural state' is a 'ruin' but also in the earlier mentioned analysis of the human faculty of thought. In Arendt's view, human thought cannot do without a specific *'de-sens[ing]'* of the world that 'must prepare the particulars given to the senses in such a way that the mind is able to handle them in their absence'.[76] Arendt explicitly takes recourse to Augustine's theory of memory to comprehend what is at stake in such a preparatory attitude of disconnection that counteracts the world's transience. In an analysis of Augustine's view of memory in the *Trinity*, she highlights the 'twofold transformation' through which a visible sense-object becomes an image and is then turned into a thought-object.[77] According to Arendt, thought releases an object or phenomenon from the passage of time and thereby allows a human being to appropriate the object or phenomenon at hand. As we have seen, for Arendt as well, thought is a distinctly human faculty that conditions the 'non-time space' that is needed for quiet reflection and deliberation. Augustine's work is Arendt's most important intellectual source to understand how such a space for liberty can be brought about. 'Thought-objects come into being only when the mind actively and deliberately remembers, recollects and selects from the storehouse of memory whatever arouses its interest sufficiently to induce concentration'.[78] In line with Augustine's views, Arendt stresses the inherent difference between *real* objects that are given to the senses and belong to a world in flux, and *thought*-objects that are of a mental nature and are thereby released from the world's transience (the latter are 'absent non-visibles'[79]).

In spite of these parallels between Augustine's philosophy of memory and Arendt's philosophy of thought, both thinkers part ways when Augustine takes recourse to the transhistorical truths of Christian faith. For apart from the memory of physical objects and experiences, Augustine does indeed mention a second type of memory: the memory of God. Like the memory of physical objects and experiences, the memory of God enables the unexpected retrieval of a kernel of enduring presence. However, God's Being is wholly *untouched by* and not just *released from* the transience of the created universe. It is likened to an eternal present and inseparable from a Word in which 'no element . . . yields place or succeeds to something else'.[80] Describing a 'Lord God of the mind', Augustine retrieves the evidence of His eternal presence within his own memory and states that he

> ha[s] not found [Him] outside it. For I have found nothing coming from you which I have not stored in my memory since the time I first learnt of you. Since the day I learnt of you, I have never forgotten you. Where I discovered the truth there I found my God, truth itself, which from the time I learnt it, I have not forgotten. And so, since the time I learnt of you, you remain in my consciousness, and there I find you when I recall you and delight in you.[81]

In contrast to the transient nature of all physical phenomena, therefore, God's presence cannot ever be wholly forgotten. Augustine distinguishes the memory of the divine from the memory of objects, emotions and the mind itself to argue that it is never impossible to recover the presence of the sole Being that is immutable and non-temporal. The rhetorical strategy of the *Confessions* rests on a deep connection between the human capacity to recollect and the existence of a Being that, by its very essence, *resists* forgetting. While a human being can be led astray and live a faithless life, the memory of God cannot be fully obliterated. Augustine's view of the memory of God is deeply puzzling: even though, in our darkest hours, we can forget God, His presence cannot actually be truly and utterly obliterated. While human beings may not always consciously recollect God's presence, they can always recapture it within their own memory. It is for this reason that Augustine, in apparent preparation of Bergson, Freud and Heidegger's later views, already states that even forgetting is something that can be remembered, thereby once again emphasizing the primacy of memory and recollection. 'I am certain that I remember forgetfulness itself', even though 'forgetfulness destroys what we remember'.[82] It is through this same paradox, moreover, that Augustine can gauge both the deeply alienating power of sin (turning away from God's memory entails forgetting something that is present within one's self) *and* the ineradicable possibility of grace (this divine presence can never fully be obliterated). While Augustine's own life, prior to his conversion, was marked by a forgetting of God (*oblivio dei*, God is being forgotten), the moment of conversion itself is cast as a retrieval of a presence that has never gone away (*memoria dei*, God is the one who remembers). 'I call upon you my God, my mercy (Ps: 58: 18). You made me and, when I forgot you, you did not forget me'.[83]

Though Augustine's view of the memory of physical objects and experience was a prime source of inspiration for Arendt's philosophy of thought, Arendt's philosophy cannot in any way accommodate his conception of the memory of God. Arendt's philosophy of history is a deeply secular one, presupposing at all times the full separation of religion and politics. It rests on a *distance* between history and transhistorical truths and the concomitant *gap* between the present, past and future. From Arendt's perspective, therefore, for all his emphasis on the impermanence of our world, 'Augustine's attitude toward secular history is essentially no different from that of the Romans'.[84] No more than Virgil is Augustine capable of coming to terms with the radical openness of history and the confidence that human action can truly change it from within.[85]

BENJAMIN'S NON-METAPHYSICS OF YOUTH

In the years leading up to the First World War, Benjamin, as well, devotes numerous essays to the concepts of youth and childhood.

In these texts, he picks up the thread of the connection between childhood on the one hand and the ability to begin on the other. 'Youth stands in the centre, where the new comes into being [*wo das Neue wird*]' (EW, 168; GS II, 72). In the essay 'Experience' (1913) Benjamin sharply opposes the adult's bleak outlook on the world to the youthful confidence in the possibility of change. The 'spirit' and 'greatness' of youth is pitted against the adult's 'long sobriety of serious life' and serves Benjamin to formulate his affirmation of meaningful renewal and innovation (SW 1, 3). Under the influence of his participation in various youth movements in the 1910s, Benjamin follows the lead of Nietzsche's essay on forgetting and explores youth as a life-giving and life-altering force. In young age, life is encountered as a realm of possibilities and opportunities that is at odds with the adult experience of 'life's drudgery' and even 'meaninglessness' (SW 1, 3-4). With reference to Zarathustra, Benjamin describes how 'youth will experience spirit, and the less effortlessly he attains greatness, the more he will encounter spirit everywhere in his wandering and in every person' (SW 1, 5).

One year later Benjamin's confidence in the creative powers of youth has undergone a drastic change. For all its greatness and 'experience of spirit'[*Erfahrung des Geistes*] (SW 1, 4; GS II, 56), it seems that the spontaneous creativity and renewal that characterizes youth has somehow *disappeared*. From 1914 onwards, Benjamin's interpretation of youth and childhood builds on the observation that childhood cannot possibly endure because it is either succeeded by premature death or adulthood. Around the time when despair about the impending war brings his twenty-year-old friend Christophe Friedrich Heinle to take his own life and in the midst of his growing dissatisfaction with the youth movement, Benjamin writes an essay entitled 'Metaphysics of Youth' (1913–1914).[86] The epitaph to the essay are the first lines of Hölderlin's poem 'The Blind Singer': 'Where are you, Youth, that always wakes me / Promptly in the morning? Where are you, Light?' The title of the essay that follows these words is confusing since in this text Benjamin rejects precisely the assumption of an *ontologized* becoming and creativity. 'Metaphysics of Youth' is the starting point of Benjamin's continuing attempt to release the concepts of youth and childhood from the *Lebensphilosophie* that underlies Nietzsche's view. Youth does now no longer only embody the possibility a beginning, but also, and to an equal degree, the *inevitability of an end*. Rather than an inexhaustible power to create and regenerate, youth evidences a transience and ephemerality that cannot seemingly be overcome.[87]

'We wish to pay heed to the sources of the unnameable despair [*unnennbaren Verzweiflung*] that flows in every soul. . . . The more [our souls] immerse themselves in the uncertain decades and broach that part of their youth which is most laden with future, the more orphaned they are in the emptiness of the present [*desto verwaister atmen sie in der leeren Gegenwart*]' (SW 1, 10; GS II, 96). Because of this impossibility to *last*, Benjamin goes as far as to emphasize the *resemblance* and not the *opposition* between the youthful experience of life on the one hand and the adult's bleak and spiritless view of life on the other. In the essay 'The Life of Students' (1915), the adult's 'philistinism' is termed 'inevitable' since 'students are not the younger generation [but] . . . the aging generation' (SW 1, 45). Benjamin takes the students to task for a deeply conservative and even reactionary lifestyle that fails to muster the belief in genuine change. For Benjamin, the student's cheerfulness and light-heartedness is deeply suspicious because it masks the meekness and submissiveness that install the status quo of bourgeois society. 'Because students have sold their souls to the bourgeoisie, along with marriage and profession, they insist on those few years of bourgeois freedom' (SW 1, 45). The life of students is in truth a foreshadowing of the adult's disenchanted worldview, and not at all its most powerful antidote.

By the twenties, Benjamin has moved so far away from Nietzsche's interpretation of youth that he associates the concept of an 'absolute childhood and adolescence' with 'bourgeois society' and 'idealist philosophy' (SW 2, 273). While Nietzsche ultimately takes recourse to a *metaphysical* and even *moral* framework to understand the regenerating powers of youth, Benjamin's own conception of youth is inseparably entwined with *social* and *economic* distinctions. In essays on the proletarian children's theatre and communist pedagogy he uses the metaphor of the child to conceptualize the essence of *politics*. 'The proletarian child is born into his class—more precisely, into the next generation of his class—rather than into a family' (SW 2, 273–74). Benjamin endows proletarian child's theatre with revolutionary powers. It entails the 'neutralization' of the moral authority of a leader and substitutes this authority by 'action and gestures' that affirm the possibility of a truly different world. The child's gesture is a 'signal', not so much of the unconscious, but 'from another world, in which the child lives and commands' (SW 2, 203–4). Decades before Arendt, Benjamin already refuses to project a principle of creativity onto life as such, discovering youth and childhood as proof that bringing about true change requires social and political action. However, in Benjamin's work, the possibility of social and political change that is metaphorized by the figure of the child cannot be made dependent on the supposed *freedom* of our thoughts and actions, as Arendt suggests. Benjamin's views on the possibility, and necessity, of political change cannot be reconciled with Arendt's non-nihilistic (and even antinihilistic) humanism and liberalism. In his essay on communist pedagogy, Benjamin appeals to a 'new, nonhumanist, and noncontemplative but active and practical universality; the universality of being-ready [*der Universalität des Bereitseins*]' (SW 2, 274; GS III, 208 [translation modified]). He thereby rejects Arendt's notion of a distinctly human ability to *escape* from the passage of time in an 'immobile quiet'. Benjamin's view is at odds with Arendt's concept for a 'space of non-time' that is released from the flux of time and he refuses to consider time as the 'thinking ego's greatest enemy'. In his 'Essay on the Religious Position of the New Youth' (1914), Benjamin had already used the metaphor of the child to imagine a productive embrace *of* transience, rather than an external counterforce *to* it.

> The new youth stands before a chaos in which the objects of its choice (the sacred ones) disappear. No 'pure' and 'impure', 'sacred' and 'taboo', light its way, but only schoolmaster words, 'permitted-prohibited'. That it feels lonely and at a loss testifies to its religious seriousness, speaks for the fact that, to its way of thinking, religion no longer signifies some form of spirit or a traversable road that crosses the path of thousands and that it, too, could travel every day. (EW, 169)

From the confrontation with the transience of history, youth musters the power to 'decide' and 'choose' and thereby *bring about* a truly meaningful experience. 'The choice itself creates its objects [*Die Wahl schafft sich ihre Gegenstände*]—this is its religion-like knowledge [*religionsnächstes Wissen*]' (EW, 169; GS II, 73 [translation modified]). Seizing a sudden opportunity for intervention in the world does not require the capacity to expand the gap between past, present and future into a 'timeless' space for undisturbed reflection and free deliberation. Rather, the 'being-ready' that Benjamin has in mind entails that one manages to think and act from *within* the passage of time. Like Benjamin's later concepts of 'presence of mind', 'attentiveness', 'distraction' or 'innervation', the concepts of a universal 'being-ready', 'decision' or 'choice' presuppose an intensified reception of a fundamentally unstable world.[88]

Around the same time, this plea for an affirmation of the world's instability by way of a 'decision', 'choice' or 'being-ready' is complemented with a theory of child's play. In several vignettes in *One Way Street* (1923–1926) and *Berlin Childhood around 1900* (1932–1934), and in the essays on children's toys (1928) and the 'mimetic faculty' (1933), Benjamin associates child's play with a creative response to an external world that cannot be wholly mastered. Benjamin describes child's play as an interaction that both repeats *and* suspends the necessities of one's surroundings. In an essay on children's toys [*Spielzeuge*], for instance, he associates child's play with an 'obscure urge to repeat' [*der dunkle Drang nach Wiederholung*] and a desire 'for the same thing again and again, a hundred, or even a thousand times'. Benjamin explicitly goes beyond the conception of repetition that Freud develops in 'Beyond the Pleasure Principle' by claiming that child's play is inseparable from experiences of *'happiness'*. It is no mere instrument to 'master frightening fundamental experiences' but enables the joyful experience of 'one's victories and triumphs over and over again with total intensity' (SW 2, 120). For Benjamin, the form of repetition that underlies child's play is no repetition of the same that reproduces a given example. Child's play restores an embodied contact with the outside world by stripping it of its seeming completeness. It is not just a 'doing as if' [*So-tun-als-ob*] but it 'creates the entire event anew and starts again right from the beginning [*schafft sich die ganze Sache von neuem, fängt noch einmal von vorn an*]' (SW 2, 120; GS III, 131). Rather than imitate a model, child's play affirms the changeability of the outside world by producing a *difference* with regard to the object or event it is engaged with. In his autobiographical writings, for instance, Benjamin describes his fondness of repeating the gesture of thrusting his hand deep within rolled up socks as if something unknown could be drawn out from within them. Most remarkable about this game is that, each time he would draw back his hand and therewith unroll the sock, the enigmatic object he was seduced by (the 'pocket' for 'a little present') would be 'unveiled' as something altogether *other* (an utterly banal sock). It is telling that Benjamin's account of this game focuses on the repetition of a specific *activity*. 'I drew [the little present] ever nearer to me, until something rather disconcerting would happen: I had brought out "the present", but "the pocket" in which it had lain was no longer there. I could not repeat the experiment on this phenomenon often enough. It taught me that form and content, veil and what is veiled, are the same' (SW 3, 374). Benjamin's view of child's play does not rest on post-romantic conceptions of an enchanted world replete with an unexhausted potential for change.[89] Such a potential for change is in his view dependent on certain *actions* and *gestures*. These actions and gestures, moreover, can even be understood as a type of 'profanation' (Agamben), overcoming the distance that pertains to mysterious, auratic experiences. The activity of play replenishes the hope for a transformation of our most immediate surroundings, but not without simultaneously dispelling the illusion that such a process of renewal could come about on its own.

In the mid-thirties, Benjamin's ideas about child's play result in the concept of a 'space-for-play' that supports his thoughts on the mechanically (re)produced image. 'Because technology aims at liberating human beings from drudgery, the individual suddenly sees his space-for-play, his field of action [*Spielraum*], immeasurably expanded' (SW 3, 124 [translation modified]).[90] Neither Benjamin's view of child's play nor his concept of a 'space-for-play' presupposes that our daily environment can somehow be reconnected to foundational truths and essences. Even though play replenishes our hope for change within history, it does not in any way disclose an inner meaningfulness on the part of life itself or an essential truth that pertains to the world as such. Benjamin opposes 'play' to 'semblance' [*Schein*] to indicate that a direct responsiveness to our surroundings can shatter the illusion of a mythic world that is complete in itself. 'What is lost in the withering of semblance and the decay of the aura in works of art is matched by a huge gain in the space-for-play' (SW 3, 127 [translation modified]). Therefore, the 'space-for-play' does not at all suppress the shortcomings of the world but makes them at once visible *and* open to be engaged with. As we have seen in the first chapter, Benjamin describes this experience as follows: 'Our bars and city streets, our offices and furnished rooms, our railroad stations and our factories seemed to close relentlessly around us. Then came film and exploded this prison-world with the dynamite of the split second, so that now we can set off calmly on journeys of adventure among its farflung debris' (SW 3, 117).

The concept of a 'space-for-play' belongs in the same category as the 'spiritual' sobriety of Hölderlin's late poems and the messianic 'restitutio' that is highlighted in Benjamin's philosophy of history (see chapter 1). In line with his descriptions of the purely 'spiritual' reality of Hölderlin's poetic constructs and the messianic 'restitutio', the 'space-for-play' that is opened in and by the photographic and filmic image sets up a *novel* sphere of existence. It entails first and foremost the construction of an *added* reality or, as Benjamin puts it in his *Artwork* essay, an '*other* nature' (SW 3, 117). For this reason, Benjamin associates the 'space-for-play' with the birth of a 'one hundred percent image space [*hundertprozentigen Bildraum*]'. Benjamin describes this 'one hundred percent image space' with exactly the same formula as the messianic 'restitutio'. The 'one hundred percent image space' is framed as the birth of a 'world of universal and integral actuality' [*die Welt allseitiger und integraler Aktualität*] (SW 2, 217; GS II, 309). In a note written in preparation for the theses 'On the Concept of History' Benjamin states that '[t]he messianic world', likewise, 'is the world of total and integral actuality'[*Die messianische Welt ist die Welt allseitiger und integraler Aktualität*] (SW 4, 404; GS I, 1238). This parallelism should not be interpreted as an argument for the claim that the playful transformation of one's daily surroundings into a 'world of universal and integral actuality' is tantamount to a divine intervention within history. Neither does it entail that, in play, one gains access to age-old standards or absolute goals for history. The 'space-for-play' can no longer 'be measured out by contemplation' and it cancels out the distance between subject and object (SW 2, 217). With the construction of a space that is truly 'other' to our surroundings, Benjamin does not refer to the recovery of images that would *inspire* our reception of the world. The construction of such a purely imagistic space *results* from our affirmation of historical change but it does not *motivate* or *underlie* it. The birth of a 'one hundred percent image space' can be understood as a redemptive intervention within history precisely because it disconnects the feeling that a truly different world is possible from the appeal to preconceived models and stereotypes. The transformation of one's surroundings into a 'one hundred percent image space' is the epitome of a direct and immediate response *to* these surroundings, *doing away* with absolute ideals for history. The 'one hundred percent image space' is a 'body-space' [*Leibraum*] in which 'no limb remains untorn' (SW 2, 217).[91]

The capacity to reopen the world in and as something 'different' is conditioned by the awareness that it is as yet *lacking in determination*. In his essay on photography, for instance, Benjamin goes so far as to suggest that it is 'the task of the photographer—descendant of the augurs and haruspices—to reveal guilt and to point out the guilty in his pictures' (SW 2, 527).[92] Benjamin makes the affirmation of historical change dependent on the confrontation with a fundamental *emptiness* or *groundlessness* that pertains to history as such, therewith rejecting both the possibility and the need to recollect supposedly immemorial or eternal values and ideals. Because it thus presupposes a fundamental incompleteness on the part of history at large, the transformation of our surroundings into 'a world of universal and integral actuality' does not at all result in the hope that everything is possible. To the contrary, such an experience does not fail to make visible the *im*possibilities in and of our world. Benjamin associates the reproduction of our world as a 'one hundred percent image space' with 'pessimism all along the line', albeit a pessimism that is 'organize[d]' [*Organisierung des Pessimismus*] (SW 2, 216; GS II, 308). It is precisely the immediate reception of the world's *forlornness* that can replenish the hope for change. Benjamin terms this deeply paradoxical experience the 'profane illumination' that can be discerned, for instance, in the surrealist interest in ruins and deserted spaces. Breton 'was the first to perceive the revolutionary energies that appear in the "outmoded"—in the first iron constructions, the first factory buildings, the earliest photos, objects that have begun to be extinct, grand pianos, the dresses of five years ago, fashionable restaurants when the vogue has begun to ebb from them' (SW 2, 210).

Like these concepts of a 'space-for-play', 'one hundred percent image space' and 'profane illumination', which entail a 'sudden transform[ation]' of 'destitution' into 'revolutionary nihilism' [*wie ... die versklavten und versklavenden Dinge in revolutionären Nihilismus umschlagen*], Benjamin's interpretation of childhood rests on a specific theory of nihilism (SW 2, 210; GS II, 299). In line with Nietzsche, Benjamin considers the child a figure of forgetting. In Benjamin's view, however, such forgetting points to a universalised annihilation and not to the natural productivity of a 'higher force that dominates and directs'. The child replenishes our hope for change, not because it shares in the spontaneous regeneration of life, but because it evidences a process of 'passing-away' that can be made productive, and this on the condition that it is *transmuted*. This is the reason why, in Benjamin's view, the child metaphorizes at once the inevitability of an end *and* the possibility of a new beginning. Benjamin's concept of the child rests on the confrontation with a forgetting that is so complete that it can forget *itself*. As Deleuze suggests, such 'complete' nihilism meets 'perishing' as an all-encompassing force that is dislodged from *within*. For Benjamin, the child's reception of the world testifies to an active and unsparing negation, first and foremost to the negation of those forces that are an obstacle to change. The child's response to the world neutralizes all those distinctions and hierarchies that go against the feeling that our daily surroundings can be revolutionized. It thereby establishes a purely 'spiritual' and non-actual, added reality. As a consequence, Benjamin connects the child's reception of the world with a 'utopian' drive that is deeply immanent. 'Just as a child who has learned to grasp stretches out its hand for the moon as it would for a ball, so every revolution sets its sights as much on currently utopian goals as on goals within reach' (SW 3, 135). Such a 'different utopian' but completely nihilistic 'will' [*ein anderer utopischer Wille*] (GS VII, 665) does not jump *beyond* the world in its current state but it continues to respond to it, albeit for the sole reason that this world can be asserted as incomplete and non-determined.

With these suggestions in mind, it ceases to surprise that Benjamin's conception of childhood revolves around the concept of *Aufgabe*. Like the *Aufgabe* of the poet, the translator, the masses, the historian and 'world-politics', the *Aufgabe* of the child consists in giving up the belief that an absolute power can be recovered from within history, be it a transhistorical ground or an infinite force of renewal. Rather than as an enchanted universe filled to the brim with marvels and mysteries, the child experiences the world as a realm that remains lacking in meaning. When Benjamin describes how children 'are irresistibly drawn by the detritus [*Abfall*] generated by building, gardening, housework, tailoring, or carpentry', much more is at stake than the claim that children are prone to fooling around with the stuff that adults throw away (SW 1, 449; GS IV, 93). Benjamin's reference to *Abfall* needs to be read alongside his suggestion that it is possible to 'capture an image of history' in 'the detritus [*Abfällen*] of present existence'.[93] In both instances, Benjamin describes how the sustained confrontation with the world's lack of meaning results in a paradoxical recovery of truth. Both references to *Abfall* indicate that, as Deleuze put it, 'negation [can be] transformed into a power of affirmation'.[94] Benjamin puts it as follows: 'In using *Abfallprodukten*, [children] do not so much imitate the works of adults as bring together, in the artifact produced in play, materials of widely differing kinds in a new, intuitive relationship. Children thus produce their own small world of things within the greater one [*Kinder bilden sich damit ihre Dingwelt, eine kleine in der großen, selbst*]' (SW 1, 449–50; GS IV, 93).[95]

The child's active negation of the world in its actual state casts light on Benjamin's idea that it has a peculiar affinity with *mechanized* movement. In his essay on the mimetic faculty, he draws attention to the fact that 'the child plays at being not only a shopkeeper or teacher, but also a windmill and a train' (SW 2, 720). In the

Passagen-Werk, he adds that 'by the interest it takes in technological phenomena, its curiosity for all sorts of inventions and machinery, every childhood binds the accomplishments of technology to the old worlds of symbols' (AP, 461). In Benjamin's *oeuvre*, the symbol stands for the 'unity of the material and the transcendent object [*die Einheit von sinnlichem und übersinnlichem Gegenstand*]' (O, 160; GS I, 336 [translation modified]), that is, for a connection between the world in which we live and a truly *different* world. The child's active response to machinery is thus believed to result in the production of archetypal meanings and images. 'Each truly new configuration of nature — and, at bottom, technology is just such a configuration —' is incorporated 'into the image stock of humanity' [*Jeder wahrhaft neuen Naturgestalt – und im Grunde ist auch die Technik eine solche, entsprechen neue 'Bilder'*] (AP, 390; GS V, 493). With this claim, Benjamin does not suggest that the child's reception of the world rests on the recollection of age-old ideals for history that can thus be renewed. The 'different utopian will' of the child is grounded in the altogether opposite belief that precisely the experience of novelties and recent inventions can amount to a puzzling force of persistence and repetition. 'The child can do what the grownup absolutely cannot: recognize the new once again [*das Neue wiedererkennen*]. For us, locomotives already have symbolic character because we met with them in childhood. Our children, however, will find this in automobiles, of which we ourselves see only the new, elegant, modern, cheeky side' (AP, 390; GS V, 493). This claim that a child's direct experience of modern technology can set up a genuinely *other* and purely *imagistic* or 'symbolic' universe should not be confused with the suggestion that our experiences of and with machines can reestablish a connection with deep truths and absolute essences. Benjamin is severely critical of the idea that modern technology is to be worshipped as the ancient gods it has replaced. In his 'Theories of German Fascism' (1930), Benjamin takes a series of German authors, including Ernst Jünger, to task for their conviction that the powers of technology can be worshipped as divinities. For Benjamin such a mythologization of technology fails to comprehend it as a historical and instable phenomenon, lacking a timeless essence. It can only lead to a 'cult of war' that is inspired by ideals and stereotypes such as 'fatefulness' and 'heroism' that have lost all legitimacy after the First World War. 'Etching the landscape with flaming banners and trenches, technology wanted to recreate the heroic features of German Idealism. It went astray. What it considered heroic were the features of Hippocrates, the features of death' (SW 2, 319). Therefore, in the second version of his *Artwork* essay, Benjamin distinguishes between a 'first' and a 'second' technology. The 'cult of war' that Benjamin denounces in his essay on fascism, and that is made palpable in Ernst Jünger's own conception of a 'complete' nihilism, is one with the 'first' technology. This type of technology seeks to bridge the distance with the beyond and 'deals with irreparable lapse or sacrificial death, which holds good for eternity [*nie wiedergutzumachende Verfehlung oder den ewig stellvertretenden Opfertod*]' (SW 3, 107; GS VII, 359). The child, however, is drawn to a wholly different type of technology. In this 'second' technology, machinic movement is cut loose from whatever type of absolute essence and endowed with the specific features of a given society and period. Its 'results . . . are wholly provisional' since 'it operates by means of experiments and endlessly varied test procedures' [*Das Einmal ist keinmal gilt für die zweite (sie hat es mit dem Experiment und seiner unermüdlichen Variierung der Versuchsanordnung zu tun)*] (SW 3, 107; GS VII, 359). This 'second' technology replaces the mystic cult of machines with the completely nihilistic, and 'different utopian will' that meets the world as groundless and, for that reason precisely, as alterable. Rather than as a force that gives meaning, the child meets technology as a force of universal negation, at odds with the idealization of nature as a realm of supposed purity and innocence. Technology entails a 'cracking open of natural teleology' (AP, 635).[96] In Benjamin's view, only the child is capable of fully embracing these neutralizing powers of technology and thereby ushering forth 'symbolic' images of a reality that can in no way be confused with any current (or possible) state of events.

DAS TAGEBUCH

As we know from the previous two chapters, the transmutation of transience into a productive force is conditioned by the inner unity and coherence of a given *construct*. In his 'Metaphysics of Youth', as well, Benjamin argues that such a redemptive 'turning of time' is dependent on the autonomous existence of a specific *work*. This is the reason why he introduces the concept of *Tagebuch* (diary, book of days) as the material expression of an all-encompassing but transmuted passing away. According to Benjamin, the activity of noting down the events of the day in a diary is constitutive of the same temporal plasticity that can be discovered in childhood. 'From day to day, second to second, the self preserves itself [*selbsterhält sich das Ich*], clinging to that instrument: time, the instrument it was supposed to play. In despair, he thus recalls his childhood [*der also Verzweifelte entsann sich seiner Kindheit*]. In those days there was time without flight and an "I" without death [*damals war noch Zeit ohne Flucht und Ich ohne Sterben*]' (SW 1, 11; GS II, 97). Like child's play, the activity of writing down the day's events in a diary does not shy away from the confrontation with a fundamental transience but it manages to replenish the hope that this transience can nevertheless be dispelled. This unexpected moment of 'liberation [*eine Befreiungstat*]' (SW 1, 11; GS II, 97) requires the 'forgetting of forgetting' that also motivated Benjamin's interpretation of Hölderlin's poem 'Blödigkeit', the messianic 'restitutio' and the expressive mode of allegory. Because childhood is an inherently ephemeral stage that cannot withstand the passage of time, it resists the powers of memory and recollection. 'The medium in which the pure melody of his youth would swell was destroyed' (SW 1, 11). It is for this reason that the temporal plasticity that characterizes both child's play and the diary is one with 'despair' [*Verzweiflung*], having nothing to do with an a-temporal innocence and purity that survives over time. When Benjamin uses the word *Ent-sinnung* to capture how the diary can nonetheless 'recall' the experience of the child, he describes a thinking-away-from-the-present, and not a moving-back-towards-the-past. Like Hölderlin's concept of *nach-denken* and Benjamin's notion of *ent-schlafen*, this unexpected retrieval of the child's 'utopian will' requires a sustained but creative affirmation of an 'emptiness of time' [*Leere der Zeit*] (SW 1, 11; GS II, 97), and even a type of 'obliviousness' [*Vergessenheit*] (SW 1, 11; GS II, 97). The writer of the diary 'gazes down and down into the current whence he had emerged and slowly, finally, he is redeemed by losing his comprehension. Amid such obliviousness, not knowing what he thinks and yet thinking himself redeemed, he begins the diary' [*Er sieht und sieht hinab in jene Strömung, aus der er aufgetaucht war, und er verliert langsam, endlich und erlösend sein Begreifen. In solcher Vergessenheit, unwissend was er meint und doch erlöster Meinung entstand das Tagebuch*] (SW 1, 11; GS II, 97).

Benjamin's ideas about the diary part ways with the common view that it conditions an intimate conversation with a stable and unified self. Unlike Elias Canetti, who emphasizes that all diaries are 'secrets' that cannot be shared with anyone else, Benjamin dismisses the view that they bring about quiet reflection and undisturbed deliberation.[97] The 'other self' (SW 1, 11) that it fashions should be considered an 'abdicating self' [*ein Ich ... der abdankt*] (SW

1, 14; GS II, 101) that 'tears away from consummation' [*riß er sich aus seiner Vollendung*] (SW 1, 15; GS II, 102). In the diary, we 'return home to ourselves as our enemy [*kehren wir zu uns heim als unser Feind*]' (SW 1, 14; GS II, 101). The diary does not allow for a further appropriation and internalization of our experiences of and activities in the world. Noting down these events does not result in a deeper understanding and it does not weave them together into the homogeneity of a continuous self. In Benjamin's view, the diary does set up the 'interval' [*Abstand*] that is needed to think, but such thinking has nothing in common with the quiet contemplation that, in a humanistic and liberal view such as Arendt's, is believed to hold the chaos and randomness of life at bay. The 'other self' that is fashioned by and in the diary is at odds with 'the murky inwardness of the self which calls me I and tortures me with its intimacies [*die trübe Innerlichkeit jenes Erlebenden der mich Ich nennt und mit Vertrautheit martert*]' (SW 1, 11; GS II, 97). It acts and thinks from *within* the passage of time and does not seek to expand the gap between the present, past and future into a stable ground for consideration and resolve. Benjamin is very clear in stating that, in the diary, the 'self relates nothing more to itself' (SW 1, 15) and that 'destiny declares its faith in us *because* we have long since ceased to relate [this destiny] to ourselves [*zu uns bekennt sich unser Schicksal, weil wir es auf uns schon längst nicht mehr bezogen*]' (SW 1, 12; GS II, 99 [emphasis added]).

Rather than bestowing an underlying ground onto the contingencies of our daily life, Benjamin's concept of diary entails the active negation of meaning that is characteristic to complete nihilism. The specific temporality that is created in the diary is 'the time of death' [*die Zeit des Todes*] (SW 1, 15; GS II, 103). The diary does not put into a place an external counter-power to the evanescence of life but it fully shares within it. It is, states Benjamin, written 'from the vantage point of our death' (SW 1, 15) and sets up an 'I [that] is entirely transposed into time [*ich bin ganz und gar in Zeit versetzt*]': Time 'irradiates in me [*strahlt mich aus*]' (SW 1, 12; GS II, 98). In an essay on the diary, the Belgian philosopher Patricia de Martelaere describes how this assertion of a lack of meaning can nonetheless grow into a replenishment of hope. Diaries, she writes, condition a 'super-temporal communication with a *later* I, that is as yet unknown and might very well differ fundamentally from the current I'.[98] Such a 'later I' is in fact our own I 'that is already dead while, a moment earlier, it was still alive and which will be the sole presence [that is granted] the longed-for overview. . . . [I]f this [I] would know *everything* that we know about ourselves, it would be able to endow the entirety of our life with meaning. In the diary we provide it, posthumously, with all the material'.[99] The activity of writing a diary always has 'a posthumous character'.[100] For Benjamin, as well, the diary is meant to preserve the past and the present but not without asserting that these are as yet *falling short in determination*. In Benjamin's view, it is nothing but the confrontation with the structural incompleteness of the past and the present that vouchsafes the possibility of a genuine, different future. The diary preserves the very groundlessness of the past and the present in order to maintain the hope that they will at some point yield to an as yet non-actualized revelation of meaning. In the diary, we reanimate the belief that 'past things have futurity' [*[D]ie Vergangenen werden zukünftig*]. 'The past of things *is* the future of the I time' [*Der Dinge Vergangenheit ist die Zukunft der Ich-Zeit*] (SW 1, 15; GS II, 102 [emphasis added]). In the diary meaning is suspended but only to make the possibility of its resolution all the more tangible. It makes the passing away of everything acutely noticeable but not without asserting the confidence that this passing away might itself at some point pass away. Such an experience can only be described with the oxymoron of 'immortal time [*unsterbliche Zeit*]' (e.g., SW 1, 11; GS II, 98). Our diaries are written for only ourselves, not because they grant us a deeper self-knowledge but because they annul and suspend everything we cling to in actual life, and thus acknowledge the possibility of a different one. In the diary, 'death [is drowned] in immortality [*in Unsterblichkeit ertränken*]' (SW 1, 14; GS II, 101).

Benjamin describes how, while going about our lives, we ceaselessly 'r[u]n past [our] fate' and are 'unable ever to encounter it' [*Niemals war er dem Schicksal begegnet, an dem er vorbei lief*] (SW 1, 15; GS II, 102). Daily existence is but a 'chain of experiences' that seem external to our sense of selfhood, resulting in the fact that we 'experience [everything] inadequately' (SW 1, 11). When noted down in a diary, this seeming randomness and inadequacy of the events of our ordinary lives is made palpable. A diary does not bestow an overarching context of meaning, much less an importance, onto our existence but it captures daily life in its very arbitrariness. Still, the diary sets up an order of its own. Benjamin likens it to a 'book *of* time [*ein Buch von der Zeit*], a book of days' (SW 1, 11; GS II, 98) that at once exposes *and* dislodges the randomness of our ordinary lives. The diary does indeed set up a rigid system that divides the haphazardness of daily life in numbered years, months, weeks and days. In contrast to our daily life, 'at whose heart an inscrutable death lies in wait' (SW 1, 11), the diary is governed by a logic so strict that it conjures a semblance of infinity. In the diary, the numbered days succeed one another in an almost mechanical manner, untroubled, it seems, by the transience that holds sway over our actual existence. Daily life is 'devoured by the countless demands of the moment' and thus hollowed out by evanescence: death 'kills daily so that life itself may go on' (SW 1, 11). The quasi automatic succession of days in the diary, for its part, sets up an experience in which time no longer 'sen[ds] us forth' but 'is flooded back toward us' [*fühlten wir Zeit, die uns aussandte, gewaltig gegen uns wieder fluten*] (SW 1, 13; GS II, 100). In spite of being devoid of an overarching context of meaning, our daily existence is thus reworked into the genuinely different and non-actual reality of a *book*. While ordinary existence is inseparable from annihilation and can only proceed by pushing away one moment after another, the diary entails a 'creation of time' [*der Schöpfung der Zeit*] (SW 1, 12; GS II, 98).

The *Tagebuch* needs to be opposed to Benjamin's concept of 'calendar' [*Kalender*]. Benjamin associates the calendar with the qualitative, deep or true memory that preserves an immemorial past (see chapter 2). Such an immemorial past is deemed worthy of being remembered because it marks an 'interval' [*Abstand*] that 'stands apart' from [*ab-stand*] the common course of the world. A calendar retains events with a significance that goes beyond their factual occurrence, introducing a truly novel era within history. In his theses on 'The Concept of History', for instance, Benjamin refers to political revolutions as instants that 'make the continuum of history explode' and thereby 'introduced a new calendar' (SW 4, 395). Such moments differ inherently from the arbitrary succession of events that makes up ordinary reality. Though revolutionary events do not come from nowhere, their significance for history retains a sense of the absolute because it cannot be gauged by reconstructing their underlying causes. The past that is inserted into a calendar no longer merely belongs to the 'eternal repetition of the same' that dominates over daily life. The singular importance of the events that are thus retained remain ungraspable for whoever considers history as a chain of moments without qualitative distinctions.[101] In Benjamin's view, the possibility that the great events of history are enshrined into the specific memory of a calendar is dependent on societal and historical elements. Benjamin underscores that we have lost the capacity to bestow a truly historical importance onto specific events. Our modern 'poverty of experience' has done away with our affinity for events that are deemed unique and worthy of being commemorated.[102] '[C]alendars do not measure time the way clocks do; they are monuments of a historical consciousness of which not the slightest trace has been apparent in Europe, it would seem, for the past hundred years' (SW 4, 395).

Even though modern man 'feels as though he has been dropped from the calendar' (SW 4, 336) the diary vouchsafes a space that 'stands apart' from the common course of life. Benjamin goes so far as to associate the activity of writing down the day's events in a diary with a moment of 'redemption' [*erlösend, erlöster*] (e.g., SW 1, 11; GS II, 97). A diary enables man to fashion a 'countermovement' [*Gegenbewegung*] to the draining experience that existence is but an empty recurrence of interchangeable instants (SW 1, 15; GS II, 102). Benjamin's argument that the diary modifies our life from within hinges on the use of the German word *widerfahren*. This term can, first of all, be translated as 'befall', thereby indicating that, in daily life, events merely happen *to* us. Because writing them down in a book entails a sustained activity on the part of man, the diary dislodges the passivity that comes over us in ordinary life. In the diary, it is no longer the case that things merely 'happen to' us since, vice versa, 'the "I" befalls all things, they gravitate toward our self' [*allen Dingen widerfährt das Ich im Tagebuche, sie leben zum Ich dahin*]. 'In the diary our self . . . impinges on everything else . . . [b]ut time no longer impinges on this self' [*allem andern geschieht unser Ich als Zeit . . . [a]ber diesem . . . geschieht Zeit nicht mehr*] (SW 1, 12; GS II, 98). Therefore, a second meaning of the word *widerfahren* points to the possibility that our daily existence is 'experienced anew' [*wider-er-fahren*] in and as the content of a diary. In the diary, the haphazardness of ordinary life is transformed into an 'experience perfected'[*sich zum Vollendeten verwandelt*] (SW 1, 11; GS II, 97). This entails that the diary reopens the very randomness of life as 'fated' (see SW 1, 15; GS II, 102). This reference to fate or destiny should not be confused with the claim that the diary recovers a more profound significance that pertains to ordinary reality. The diary does not set up a connection between the contingency of our daily life on the one hand and an absolute significance or inherent meaningfulness on the other. Such a pseudo-transcendent ground is fully lacking and it would be at odds with the irreducible arbitrariness and transience of everything historical. In its 'perfected' shape, ordinary reality does not shed its arbitrary nature. Still, in the diary, ordinary reality is put into writing exactly as what it is: a tangible, accessible and changeable realm that can be responded to, acted upon and decided about. Reworking the occurrences of our lives in the novel unity of the diary, however arbitrary these occurrences may be, restores a 'time of the self' [*Zeit des Ich*] in which the most random thing can 'come to meet [us] [*begegnet . . . uns*]' (SW 1, 15 and 14; GS II, 102 and 101).

NOTES

1. Virgil, *Aeneid*, transl. by Frederick Ahl (Oxford and New York: Oxford University Press, 2007), 50–51 (II, 707–10).
2. For more on this issue, see Philippe Ariès's claim that '[i]n medieval society the idea of childhood did not exist', and that the awareness of the special nature of childhood only arose around the end of the sixteenth century. In *Centuries of Childhood. A Social History of Family Life*, transl. by Robert Baldick (New York: Alfred A. Knopf, 1962), 128.
3. Compare, however, Wordsworth's 'The Rainbow' to the much more melancholy 'Ode, Intimations of Immortality from Recollections of Early Childhood', that includes lines such as 'It is not now as it hath been of yore;— / Turn wheresoe'er I may, / By night or day. / The things which I have seen I now can see no more'.
4. Friedrich Nietzsche, 'On the Uses and Disadvantages of History for Life', 64.
5. Ibid., 62.
6. Ibid., 61.
7. Friedrich Nietzsche, *Thus Spoke Zarathustra*, 17.
8. Ibid., 52.
9. 'Cheerfulness, the good conscience, the joyful deed, confidence in the future—all of them depend, in the case of the individual as of a nation, on the existence of a line dividing the bright and discernible from the unilluminable and dark; on one's being just as able to forget at the right time as to remember at the right time; on the possession of a powerful instinct for sensing when it is necessary to feel historically and when unhistorically'. In Friedrich Nietzsche, 'On the Uses and Disadvantages of History for Life', 63.
10. 'The historical sense makes its servants passive and retrospective; and almost the only time the sufferer from the fever of history becomes active is when this sense is in abeyance through momentary forgetfulness'. In ibid., 102.
11. Ibid., 67 and 76.
12. See Deleuze, *Nietzsche and Philosophy*, 68–69. See chapter 1.
13. Nietzsche, 'On the Uses and Disadvantages of History for Life', 115.
14. Ibid., 103 and 115.
15. Ibid., 117.
16. Ibid., 118 and 121.
17. Ibid., 67.
18. Ibid., 120.
19. Compare with Benjamin's concept of *Auf-gabe* [to give up], cf. chapter 1.
20. Hannah Arendt, *The Life of the Mind / Willing*, 217.
21. Hannah Arendt, *The Human Condition*, 246–47.
22. Hannah Arendt, *The Life of the Mind / Willing*, 217.
23. Hannah Arendt, *The Human Condition*, 246 (emphasis added).
24. Ibid., 247.

What Is the Child? Or How Can We Begin Anew? 177

25. Ibid., 246. In this context, see also Seyla Benhabib's reference to a 'melancholia in Hannah Arendt's work', in *The Reluctant Modernism of Hannah Arendt* (Lanham, MD: Rowman & Littlefield, 2003), 193.
26. Hannah Arendt, 'The Concept of History: Ancient and Modern', in *Between Past and Future: Six Exercises in Political Thought* (New York: Viking Press, 1961), 41–90.
27. Ibid., 63.
28. Ibid., 62.
29. Hannah Arendt, 'Preface: The Gap Between Past and Future', in *Between Past and Future*, 11.
30. Hannah Arendt, 'The Concept of History', 65.
31. Ibid., 84.
32. Hannah Arendt, *The Life of the Mind / Thinking*, 209.
33. Ibid., 206.
34. Ibid., 205.
35. Hannah Arendt, 'Preface: The Gap Between Past and Future', 14. This view of human freedom as the outcome of the disruption of a cosmic dynamic of loss and annihilation explains Arendt's emphasis on the importance of the human faculties to forgive and to make and keep promises. Forgiving and promising are exceptional because they interrupt a dynamic of passing-away that cannot be entirely overcome. They are 'isolated islands of certainty in an ocean of uncertainty' (in Hannah Arendt, *The Human Condition*, 244). They remain but a 'remedy' against the 'irreversibility of action' and the 'unpredictability of the future' (ibid., 237). 'It is the insertion of man with his limited life span that transforms the continuously flowing stream of sheer change . . . into time as we know it' (in Hannah Arendt, *The Life of the Mind / Thinking*, 203).
36. Hannah Arendt, *The Life of the Mind / Thinking*, 202.
37. Ibid., 205.
38. Ibid.
39. Ibid., 208.
40. Ibid., 210.
41. Hannah Arendt, 'Preface: The Gap Between Past and Future', 12.
42. Hannah Arendt, *The Life of the Mind / Thinking*, 209.
43. Virgil, 'Fourth Eclogue', in *Eclogues, Georgics, Aeneid I–VI*, transl. by H. Rushton Fairclough, revised by G. P. Goold (Cambridge, MA: Harvard University Press, 1999), 49.
44. Ibid., 53.
45. Hannah Arendt, *The Life of the Mind / Willing*, 212.
46. Hannah Arendt, 'The Concept of History', 64.
47. Hannah Arendt, *The Life of the Mind / Willing*, 212.
48. Ibid., 212.
49. Ibid., 213.
50. Ibid., 212.
51. Ibid., 214–15.
52. Hannah Arendt, 'Preface: The Gap Between Past and Future', 6. See also Arendt's remarks about the importance of recollection in *The Life of the Mind / Thinking*, 76–77. For more on the importance of recollection for Arendt's (political) philosophy, see Irene McMullin, 'The Amnesia of the Modern: Arendt on the Role of Memory in the Constitution of the Political', in *Philosophical Topics* 39 (2) (Fall 2011): 91–116.
53. Hannah Arendt, *The Life of the Mind / Willing*, 214.
54. Hannah Arendt, *The Life of the Mind / Willing*, 213. See also the final lines about 'the sorts of wine' in Book Two of the *Georgics*: 'But there's no number for

the sorts of wine nor names / for each of them, and little to be gained by trying to concoct / the list'. In Virgil, 'Book Two', in *Georgics*, transl. by Peter Fallon (Oxford and New York: Oxford University Press, 2006), 30 (lines 103–5).

55. See Arendt's statement about Virgil: 'Whatever lay prior to th[e] first foundation [of Rome], itself the resurgence of some definite past, was situated outside of history; it was nature, whose cyclical sempiternity might provide a refuge from the onward march of time . . . but whose own origin was of no interest because it was beyond the scope of action'. In Hannah Arendt, *The Life of the Mind / Willing*, 215.

56. In her essay on Arendt's reading of Virgil, Catherine Frost highlights the role of sacrifice, suffering and death in the *Aeneid* and thereby complicates Arendt's reading of Virgil as an author of 're-births'. See Catherine Frost, 'Birth, death and survival: sources of political renewal in the work of Hannah Arendt and Virgil's *Aeneid*', in *Mortality*, Routledge, 5 October 2017, doi:10.1080/13576275.2017.1377167.

57. Augustine, quoted in Hannah Arendt, *The Life of the Mind / Willing*, 217. The original phrase comes from Augustine, *The City of God*, book 12, chapter 21 (Arendt incorrectly refers to chapter 20). For a discussion of Arendt's use of this phrase, and the connection between her early thesis on Augustine and her later writings, see Stephan Kampowski, *Arendt, Augustine and the New Beginning: The Action Theory and Moral Thought of Hannah Arendt in the Light of her Dissertation on St. Augustine* (Grand Rapids, MI: Eerdmans, 2008). Kampowski's discussion of the sentence 'Hoc ergo ut esset, creatus est homo, ante quem nullus fuit' can be found on pp. 47–54.

58. Hannah Arendt, *The Life of the Mind / Willing*, 108-9.

59. Ibid., 108.

60. Augustine, quoted in ibid., 108. The original phrase can be found in *The City of God*, Book 11, Chapter 6.

61. Augustine, *Confessions*, transl. Henry Chadwick (Oxford: Oxford University Press, 2008), 222 (Book 11 (2: 3)).

62. Ibid., 231 (Book 11 (14: 17)). See also the statement that '[t]ime flies so quickly from future into past that it is an interval with no duration. If it has duration, it is divisible into past and future. But the present occupies no space'. In ibid., 233 (Book 11 (15: 20)).

63. Augustine, quoted in *The Life of the Mind / Willing*, 91. The original phrase can be found in *On the Free Choice of the Will*, Book 3, Chapter 7.

64. Augustine, quoted in *The Life of the Mind / Willing*, 109. The original phrase can be found in *The City of God*, Book 13, Chapter 10.

65. For more on Augustine's view of memory and recollection, see Paige E. Hochschild, *Memory in Augustine's Theological Anthropology* (Oxford: Oxford University Press, 2012). The third part, which contains a close-reading of books 10–13 of the *Confessions* is particularly revealing.

66. Hannah Arendt, *The Life of the Mind / Willing*, 101

67. Ibid., 109.

68. Hannah Arendt, 'The Concept of History', 73.

69. Hannah Arendt, *The Life of the Mind / Willing*, 117.

70. Ibid., 117.

71. Augustine, *Confessions*, 185 (Book 10 (8: 12)), 186 (Book 10 (8: 13)), 192 (Book 10 (14: 21)).

72. Ibid., 186 (Book 10 (8: 13)).

73. 'Who can deny that the past does not now exist? Yet there is still in the mind a memory of the past. None can deny that present time lacks any extension because it passes in a flash. Yet attention is continuous, and it is through

this that what will be present progresses towards being absent'. In ibid., 244 (Book 11 (28: 37)). See also ibid., 234 (Book 11 (18: 23)): 'Thus my boyhood, which is no longer, lies in past time which is no longer. But when I am recollecting and telling my story, I am looking on its image in present time, since it is still in my memory'.

74. Ibid., 242 (Book 11 (27: 36)).
75. In this context Augustine speaks about 'a present of things past' and describes memory as 'the present considering the past'. In ibid., 235 (Book 11 (20: 26)).
76. Hannah Arendt, *The Life of the Mind / Thinking*, 77.
77. Ibid., 77.
78. Ibid.
79. Ibid., 203.
80. Augustine, *Confessions*, 226 (Book 11 (7: 9)).
81. Ibid., 200 (Book 10 (24: 35)).
82. Ibid., 194 (Book 10 (16: 25)).
83. Augustine, *Confessions*, 274 (Book 13 (1: 1)). See also Harald Weinrich's comment of this line. As he puts it, 'to seek God thus means seeking, in the forgetfulness of God (*oblivio dei*, understood as a genitivus objectivus), the signs of God's remembrance (*memoria Dei*, understood as a genitivus subjectivus) and allowing oneself to be led by the "traces" on the path returning to God'. In Harald Weinrich, *Lethe*, 24.
84. Hannah Arendt, 'The Concept of History', 66.
85. See Peter Eli Gordon's statement that it was Arendt's 'cardinal belief that politics could only come into its own once it abandoned the philosophical search for eternal verities and embraced without regret the realm of doxa and appearance'. In Peter Eli Gordon, 'The Concept of the Apolitical: German Jewish Thought and Weimar Political Theology', in *Social Research* 74 (3) (2007): 872. See also Seyla Benhabib, *The Reluctant Modernism of Hannah Arendt*, 193–98.
86. A pivotal essay to capture the moment of Benjamin's disappointment with the Youth Movement is 'Youth was Silent' in EW, 135–38. About this issue, see the chapter 'Metaphysics of Youth: Berlin and Freiburg, 1912–1914', in Howard Eiland and Michael W. Jennings, *Walter Benjamin: A Critical Life* (Cambridge and London: Harvard University Press, 2014). See also Martin Jay, 'Remembrance and the First World War', in *Benjamin Studien*, ed. Helga Geyer-Ryan, Paul Koopman, and Klaas Yntema (Amsterdam: Rodopi, 2002), 187–208 and Johannes Steizinger, *Revolte, Eros und Sprache: Walter Benjamin's 'Metaphysik der Jugend'* (Berlin: Kulturverlag Kadmos, 2013).
87. See also Johannes Steizinger, 'Geist, Geschichte und Melancholie. Benjamins Idee der Jugend', in *Revolte, Eros und Sprache*, for example, the discussion of youth's 'impossible awakening' on pp. 61–66.
88. For an analysis of the non-humanist, neurological understanding of modern experience that is at stake in these concepts, see Susan Buck-Morss, 'Aesthetics and Anaesthetics: Walter Benjamin's Artwork Essay Reconsidered'.
89. See also the discussion of Benjamin's concept of childhood (and the relation with Piaget) in Susan Buck-Morss, *Dialectics of Seeing*, 262–70. Buck-Morss, as well, rejects 'the romanticizing of childhood innocence' (p. 265).
90. On the concept of 'space-for-play', see the work of Miriam Bratu Hansen, esp. chapter 7 of *Cinema and Experience*.
91. See also the statement that '[w]here an action puts forth its own image and exists, absorbing and consuming it, where nearness looks with its own eyes, the long-sought image space is opened' (SW 2, 217). For an analysis of Benjamin's concepts of 'body- and image-space', 'one hundred percent image space',

and 'world of universal and integral actuality', see Sigrid Weigel, *Body- and Image-Space: Re-reading Walter Benjamin*, esp. Chapters 1 and 2.

92. See also chapter 1.

93. See chapter 1. The reference comes from Benjamin, *Gesammelte Briefe. Band V. 1935–1937*, 138.

94. Gilles Deleuze, *Nietzsche and Philosophy*, 71.

95. For the same passage, see also the essay on 'Old Forgotten Children's Books' (SW 1, 408).

96. See also 'The origin of the second technology lies at the point where, by an unconscious ruse, human beings first began to distance themselves from nature. It lies, in other words, in play' (SW 3, 107).

97. Elias Canetti, 'Dialog mit dem grausamen Partner', in *Das Gewissen der Worte: Essays* (Munich: Hanser, 1976), 54–71.

98. Patricia de Martelaere, 'Het dagboek en de dood', in *Een verlangen naar ontroostbaarheid. Over leven, kunst en dood* (Amsterdam: Meulenhoff, 2008), 161.

99. Ibid., 165.

100. Ibid. See also the following sentence: 'Diaries are, in that sense, always more than mere books-of-the-day (why would a *day* matter so much to an individual): they simultaneously try to become a type of life-books, in which insignificant or surprising experiences are preserved, for the benefit of later eye that will have a better overview and that might be capable of discerning a continuity within everything disparate'. In ibid., 161.

101. This distinction between an empty, measurable, divisible and quantifiable temporal succession on the one hand, and a qualitative memory that retains unique and significant events, is, of course, borrowed from Bergson's duality between space-time (mechanical clock-time) and duration (the indivisible stream of time). According to Bergson, as well, the immemorial past that 'stands out' involves 'memory-images' that differ inherently from those images that are summoned by the present with the help of perception and consciousness. See, for example, Henri Bergson, *Matter and Memory*, 153.

102. See chapter 2.

By Way of Conclusion

A Note on Shadows

Somewhere in the Hiroshima Peace Memorial Museum, two objects are brought on display that seem not at all in their right place among the other material remains, documents and artworks that bear witness to the explosion of the atomic bomb. One of them is a wooden panel that upon first sight does not really seem to differ from any ordinary wooden panel that one can find, especially in a country like Japan, by the thousands. The second one is made of stone and shaped like the steps that are used for a house or a public building. Again, there is nothing striking about these steps and it is not unlike the kind of steps that any person, in Japan or elsewhere, would use whenever entering a house or shop. Yet, a pattern of leaves is clearly noticeable on the wooden panel and, on the steps, there is a large dark stain. These are not drawings, inscriptions or zones of color that have been added at a later moment, but the shadows of branches and a human body that have somehow 'attached' themselves to these objects.

On 6 August 1945, at 8:15 a.m., Hiroshima was hit by the most atrocious event that was ever planned by human minds and made real by human hands. On the day of the explosion, approximately seventy thousand people died, and, in the months to come, at least another seventy thousand succumbed to the effects of nuclear radiation. The wooden panel and the stone steps that are on display in the Peace Memorial Museum are material remains of that specific moment and that specific place: the shadows that are engraved onto them were cast by a branch with leaves somewhere in the city of Hiroshima and by a woman or man who on that summer morning was waiting for the bank to open. The process through which these shadows were transfixed onto the panel and steps is the result of the explosion of the bomb itself. This explosion was accompanied by such an extreme flash of light that it generated the same effect as a photo camera: a banal and fleeting moment was preserved forever, albeit not on a sensitive plate but on the harsh and natural material of wood or stone.[1]

The use of atomic weapons added a wholly new dimension to the age-old human capacity to destroy. This new dimension cannot be measured by the number of casualties alone, however high this number turned out to be. It results from the specific temporal structure that is characteristic to atomic destruction. While the actual explosion of an atomic bomb lasts less than a microsecond, its radiation generates effects that are of a much more extended and expanded nature. Nuclear fallout led to a sharp increase of various lingering diseases, some of them only becoming manifest ten years later. Moreover, the use of atomic bombs is often cited as the starting point of a new geological era, the Anthropocene, in which human beings are believed to have modified nature in ways that cannot possibly be undone. With the nuclear blasts the artificial isotopes caesium-137 and strontium-90 became a permanent presence in the earth's soil. For this reason, the explosion of the atomic bomb should not just be considered as an *event* in history but, first and foremost, as the beginning of a novel, and irreversible, *epoch*. However, due to the irreversible nature of the effects of the atomic bomb, its explosion can equally be understood as the *opposite* of the beginning of a novel epoch, that is, as an event that closed off the possibility of a genuine future. For when no human action or natural process will ever succeed in filtering out the fallout that was left behind by nuclear tests and bombs, how can we imagine a world that will have truly moved beyond it? On the sole basis of events that happened in the *past*, at least one fundamental assumption about the *future* can already be asserted: it will always bear *some* trace of the radiation that was released in the period between 1945 and 1963. Rather than saying that, after this period, nothing was the same anymore, it seems in fact more accurate to say that, as to the presence of radiation, nothing will ever be allowed to become truly 'other' again. The nuclear fallout is a perpetual reminder of the fact that nothing that is either natural or manmade, not even the very opposition between what is natural and what is manmade, is inherently immune to being destroyed. With the invention of weapons that can reduce the entirety of our planet to nothingness, a power to obliterate was introduced that knows no antithesis. This is how Günther Anders puts it in the first paragraph of his *Reflections on the H-Bomb*:

If there is anything that modern man regards as infinite, it is no longer God; nor is it nature, let alone morality or culture; it is his own power. *Creatio ex nihilo*, which was once the mark of omnipotence, has been supplanted by its opposite, *potestas annihilationis* or *reductio ad nihil*; and this power to destroy, to reduce to nothingness lies in our own hand. The Promethean dream of omnipotence has at long last come true, though in an unexpected form. Since we are in a position to inflict absolute destruction on each other, we have apocalyptic powers. It is we who are the infinite.[2]

The awareness that only the power to destroy might deserve to be called indestructible comes with a specific importance to the issue of forgetting. When we are unable to retrieve a genuine counter-principle to destruction, this means that even the human faculty of remembrance is ultimately deemed incapable of going against an all-encompassing force of annihilation. With the surfacing of an infinite power to destroy, even our capacity to overcome loss by way of memory and recollection is deeply affected. In the testimonies of victims we can find one of the clearest indications that not even the confidence in the redemptive potential of commemoration was granted survival in the face of the atomic bomb. 'I suspect that the A-bomb planners thought in such a way', one of them told the Nobel Prize–winning novelist Kenzaburo Oe, 'that in making the final decision, they trusted too much in the enemy's human strength to cope with the hell that would follow the dropping of the atomic bomb. If so, theirs was a most paradoxical humanism'.[3] What is indeed often overlooked when we examine the moral obligation to commemorate past injustices is that, for not a few of the survivors—though by no means for all of them—this urge to commemorate is not only a rather meaningless but even an unbearable endeavour. What matters much more to these victims than the awareness that their suffering will be remembered in the future is the recognition that the powers they were up against were infinitely stronger than even the human faculty of memory:

> My nightmare stems from a suspicion that a certain 'trust in human strength', or 'humanism', flashed across the minds of the American intellectuals who decided upon the project that concluded with the dropping of the atomic bomb on Hiroshima. That 'humanism' ran as follows: If this absolutely lethal bomb is dropped on Hiroshima, a scientifically predicable hell will result. But the hell will not be so completely beyond the possibility of human recovery that all mankind will despise their humanity merely at the thought of it.[4]

It is only with these observations in mind that the wooden panel and stone steps in the Hiroshima Peace Memorial Museum can be given the expressiveness that is their due. These objects are no objects of commemoration. Nothing in them bespeaks any capacity to counter-act disappearance or mediate loss. They do not evidence whatever 'trust in human strength'.[5] Shadows, that is, are marked illustrations of precariousness and vulnerability. They exemplify a transience that is irremediable. They are ephemeral and cannot be transfixed. They cannot stand on their own and always depend on something that inevitably remains external; the object or human being they are a shadow of and the rays of light through which they are produced. Everything about shadows exposes that they do not act but are acted *upon*: they do not carry anything but *fall*. They are dependent on movements and changes coming from *elsewhere*. A shadow is the only phenomenon that is both real and entirely two-dimensional, irreducibly distinct from the very phenomenon from which it originates. A shadow, in other words, can be endowed only with the status of being residual and displaced: it is always redundant or 'too much' vis-à-vis the entity it derives its existence from—always on the way to being forgotten.

And yet, in Hiroshima, shadows *do* seem to stand on their own. The wooden panel and the stone steps that are kept in the Peace Memorial Museum are indicative of a moment in time that is at once deeply transient *and* strangely persistent. While everything about them evidences an *in*capacity to endure and an *in*ability to become independent, these shadows, unlike their referents, *did* in fact survive over time. What is more, while shadows that have detached themselves from human bodies are, in Western history, associated either with illusion (Plato's cave) or death (Dante's Hell), the shadows in Hiroshima set up a dynamic of unsuspected change and a continued life. In his important philosophical pamphlet *In Praise of Shadows* (1933), the Japanese writer Junichiro Tanizaki had already famously proclaimed that Japanese culture 'find[s] beauty not in the thing itself but in the patterns of shadows, the light and the darkness, that one thing against another creates'.[6] Effigies or flower arrangements in the alcove of Japanese houses, for instance, do not merit our attention by virtue of the way they look in themselves or when isolated from their environment but only to the extent that they 'set off to unexpected advantage both [themselves] and [their] surroundings'.[7] In Japanese aesthetics, in other words, shadows are no mere indices and they do not have a merely secondary significance vis-à-vis the objects they are a shadow of. On the contrary, shadows are endowed with a capacity to *modify* their referents. They release objects from their rigid isolation and self-identity and they are believed to allow them to join in an unanticipated and ever-changing variation alongside and together with their surroundings. 'The beauty of a Japanese room', writes Tanizaki, 'depends on a variation of shadows, heavy shadows against light shadows—it has nothing else'.[8] Shadows thus succeed in creating a surprising and playful choreography out of entities that, when experienced in isolation from each other, are firmly rooted and immutable. They inject time and the change of light in an otherwise self-absorbed and strictly organized universe.

This is precisely the effect of the transfixed shadows in Hiroshima. Evidencing a scene that cannot be mistaken for a historical possibility (no actual shadow can be detached from its referent), the transfixed shadows are the result of a specific *work*. They act upon their own moment of origination and bring about an *added, non-actual reality*. On the one hand, they are material remnants of the *im*possibilities of history and the deeply rooted forces of annihilation that hold sway over it. However autonomous they have seemingly become, the shadows on the wooden panel and the stone steps are in no way *external* to the destruction caused by the atomic bomb; they make palpable the relentlessness and indifference of universal annihilation. For this reason, they are indicative of a specific type of despair. But, on the other hand, these shadows have also dislodged the atomic bomb's infinite power to destroy. The wooden panel and the stone steps grant the most random event and the most precarious object an awkward capacity to persist. For this reason the despair they materialize cannot be separated from a puzzling type of hope. Having been created *by* the actual flash of the explosion, these engraved shadows result *from* destruction and they originated *in* annihilation. In the transfixed shadows in Hiroshima, destruction and annihilation have been transmuted into a force that has ultimately destroyed and annihilated *itself*. Here, obliteration turned toward itself and became *productive*. As a consequence, the transfixed shadows embody the *internal* limits of even the most unsparing violence and this precisely *because* they make this unsparingness visible. When all-encompassing obliteration is thus brought to take itself as object, its fundamental void and groundlessness becomes clear for all to see.

Perhaps it is only this remarkable capacity to experience the inseparability of destruction and productivity, forgetting and persistence, which conditions the possibility of a genuine future. Such a future does not require a certain grasp of what lies await or should be done. It would be inseparable from a 'hope in the past' (see SW 4, 391). The work of thought that restores an unsuspected dimension of hope is capable of doing more than denouncing past suffering and injustice. It does not result in the 'silence' (Adorno, Steiner) that commemorates suffering as an undeniable presence that should nonetheless have been avoided. When a moment of creation is uncovered within the heart of an infinite force of annihilation, the moral impulse to negate the suffering from the past is complemented with the unsuspected retrieval of a moment of 'happiness' (Benjamin, Proust). It is perhaps only in this moment of 'happiness' that the suffering of the past is shown off as radically incomplete and, finally, allowed to pass away.

NOTES

1. See also Paul Virilio's comparison of these shadows with the photographs of Niepce and Daguerre in Paul Virilio, *War and Cinema: The Logistics of Perception*, transl. by Patrick Camiller (London: Verso, 1989), 81.
2. Günther Anders, 'Reflections on the H-Bomb', in *Dissent* 3 (2) (1956): 146.
3. Kenzaburo Oe, *Hiroshima Notes*, transl. by David L. Swain and Toshi Yonezawa (New York: Grove Press, 1996), 116.
4. Ibid., 115.
5. For an interesting analysis of these shadows, inspired by Derrida, see Akira Mizuta Lippit, *Atomic Light (Shadow Optics)* (Minneapolis and London: University of Minnesota Press, 2005), 95.
6. Junichiro Tanizaki, *In Praise of Shadows*, transl. by Thomas J. Harper and Edward G. Seidensticker (London: Vintage Books, 2001), 46.
7. Ibid., 31.
8. Ibid., 29.

Abbreviations and Translations

The following abbreviations are used throughout the text and notes:

AP Benjamin, Walter. 2002. *The Arcades Project*. Translated by Howard Eiland. Cambridge, MA: Harvard University Press.

EW Benjamin, Walter. 2011. *Early Writings. 1910–1917*. Translated by Howard Eiland and others. Cambridge, MA: Harvard University Press.

GS I–VII Benjamin, Walter. 1995. *Gesammelte Schriften*. Edited by Rolf Tiedemann and Herman Schweppenhäuser. 7 vols. Frankfurt am Main: Suhrkamp Verlag.

O Benjamin, Walter. 1998. *The Origin of German Tragic Drama*. Translated by John Osborne. London: Verso Books.

SW 1–4 Benjamin, Walter. 2004. *Selected Writings*. Edited by Marcus Bullock, Howard Eiland, and Michael W. Jennings. 4 vols. Cambridge, MA: Harvard University Press.

Bibliography

Adorno, Theodor. 2002. *Essays on Music*. Edited by Richard Leppert. Translated by Susan H. Gillespie. Berkeley and Los Angeles: University of California Press.
———. 2008. *Lectures on Negative Dialectics: Fragments of a Lecture Course 1965/1966*. Edited by Rolf Tiedemann. Translated by Rodney Livingstone. Cambridge: Polity Press.
———. 2005. *Minima Moralia: Reflections on a Damaged Life*. Translated by E. F. N. Jephcott. London and New York: Verso.
———. 2007. *Negative Dialectics*. Translated by E. B. Ashton. London and New York: Continuum.
———. 2005. 'The Meaning of Working through the Past'. In *Critical Models: Interventions and Catchwords*. Translated by Henry W. Pickford. New York: Columbia University Press.
Agamben, Giorgio. 2000. *Remnants of Auschwitz*. Translated by Daniel Heller-Roazen. New York: Zone Books.
———. 2005. *The Time that Remains: A Commentary on the Letter to the Romans*. Translated by Patricia Dailey. Stanford, CA: Stanford University Press.
Al-Saji, Alia. 2004. 'The Memory of Another Past: Bergson, Deleuze and a New Theory of Time'. *Continental Philosophy Review* 37 (2): 203–39.
———. 2007. 'The Temporality of Life: Merleau-Ponty, Bergson, and the Immemorial Past'. *The Southern Journal of Philosophy* 45 (2): 177–206.
Alter, Robert. 1991. *Necessary Angels: Tradition and Modernity in Kafka, Benjamin, and Scholem*. Cambridge, MA: Harvard University Press.
Anders, Günther. 1956. 'Reflections on the H-Bomb'. *Dissent* 3 (2): 146–55.
Arendt, Hannah. 1961. 'Preface: The Gap between Past and Future'. In *Between Past and Future: Six Exercises in Political Thought*. New York: Viking Press.
———. 1961. 'The Concept of History: Ancient and Modern'. In *Between Past and Future: Six Exercises in Political Thought*. New York: Viking Press.
———. 1998. *The Human Condition*. Chicago and London: The University of Chicago Press.
———. 1978. *The Life of the Mind*. San Diego, New York, London: Harcourt.
Ariès, Philippe. 1962. *Centuries of Childhood: A Social History of Family Life*. Translated by Robert Baldick. New York: Alfred A. Knopf.
Aristotle. 1941. 'De Memoria et Reminiscentia (On Memory and Reminiscence)'. In *The Basic Works of Aristotle*. Edited by Richard McKeon. Translated by J. I. Beare. New York: Random House.
Assmann, Aleida. 2011. *Cultural Memory and Western Civilization: Arts of Memory*. Cambridge: Cambridge University Press.
———. 2006a. 'Die Zukunft der Erinnerung an den Holocaust'. In *Der lange Schatten der Vergangenheit. Erinnerungskultur und Geschichtspolitik*. München: C. H. Beck.
———. 2006b. 'Europa als Erinnerungsgemeinschaft'. In *Der lange Schatten der Vergangenheit. Erinnerungskultur und Geschichtspolitik*. München: C. H. Beck.

Augustine. 2008. *Confessions*. Translated by Henry Chadwick. Oxford: Oxford University Press.
———. 2010. *On the Free Choice of the Will*. In *On the Free Choice of the Will, On Grace and Free Choice, and Other Writings*. Translated by Peter King. Cambridge: Cambridge University Press.
———. 1998. *The City of God against the Pagans*. Translated by R. W. Dyson. Cambridge: Cambridge University Press.
Barash, Jeffrey Andrew. 2016. *Collective Memory and the Historical Past*. Chicago and London: The University of Chicago Press.
———. 2003. *Martin Heidegger and the Problem of Historical Meaning*. New York: Fordham University Press.
Baudelaire, Charles. 1982. *Les Fleurs du Mal*. Translated by Richard Howard. Boston: David R. Godine.
Benhabib, Seyla. 2003. *The Reluctant Modernism of Hannah Arendt*. Lanham, MD: Rowman & Littlefield.
Benjamin, Andrew. 2005. 'Boredom and Distraction: The Moods of Modernity'. In *Walter Benjamin and History*. Edited by Andrew Benjamin. London and New York: Continuum.
———. 2002. 'The Absolute as Translatability: Working through Walter Benjamin on Language'. In *Walter Benjamin and Romanticism*. Edited by Beatrice Hanssen and Andrew Benjamin. New York: Continuum.
———. 2015. 'Time and Task: Benjamin and Heidegger Showing the Present'. In *Sparks Will Fly: Benjamin and Heidegger*. Edited by Andrew Benjamin and Dimitris Vardoulakis. Albany: State University of New York Press.
Benjamin, Walter. 1928. 'Altes Spielzeug'. In *GS IV*, 511–15. Translated into English as 'Old Toys'. In *SW 2*, 98–102.
———. 1934. 'Berliner Kindheit um Neunzehnhundert'. In *GS IV*, 235–304. Translated into English as 'Berlin Childhood around 1900 (1934 Version)'. In *SW 3*, 344–413.
———. 1938. 'Brief an Gershom Scholem'. In *Gesammelte Briefe VI, 1938–1940*, edited by Christoph Gödde and Henri Lonitzs, 105–14. Frankfurt am Main: Suhrkamp Verlag, 2000. Translated into English as 'Letter to Gershom Scholem on Franz Kafka'. In *SW 3*, 322–29.
———. 1938. 'Briefwechsel Theodor W. Adorno und Walter Benjamin'. In *Briefwechsel, 1928–1940*, 364–86. Frankfurt am Main: Suhrkamp Verlag, 1994. Translated into English as 'Exchange with Theodor W. Adorno on "The Paris of the Second Empire in Baudelaire"'. In *SW 4*, 99–115.
———. 1939. 'Das Kunstwerk im Zeitalter seiner technischen Reproduzierbarkeit, Das "Dritte Fassung"'. In *GS I*, 471–508. Translated into English as 'The Work of Art in the Age of Its Technological Reproducibility: Third Version'. In *SW 4*, 251–83.
———. 1936. 'Das Kunstwerk im Zeitalter seiner technischen Reproduzierbarkeit, Das "Zweite Fassung"'. In *GS VII*, 350–84. Translated into English as 'The Work of Art in the Age of Its Technological Reproducibility: Second Version'. In *SW 3*, 101–33.
———. 1915. 'Das Leben der Studenten'. In *GS II*, 75–87. Translated into English as 'The Life of Students'. In *SW 1*, 37–47.
———. 1938. 'Das Paris des Second Empire bei Baudelaire'. In *GS I*, 511–604. Translated into English as 'The Paris of the Second Empire in Baudelaire'. In *SW 4*, 3–92.
———. 2002. 'Das Passagen-Werk'. In *GS V-6*. Translated into English as *The Arcades Project*. Translated by Howard Eiland. Cambridge, MA: Harvard University Press.

———. 1914. 'Das religiöse Stellung der neuen Jugend'. In *GS II*, 72-4. Translated into English as 'The Religious Position of the New Youth'. In *EW*, 168–70.
———. 1919. 'Der Begriff der Kunstkritik in der Deutschen Romantik'. In *GS I*, 7–122. Translated into English as 'The Concept of Criticism in German Romanticism'. In *SW 1*, 116–200.
———. 1931. 'Der destruktive Charakter'. In *GS IV*, 396–98. Translated into English as 'The Destructive Character'. In *SW 2*, 541–42.
———. 1936. 'Der Erzähler'. In *GS II*, 438–65. Translated into English as 'The Storyteller'. In *SW 3*, 143–66.
———. 1917. '"Der Idiot" von Dostojewskij'. In *GS II*, 237–41. Translated into English as 'Dostoevsky's *The Idiot*'. In *SW 1*, 78–81.
———. 1929. 'Der Sürrealismus'. In *GS II*, 295–310. Translated into English as 'Surrealism'. In *SW 2*, 207–21.
———. 1921a. 'Die Aufgabe des Übersetzers'. In *GS IV*, 9–21. Translated into English as 'The Task of the Translator'. In *SW 1*, 253–63.
———. 1921b. 'Die Bedeutung der Zeit in der moralischen Welt'. In *GS VI*, 97–98. Translated into English as 'The Meaning of Time in the Moral Universe'. In *SW 1*, 286–87.
———. 1936. 'Die Bedeutung des schönen Scheins'. In *GS VII*, 667–68. Translated into English as 'The Significance of Beautiful Semblance'. In *SW 3*, 137–38.
———. 1923–1926. *Einbahnstraße*. In *GS IV*, 83–148. Translated into English as *One-Way Street*. In *SW 1*, 444–88.
———. 1929. 'Eine kommunistische Pädagogik'. In *GS III*, 206–9. Translated into English as 'A Communist Pedagogy'. In *SW 2*, 273–75.
———. 1913–1914. 'Erfahrung'. In *GS II*, 54–56. Translated into English as 'Experience'. In *SW 1*, 3–5.
———. 1934. 'Franz Kafka'. In *GS II*, 409–38. Translated into English as 'Franz Kafka'. In *SW 2*, 794–818.
———. 1999. *Gesammelte Briefe. Band V. 1935-1937*. Edited by Christoph Gödde and Henri Lonitz. Frankfurt am Main: Suhrkamp
———. 1924–1925. 'Goethes Wahlverwandtschaften'. In *GS I*, 123–201. Translated into English as 'Goethe's Elective Affinities'. In *SW 1*, 297–360.
———. 1935–1936. 'Im übrigen bricht in den Revolutionen . . .'. In *GS VII*, 665–66. Translated into English as 'A Different Utopian Will'. In *SW 3*, 134–36.
———. 1931. 'Kleine Geschichte der Photographie'. In *GS II*, 368–85. Translated into English as 'Little History of Photography'. In *SW 2*, 507–30.
———. 1914. 'Metaphysik der Jugend'. In *GS II*, 91–104. Translated into English as 'Metaphysics of Youth'. In *SW 1*, 6–17.
———. 1940. 'Paralipomena to "On the Concept of History"'. In *SW 4*, 401–11. Fragments translated from German in *GS I*, 1230–5, 1237–38, 1240–1, 1245–46.
———. 1935. 'Paris, die Hauptstadt des XIX. Jahrhunderts'. In *GS V*, 45–59. Translated into English as 'Paris, the Capital of the Nineteenth Century'. In *SW 3*, 32–49.
———. 1928–1929. 'Programm eines proletarischen Kindertheaters'. In *GS II*, 763–69. Translated into English as 'Program for a Proletarian Children's Theater'. In *SW 2*, 201–6.
———. 1929. 'Robert Walser'. In *GS II*, 324–28. Translated into English as 'Robert Walser'. In *SW 2*, 257–61.
———. 1919. 'Schicksal und Charakter'. In *GS II*, 171–79. Translated into English as 'Fate and Character'. In *SW 1*, 201–6.
———. 1921. 'Schönheit und Schein'. In *GS VI*, 129. Translated into English as 'Beauty and Semblance'. In *SW 1*, 283.

———. 1928. 'Spielzeug und Spielen'. In *GS III*, 127–32. Translated into English as 'Toys and Play'. In *SW 2*, 117–21.
———. 1994. *The Correspondence of Walter Benjamin 1910-1940*. Edited by Gershom Scholem and Theodor W. Adorno. Translated by Manfred R. Jacobson and Evelyn M. Jacobson. Chicago and London: The University of Chicago Press.
———. 1989. *The Correspondence of Walter Benjamin and Gershom Scholem 1932-1940*. Edited by Gershom Scholem. Translated by Gary Smith and Andre Lefevere. New York: Schocken Books.
———. 1921. 'Theologisch-Politisches Fragment'. In *GS II*, 203–4. Translated into English as 'Theological-Political Fragment'. In *SW 3*, 305–6.
———. 1930. 'Theorien des deutschen Faschismus'. In *GS III*, 238–50. Translated into English as 'Theories of German Fascism'. In *SW 2*, 312–21.
———. 1916. 'Trauerspiel und Tragödie'. In *GS II*, 133–37. Translated into English as '*Trauerspiel* and Tragedy'. In *SW 1*, 55–57.
———. 1933. 'Über das mimetische Vermögen'. In *GS II*, 210–13. Translated into English as 'On the Mimetic Faculty'. In *SW 2*, 720–22.
———. 1918. 'Über das Programm der kommenden Philosophie'. In *GS II*, 157–71. Translated into English as 'On the Program of the Coming Philosophy'. In *SW 1*, 100–110.
———. 1940. 'Über den Begriff der Geschichte'. In *GS I*, 691–704. Translated into English as 'On the Concept of History'. In *SW 4*, 389–400.
———. 1939. 'Über einige Motive bei Baudelaire'. In *GS I*, 605–53. Translated into English as 'On Some Motifs in Baudelaire'. In *SW 4*, 313–55.
———. 1920. 'Über "Schein"'. In *GS I*, 831–33. Translated into English as 'On Semblance'. In *SW 1*, 223–25.
———. 1916. 'Über Sprache überhaupt und über die Sprache des Menschen'. In *GS II*, 140–57. Translated into English as 'On Language as Such and on the Language of Man'. In *SW 1*, 62–74.
———. 1998. *Ursprung des Deutschen Trauerspiels* (1925). In *GS I*, 203–430. Translated into English as *The Origin of German Tragic Drama*. Translated by John Osborne. London: Verso Books.
———. 1938–1939. 'Zentralpark'. In *GS I*, 655–90. Translated into English as 'Central Park'. In *SW 4*, 161–99.
———. 1929. 'Zum Bilde Prousts'. In *GS II*, 310–24. Translated into English as 'On the Image of Proust'. In *SW 2*, 237–47.
———. 1921. 'Zur Kritik der Gewalt'. In *GS II*, 179–203. Translated into English as 'Critique of Violence'. In *SW 1*, 236–52.
———. 1915. 'Zwei Gedichte von Friedrich Hölderlin'. In *GS II*, 105–26. Translated into English as 'Two Poems by Friedrich Hölderlin'. In *SW 1*, 18–36.
Bergson, Henri. 1944. *Creative Evolution*. Translated by Arthur Mitchell. New York: Modern Library.
———. 1991. *Matter and Memory*. Translated by Nancy Margaret, Paul and William Scott Palmer. New York: Zone Books.
———. 2002. 'Memory of the Present and False Recognition'. In *Mind Energy, Key Writings*. Edited by Keith Ansell Pearson and John Mullarkey. Translated by Melissa McMahon. London: Continuum.
Bloch, Ernst. 1995. *The Principle of Hope*. Translated by Neville Plaice, Stephen Plaice and Paul Knight. Cambridge, MA: The MIT Press.
———. 2000. *The Spirit of Utopia*. Translated by Anthony A. Nassar. Stanford, CA: Stanford University Press.
Blond, Louis P. 2010. *Heidegger and Nietzsche. Overcoming Metaphysics*. London and New York: Continuum.

Buck-Morss, Susan. 1992. 'Aesthetics and Anaesthetics: Walter Benjamin's Artwork Essay Reconsidered'. *October* 62: 3–41.
———. 1989. *Dialectics of Seeing: Walter Benjamin and the Arcades Project*. Cambridge and London: The MIT Press.
———. 2006. 'The Flâneur, the Sandwichman and the Whore: The Politics of Loitering'. In *Walter Benjamin and the Arcades Project*. Edited by Beatrice Hanssen. London and New York: Continuum.
———. 1997. *The Origin of Negative Dialectics: Theodor W. Adorno, Walter Benjamin, and the Frankfurt Institute*. New York: The Free Press.
Butler, Judith. 2016. 'One Time Traverses Another: Benjamin's "Theological-Political Fragment"'. In *Walter Benjamin and Theology*, edited by Colby Dickinson and Stéphane Symons. New York: Fordham University Press.
Canetti, Elias. 1976. 'Dialog mit dem grausamen Partner'. In *Das Gewissen der Worte: Essays*. Munich: Hanser.
Chrétien, Jean-Louis. 2002. *The Unforgettable and the Unhoped For*. Translated by Jeffrey Bloechl. New York: Fordham University Press.
Clark, T. J. 2012. 'For a Left with No Future'. *New Left Review* 74 (March-April): 53–75.
Comay, Rebecca. 2005. 'The Sickness of Tradition: Between Melancholia and Fetishism'. In *Walter Benjamin and History*. Edited by Andrew Benjamin. London and New York: Continuum.
Dallmayr, Fred. 1993. 'Heidegger and Freud'. *Political Psychology* 14 (2): 235–53.
Daney, Serge. 2004. 'The Tracking Shot in *Kapò*'. *Senses of Cinema* 30 (January-March). Translated by Laurent Kretzschmar.
Dastur, Françoise. 1999. *Heidegger and the Question of Time*. Translated by François Raffoul and David Pettigrew. New York: Humanity Books.
Deleuze, Gilles. 1991a. *Bergsonism*. Translated by Hugh Tomlinson and Barbara Habberjam. New York: Zone Books.
———. 1991b. 'Coldness and Cruelty'. In *Masochism*. Translated by Jean McNeill. New York: Zone Books.
———. 1985. *Cinéma 2. L'image-temps*. Paris: Les Éditions de Minuit.
———. 1989. *Cinema 2. The Time-Image*. Translated by Hugh Tomlinson and Robert Galeta. London: The Athlone Press.
———. 1994. *Difference and Repetition*. Translated by Paul Patton. London and New York: Continuum.
———. 2011. *Différence et Répétition*. Paris: Presses Universitaires de France.
———. 1990. *Logic of Sense*. Translated by Mark Lester. London: The Athlone Press.
———. 1997. *Negotiations, 1972–1990*. Translated by Martin Joughin. New York: Columbia University Press.
———. 2006. *Nietzsche and Philosophy*. Translated by Hugh Tomlinson. New York: Columbia University Press.
———. 1983. *Nietzsche et la philosophie*. Paris: Presses Universitaires de France.
———. 2008. *Proust and Signs*. Translated by Richard Howard. London and New York: Continuum.
de Martelaere, Patricia. 2008. 'Het dagboek en de dood'. In *Een Verlangen naar ontroostbaarheid: Over leven, kunst en dood*. Amsterdam: Meulenhoff.
Derrida, Jacques. 1990. *Force de loi; le fondement mystique de l'autorité / Force of Law: The Mystical Foundation of Authority*. Translated by Mary Quaintance. New York: Cardozo Law Review.
———. 1982. '*Ousia* and *Gramme*: Note on a Note from *Being and Time*'. In *Margins of Philosophy*. Translated by Alan Bass. Sussex: The Harvester Press.

———. 1994. *Specters of Marx: The State of the Debt, the Work of Mourning, and the New International*. Translated by Peggy Kamuf. New York and London: Routledge.

Didi-Huberman, Georges. 2008. *Images in Spite of All: Four Photographs from Auschwitz*. Translated by Shane B. Lillis. Chicago: The University of Chicago Press.

Düttmann, Alexander García. 2000. *The Gift of Language. Memory and Promise in Adorno, Benjamin, Heidegger and Rosenzweig*. London: The Athlone Press.

Eco, Umberto. 1988. 'An *Ars Oblivionalis*? Forget It'. *PMLA* 103: 254–61.

Eiland, Howard. 2003. 'Reception in Distraction'. *boundary 2* 30 (1): 51–66.

Eiland, Howard, and Michael W. Jennings. 2014. *Walter Benjamin. A Critical Life*. Cambridge, MA, and London: Harvard University Press.

Fenves, Peter. 2016. 'Completion Instead of Revelation: Toward the "Theological-Political Fragment"'. In *Walter Benjamin and Theology*, edited by Colby Dickinson and Stéphane Symons. New York: Fordham University Press.

Ferber, Ilit. 2013. *Philosophy and Melancholy. Benjamin's Early Reflections on Theater and Language*. Stanford, CA: Stanford University Press.

Freud, Sigmund. 1956–1974. 'An Autobiographical Study'. In *Standard Edition. Volume XX*. Edited and Translated by James Strachey, in collaboration with Anna Freud. Assisted by Alix Strachey and Alan Tyson. London: The Hogarth Press.

———. 1956–1974. 'A Note Upon the "Mystic Writing-Pad"'. In *Standard Edition. Volume XIX*. Edited and Translated by James Strachey, in collaboration with Anna Freud. Assisted by Alix Strachey and Alan Tyson. London: The Hogarth Press.

———. 1956–1974. 'Beyond the Pleasure Principle'. In *Standard Edition. Volume XVIII*. Edited and Translated by James Strachey, in collaboration with Anna Freud. Assisted by Alix Strachey and Alan Tyson. London: The Hogarth Press.

———. 1956–1974. 'Draft H – Paranoia'. In *Standard Edition. Volume I*. Edited and Translated by James Strachey, in collaboration with Anna Freud. Assisted by Alix Strachey and Alan Tyson. London: The Hogarth Press.

———. 1956–1974. 'New Introductory Lectures on Psychoanalysis. Lecture XXXV. The Question of a Weltanschauung'. in *Standard Edition. Volume XXII*. Edited and Translated by James Strachey, in collaboration with Anna Freud. Assisted by Alix Strachey and Alan Tyson. London: The Hogarth Press.

———. 1956–1974. 'Notes Upon a Case of Obsessional Neurosis'. In *The Standard Edition of the Complete Psychological Works of Sigmund Freud. Volume X*. Edited and Translated by James Strachey, in collaboration with Anna Freud. Assisted by Alix Strachey and Alan Tyson. London: The Hogarth Press.

———. 1956–1974. 'On the History of the Psycho-Analytic Movement'. In *Standard Edition. Volume XIV*. Edited and Translated by James Strachey, in collaboration with Anna Freud. Assisted by Alix Strachey and Alan Tyson. London: The Hogarth Press.

———. 1956–1974. 'On Transience'. in *Standard Edition. Volume XIV*. Edited and Translated by James Strachey, in collaboration with Anna Freud. Assisted by Alix Strachey and Alan Tyson. London: The Hogarth Press.

———. 1956–1974. 'The Ego and the Id'. In *Standard Edition. Volume XIX*. Edited and Translated by James Strachey, in collaboration with Anna Freud. Assisted by Alix Strachey and Alan Tyson. London: The Hogarth Press.

———. 1956–1974. 'The Psychical Mechanism of Forgetfulness'. In *Standard Edition. Volume III*. Edited and Translated by James Strachey, in collaboration

with Anna Freud. Assisted by Alix Strachey and Alan Tyson. London: The Hogarth Press.
———. 1956–1974. 'The Psychopathology of Everyday Life'. In *Standard Edition. Volume VI*. Edited and Translated by James Strachey, in collaboration with Anna Freud. Assisted by Alix Strachey and Alan Tyson. London: The Hogarth Press.
———. 1956–1974 'The Unconscious'. In *Standard Edition. Volume XIV*. Edited and Translated by James Strachey, in collaboration with Anna Freud. Assisted by Alix Strachey and Alan Tyson. London: The Hogarth Press.
———. 1956–1974. 'Three Essays on Sexuality'. In *Standard Edition. Volume VII*. Edited and Translated by James Strachey, in collaboration with Anna Freud. Assisted by Alix Strachey and Alan Tyson. London: The Hogarth Press.
———. 1956–1974. 'Two Principles of Mental Functioning'. In *Standard Edition. Volume XII*. Edited and Translated by James Strachey, in collaboration with Anna Freud. Assisted by Alix Strachey and Alan Tyson. London: The Hogarth Press.
Friedlander, Eli. 2012. *Walter Benjamin: A Philosophical Portrait*. Cambridge, MA: Harvard University Press.
Frost, Catherine. 2017. 'Birth, Death and Survival: Sources of Political Renewal in the Work of Hannah Arendt and Virgil's *Aeneid*'. *Mortality*, 5 October. doi:10.1080/13576275.2017.1377167.
Glazova, Anna, and Paul North, eds. 2014. *Messianic Thought Outside Theology*. New York: Fordham University Press.
Gordon, Peter Eli. 2016. *Adorno and Existence*. Cambridge, MA, and London: Harvard University Press.
———. 2007. 'The Concept of the Apolitical: German Jewish Thought and Weimar Political Theology'. *Social Research* 74 (3): 855–78.
———. 2016. 'The Odd Couple'. *The Nation*, June 9.
Hansen, Miriam Bratu. 1987. 'Benjamin, Cinema and Experience: "The Blue Flower in the Land of Technology"'. *New German Critique* 40: 179–224.
———. 2012. 'Play-Form of Second Nature'. In *Cinema and Experience: Siegfried Kracauer, Walter Benjamin, and Theodor W. Adorno*. Berkeley: University of California Press.
———. 2004. 'Room-for-Play. Benjamin's Gamble with Cinema'. *October* 109: 3–45.
———. 1997. '"Dichtermut" and "Blödigkeit": Two Poems by Hölderlin Interpreted by Walter Benjamin'. *MLN* 112 (5): 786–816.
Heidegger, Martin. 1996. *Being and Time*. Translated by Joan Stambaugh. New York: State University of New York Press.
———. 2012. *Contributions to Philosophy (Of the Event)*. Translated by Richard Rojcewicz and Daniela Vallega-Neu. Bloomington and Indianapolis: Indiana University Press.
———. 1998. *Gesamtausgabe. Band 69. Die Geschichte des Seyns*. Frankfurt am Main: Vittorio Klostermann.
———. 2000. *Introduction to Metaphysics*. Revised and expanded. Translated by Gregory Fried and Richard Polt. New Haven, CT, and London: Yale University Press.
———. 1991a. *Nietzsche. Volumes One and Two*. Translated by David Farrell Krell. San Francisco: Harper Collins.
———. 1991b. *Nietzsche. Volumes Three and Four*. Translated by Joan Stambaugh, David Farrell Krell and Frank A. Capuzzi. San Francisco: Harper Collins.
———. 2010. 'On the Question of Being'. In *Pathmarks*. Edited and translated by William McNeill. Cambridge: Cambridge University Press.

———. 1992. *Parmenides*. Translated by André Schuwer and Richard Rojcewicz. Bloomington and Indianapolis: Indiana University Press.
———. 2000. 'Remembrance'. In *Elucidations of Hölderlin's Poetry*. Translated by Keith Hoeller. New York: Humanity Books.
———. 1997. 'The End of Philosophy and the Task of Thinking'. In *Basic Writings: From Being and Time (1929) to The Task of Thinking (1964)*. Edited and introduced by David Farrell Krell. San Francisco: Harper Collins.
———. 2015. *The History of Beyng*. Translated by Jeffrey Powell and William McNeill. Bloomington and Indianapolis: Indiana University Press.
———. 1977. 'The Word of Nietzsche: 'God is Dead''. In *The Question Concerning Technology and Other Essays*. Translated and Introduced by William Lovitt. New York and London: Garland Publishing.
———. 1972. 'Time and Being'. In *On Time and Being*. Translated by Joan Stambaugh. New York and London: Harper Torchbooks.
———. 2001. *Zollikon Seminars Protocols-Conversations-Letters*. Edited by Medard Boss. Translated by Franz Mayr and Richard Askay. Evanston: Northwestern University Press.
Hochschild, Paige E. 2012. *Memory in Augustine's Theological Anthropology*. Oxford: Oxford University Press.
Hodge, Joanna. 2015. 'Sobriety, Intoxication, Hyperbology: Benjamin and Heidegger Reading Hölderlin'. In *Sparks Will Fly: Benjamin and Heidegger*. Edited by Andrew Benjamin and Dimitris Vardoulakis. Albany: State University of New York Press.
Huyssen, Andreas. 1986. 'Mapping the Postmodern'. In *After the Great Divide: Modernism, Mass Culture, Postmodernism*. Bloomington: Indiana University Press.
———. 2005. *Present Pasts. Urban Palimpsests and the Politics of Memory*. Stanford, CA: Stanford University Press.
———. 1986. 'The Search for Tradition'. In *After the Great Divide: Modernism, Mass Culture, Postmodernism*. Bloomington: Indiana University Press.
———. 1995. *Twilight Memories. Marking Time in a Culture of Amnesia*. New York and London: Routledge.
Jacobson, Eric. 2003. *Metaphysics of the Profane: The Political Theology of Walter Benjamin and Gershom Scholem*. New York: Columbia University Press.
Jay, Martin. 2002. 'Remembrance and the First World War'. In *Benjamin Studien*. Edited by Helga Geyer-Ryan, Paul Koopman, and Klaas Yntema. Amsterdam: Rodopi.
Johnston, Nicholas. 2017. 'Total Mobilization and Standing Reserve: Ernst Jünger and Martin Heidegger on Technology and History'. Unpublished MA Thesis. Institute of Philosophy, KU Leuven.
Judt, Tony. 2005. *Postwar: A History of Europe since 1945*. New York: Penguin Books.
Jünger, Ernst. 2016. 'Across the Line'. In *Martin Heidegger and Ernst Jünger. Correspondence 1949-1975*. Translated by Timothy Sean Quinn. New York and London: Rowman & Littlefield International.
Kampowski, Stephan. 2008. *Arendt, Augustine, and the New Beginning: The Action Theory and Moral Thought of Hannah Arendt in the Light of Her Dissertation on St. Augustine*. Grand Rapids, MI: Eerdmans.
Kisiel, Theodore J. 1993. *The Genesis of Heidegger's* Being and Time. Berkeley, Los Angeles, London: University of California Press.
Kittler, Wolf. 2008. 'From Gestalt to Ge-Stell: Martin Heidegger Reads Ernst Jünger'. *Cultural Critique* 69 (Spring): 79–97.

Koch, Gertrud. 1994. 'Cosmos in Film: On the Concept of Space in Walter Benjamin's "Work of Art" Essay'. In *Walter Benjamin's Philosophy: Destruction and Experience*. Edited by Andrew Benjamin and Peter Osborne. London: Routledge.
Koselleck, Reinhart. 2004. *Futures Past: On the Semantics of Historical Time*. Translated by Keith Tribe. New York: Columbia University Press.
Kracauer, Siegfried. 1995. *History: The Last Things Before the Last*. Edited by Paul Oskar Kristeller. Princeton: Markus Wiener Publishers.
Krell, David Farrell. 1986. *Intimations of Mortality: Time, Truth, and Finitude in Heidegger's* Thinking of Being. University Park and London: The Pennsylvania State University Press.
Lapoujade, David. 2017. *Aberrant Movements: The Philosophy of Gilles Deleuze*. Translated by Joshua David Jordan. South Pasadena, CA: Semiotext(e).
Lazier, Benjamin. 2008. *God Interrupted: Heresy and the European Imagination between the World Wars*. Princeton, NJ: Princeton University Pres.
Lebovic, Nitzan. 2013. *The Philosophy of Life and Death: Ludwig Klages and the Rise of a Nazi Biopolitics*. New York: Palgrave Macmillan.
Leslie, Esther. 2006. 'Ruin and Rubble in the Arcades'. In *Walter Benjamin and the Arcades Project*. Edited by Beatrice Hanssen. London: Continuum.
Levi, Primo. 1993. *Survival in Auschwitz. The Nazi Assault on Humanity*. Translated by Stuart Woolf. New York: Collier.
———. 2017. *The Drowned and the Saved*. Translated by Raymond Rosenthal. New York: Simon & Schuster.
Levinas, Emmanuel. 1981. *Otherwise than Being, Or, Beyond Essence*. Translated by Alphonso Lingis. Boston: Kluwer.
Lippit, Akira Mizuta. 2005. *Atomic Light (Shadow Optics)*. Minneapolis and London: University of Minnesota Press.
Marcuse, Herbert. 1966. *Eros and Civilization: A Philosophical Inquiry into Freud*. Boston: Beacon Press.
Margalit, Avishai. 2004. *The Ethics of Memory*. Cambridge, MA, and London: Harvard University Press.
McFarland, James. 2013. *Constellation: Friedrich Nietzsche and Walter Benjamin in the Now-Time of History*. New York: Fordham University Press.
McMullin, Irene. 2011. 'The Amnesia of the Modern: Arendt on the Role of Memory in the Constitution of the Political. *Philosophical Topics* 39 (2) (Fall): 91–116.
Merleau-Ponty, Maurice. 1968. *The Visible and the Invisible*. Edited by Claude Lefort. Translated by Alphonso Lingis. Evanston, IL: Northwestern University Press.
Moses, Stéphane. 1996. 'Benjamin, Nietzsche et l'idée de l'éternel retour'. *Europe, revue littéraire mensuelle* 74 (804): 140–58.
———. 1999. 'Gershom Scholem's Reading of Kafka: Literary Criticism and Kabbalah'. *New German Critique* 77: 149–67.
———. 2009. *The Angel of History: Rosenzweig, Benjamin, Scholem*. Translated by Barbara Harshav. Stanford, CA: Stanford University Press.
Moyaert, Paul. 2014. *Opboksen tegen het inerte. De doodsdrift bij Freud*. Nijmegen: Vantilt.
Nägele, Rainer. 1986. 'Benjamin's Ground'. In *Benjamin's Ground: New Readings of Walter Benjamin*. Edited by Rainer Nägele. Detroit, MI: Wayne State University Press.
New German Critique 44, special issue on the *Historikerstreit* (Spring/Summer 1988).

Nietzsche, Friedrich. 1997. 'On the Uses and Disadvantages of History for Life'. In *Untimely Meditations*. Translated by R. J. Hollingdale. Cambridge: Cambridge University Press.

———. 2006. *Thus Spoke Zarathustra: A Book for All and None*. Translated by Adrian del Caro. New York: Cambridge University Press.

Oe, Kenzaburo. 1996. *Hiroshima Notes*. Translated by David L. Swain and Toshi Yonezawa. New York: Grove Press.

Pensky, Max. 2006. '*Geheimmittel*: Advertising and Dialectical Images in Benjamin's Arcades Project'. In *Walter Benjamin and the Arcades Project*. Edited by Beatrice Hanssen. London: Continuum.

Philipsen, Bart. 2012. '»ein gelobtes Land« . Hölderlins Nüchternheit zu Ende gelesen (mit Benjamin, Adorno, Szondi, Agamben)'. In *Gattung und Geschichte. Literatur- und medienwissenschaftliche Ansätze zu einer neuen Gattungstheorie*. Edited by C. Liebrand and O. Kohns. Bielefeld: Transcript Verlag.

Plato. 1992. *Theaetetus*. Translated by M. J. Levett. Indianapolis, IN, Cambridge, MA: Hackett Publishing Company.

Ponzi, Mauro. 2017. *Nietzsche's Nihilism in Walter Benjamin*. Cham: Palgrave Macmillan.

Proust, Marcel. 2003. *The Fugitive*. In *In Search of Lost Time. Volume V*. Translated and introduced by Peter Collier. London: Penguin.

———. 2003. *Time Regained*. In *In Search of Lost Time. Volume VI*. Translated by Andreas Mayor and Terence Kilmartin, revised by D. J. Enright. New York: Modern Library.

Richardson, William J. 2003. 'Heidegger and Psychoanalysis'. *Natureza humana* 5 (1): 9–38.

Ricoeur, Paul. 2004. *Memory, History, Forgetting*. Translated by Kathleen Blamey and David Pellauer. Chicago and London: The University of Chicago Press.

Rieff, David. 2016. *In Praise of Forgetting: Historical Memory and Its Ironies*. New Haven, CT: Yale University Press.

Rothberg, Michael. 2009. *Multidirectional Memory. Remembering the Holocaust in the Age of Decolonization*. Stanford, CA: Stanford University Press.

Sanyal, Debarati. 2006. *The Violence of Modernity: Baudelaire, Irony, and the Politics of Form*. Baltimore, MD: Johns Hopkins University Press.

Sartre, Jean-Paul. 1992. *Notebooks for an Ethics*. Translated by David Pellauer. Chicago: The University of Chicago Press.

Schild, Alexandre. 2013. 'Oubli de l'être'. In *Le Dictionnaire Martin Heidegger*. Edited by Philippe Arjakovsky, François Fédier and Hadrien France-Lanord. Paris: Les Éditions du Cerf.

Scholem, Gershom. 1995a. 'Redemption Through Sin'. In *The Messianic Idea in Judaism and Other Essays on Jewish Spirituality*. New York: Schocken Books.

———. 1995b. 'Toward an Understanding of the Messianic Idea'. In *The Messianic Idea in Judaism and Other Essays on Jewish Spirituality*. New York: Schocken Books.

———. 1981. *Walter Benjamin. The Story of a Friendship*. Translated by Harry Zohn. New York: Schocken Books.

Sheehan, Thomas. 2001. '*Kehre* and *Ereignis*: A Prolegomenon to *Introduction to Metaphysics*'. In *A Companion to Heidegger's Introduction to Metaphysics*. Edited by Richard Polt and Gregory Fried. New Haven, CT, and London: Yale University Press.

Sholl, Jonathan. 2012. 'Thought and Repetition in Bergson and Deleuze'. *Deleuze Studies* 6 (4): 544–63.

Sluga, Hans. 2010. 'Heidegger's Nietzsche'. In *A Companion to Heidegger*. Edited by Hubert L. Dreyfus and Mark A. Wrathall. Oxford: Blackwell Publishing.

Somers-Hall, Henry. 2013. *Deleuze's Difference and Repetition*. Edinburgh: Edinburgh University Press.
Steizinger, Johannes. 2013. *Revolte, Eros und Sprache. Walter Benjamin's "Metaphysik Der Jugend"*. Berlin: Kulturverlag Kadmos.
Styfhals, Willem. 2019. *No Spiritual Investment in the World: Gnosticism and Postwar German Philosophy*. Ithaca, NY: Cornell University Press.
Symons, Stéphane. 2013. 'In Praise of Shadows. Commemorative Images and the Atomic Bomb'. *Image and Narrative* 14 (1): 19–34.
———. 2017. *More than Life: Georg Simmel and Walter Benjamin on Art*. Evanston, IL: Northwestern University Press.
———. 2018. 'Wo bist du Nachdenkliches! Sobriety and Poetic Determinability in Hölderlin and Walser'. In *Benjamin, Adorno and the Experience of Literature*. Edited by Nathan Ross and Corey McCall. New York and London: Routledge.
Tanizaki, Junichiro. 2001. *In Praise of Shadows*. Translated by Thomas J. Harper and Edward G. Seidensticker. London: Vintage Books.
Thiem, Annika. 2016. 'Benjamin's Messianic Metaphysics of Transience'. In *Walter Benjamin and Theology*. Edited by Colby Dickinson and Stéphane Symons. New York: Fordham University Press.
Tiedemann, Rolf. 1973. *Studien zur Philosophie Walter Benjamins*. Frankfurt Am Main: Suhrkamp Verlag.
Todorov, Tzvetan. 2010. *Memory as a Remedy for Evil*. Translated by Gila Walker. London: Seagull Books.
Traverso, Enzo. 2016. *Left-Wing Melancholia. Marxism, History, and Memory*. New York: Columbia University Press.
van Reijen, Willem. 1998. *Der Schwarzwald und Paris. Heidegger und Benjamin*. München: Wilhelm Fink Verlag.
Virgil. 2007. *Aeneid*. Translated by Frederick Ahl. Oxford and New York: Oxford University Press.
———. 1999. *Eclogues, Georgics, Aeneid I–VI*. Translated by H. Rushton Fairclough. Revised by G. P. Goold. Cambridge, MA: Harvard University Press.
———. 2006. *Georgics*. Translated by Peter Fallon. Oxford and New York: Oxford University Press.
Virilio, Paul. 1989. *War and Cinema: The Logistics of Perception*. Translated by Patrick Camiller. London: Verso.
Weber, Samuel. 2008. *Benjamin's -abilities*. Cambridge, MA, and London: Harvard University Press.
———. 2008. 'Benjamin's "-abilities": Mediality and Concept Formation in Benjamin's Early Writings'. In *Benjamin Studien* 1. Edited by Daniel Weidner and Sigrid Weigel. München: Wilhelm Fink.
———. 2004. 'Storming the Work: Allegory and Theatricality in Benjamin's *Origin of the German Mourning Play*'. In *Theatricality as Medium*. New York: Fordham University Press.
Weigel, Sigrid. 1996. *Body- and Image-space: Re-reading Walter Benjamin*. Translated by Georgina Paul, with Rachel McNicholl and Jeremy Gaines. London: Routledge.
———. 2013. *Walter Benjamin: Images, the Creaturely, and the Holy*. Translated by Chadwick Smith. Stanford, CA: Stanford University Press.
Weinrich, Harald. 2004. *Lethe: The Art and Critique of Forgetting*. Translated by Steven Rendall. Ithaca, NY: Cornell University Press.
Widder, Nathan. 2012. 'Deleuze on Bergsonian Duration and Nietzsche's "Eternal Return"'. In *Time and History in Deleuze and Serres*. Edited by Bernd Herzogenrath. London and New York: Continuum.

Wohlfarth, Irving. 1986. 'Et Cetera. The Historian as Chiffonnier'. *New German Critique* 39: 142–68.
———. 2005. 'Nihilismus kontra Nihilismus. Walter Benjamins 'Weltpolitik' aus heutiger Sicht'. In *Theologie und Politik. Walter Benjamin, ein Paradigma der Moderne*. Edited by Bernd Witte and Mauro Ponzi. Berlin: Erich Schmidt Verlag.
———. 1978. 'No-Man's Land: On Walter Benjamin's "Destructive Character"'. *Diacritics* 8 (2): 47–65.
Wood, David. 2001. *The Deconstruction of Time*. Evanston, IL: Northwestern University Press.
Wordsworth, William. 2006. *Ode: Intimations of Immortality from Recollections of Early Childhood*. Whitefish, MT: Kessinger Publishing.
Wrathall, Mark A. 2005. 'Unconcealment'. In *A Companion to Heidegger*. Edited by Hubert L. Dreyfus and Mark A. Wrathall. Oxford and Cambridge: Blackwell Publishing.
Wrathall, Mark A. and Max Murphey. 2013. 'An Overview of *Being and Time*'. In *The Cambridge Companion to Heidegger's Being and Time*. Edited by Mark A. Wrathall. New York: Cambridge University Press.
Zimmerman, Michael E. 1990. *Heidegger's Confrontation with Modernity: Technology, Politics and Art*. Bloomington: Indiana University Press.
Zourabichvili, François. 2012. *Deleuze: A Philosophy of the Event*. Edited by Gregg Lambert and Daniel W. Smith. Translated by Kieran Aarons. Edinburgh: Edinburgh University Press.

Index

Abfall (garbage), 80, 147, 168; and dialectical images, 80. *See also Müll* (detritus)
abandonment by being (*Seinsverlassenheit*), 25, 102, 103, 141n102. *See also* being
about-turn, 49, 92, 122–123, 129, 142n113
absolute truth, 16, 33, 34, 40–43, 46, 82n8, 117
Adorno, Theodor, 9, 29n22, 30n35, 53, 76–81, 81n2, 82n7, 87n68–88n90; and Walter Benjamin, 78–80, 82n7
affirmation, 23, 34, 55–60, 62–67; of change, 72–73, 77, 83n11, 134, 150; of freedom, 84n30; of transience, 54, 92, 108–109
afterlife (*Fortleben*), 14, 40, 92, 95; unconscious, 100; of a lost and defeated past, 10
Agamben, Giorgio, 21, 31n45, 82n5, 85n43, 88n90, 147, 165
allegory, 24, 26, 92, 120–124, 141n112, 142n114, 170; and creativity, 24, 26, 122; as apparat de destruction, 121; as literary mode of the baroque, 120–122; Baudelaire's use of, 122; of resurrection, 122
Al-Saji, Alia, 85n44, 134n5, 134n8
Alter, Robert, 85n40
amnesia, 8, 11, 16, 69, 135n11, 177n52; culture of, 28n15
Anders, Günther, 182, 186n2
annihilation, 9, 13–14; force of, 14, 18, 183, 185; rhythm of, 13

Arendt, Hannah, 26, 31n57, 145–146, 147, 147–163, 172, 176n20, 176n23–179n86; and Friedrich Nietzsche, 150–152; and Walter Benjamin, 162–163, 171–172; capacity to begin, 26, 150, 152–156; law of mortality, 146, 150, 155–156; on memory, 155–156; philosophy of thought, 158–160
Ariès, Philippe, 176n2
Aristotle, 12, 30n31, 93–96; metaphor of wax, 95; on memory, 95
artworks, 38–39, 43, 123, 128–130, 141n110, 181
Assmann, Aleida, 28n8
atomic bomb, 21, 87n86, 181–185. *See also* Hiroshima
Aufgabe, 25, 38–48, 53–54, 58–59, 62–67, 80, 82n8, 106, 139n71, 147, 168. *See also* task
Augustine, 26, 86n67, 145, 151, 153–160, 178n57, 179n83
Auschwitz, 3, 18, 30n37, 31n44, 78–80. *See also* Holocaust
awakening, 73, 179n87

Barash, Jeffrey Andrew, 8, 29n19, 138n70, 140n82
baroque, 120–122
Baudelaire, Charles, 26, 92, 114–127, 141n107, 142n115
Benhabib, Seyla, 177n25, 179n85
being, 25, 92, 100–111; abandonment by, 102, 141n102; concept of, 112; forgetfulness of,

92, 101–103; question of being, 92, 101–103, 111, 137n51, 141n101
Benjamin, Walter, 9, 13–16, 23–27, 30n33, 33–67, 73–81, 81n1–88n90, 89–92, 98, 103, 105–106, 112–130, 138n70–139n71, 141n106–142n121, 145, 147, 160–175, 176n19, 179n86–179n91, 185
Bergson, Henri, 69, 85n44, 86n49, 89–92, 97, 103–104, 112–115, 129–130, 134n1–135n12, 180n101
Bloch, Ernst, 10, 29n25
Blödigkeit, 34–37, 40, 45–53, 60, 67, 81n2, 171
Blond, Louis, 139n76
Buck-Morss, Susan, 86n67, 88n89, 141n110, 179n89
Butler, Judith, 83n12

Canetti, Elias, 171, 180n97
capacity to begin anew, 26, 150, 152–156
childhood, 26, 40, 94, 97, 145–147, 147, 153, 160–164, 167–171, 176n2, 179n89
Chrétien, Jean-Louis, 86n67, 87n68
Clark, T. J., 10, 29n27
Comay, Rebecca, 142n113
commemoration (*Gedächtnis*), 3, 10, 12–14, 66, 83n11, 112, 115, 151, 155, 183, 184
compact mass, 43, 141n109
constellation, 24, 67, 73, 76
creativity, 23–24, 26, 49, 57, 84n30, 146–150, 161–162; of forgetting, 122, 149; of life, 26, 148, 150

Dallmayr, Fred, 136n50
Daney, Serge, 30n42, 30n43
Dastur, François, 140n82
De Martelaere, Patricia, 172, 180n98
death drive, 25, 92, 97–100, 108, 135n28, 136n37

death, 1, 8, 27, 28n18, 34, 50, 75, 83n10, 84n31, 90, 99, 120, 123–124, 127, 130–131; instinct, 130, 136n42. *See also* passing-away
Deleuze, Gilles, 34, 54–58, 60, 62, 69–72, 79, 83n13, 85n44, 86n49, 87n84, 89, 98–99, 108–109, 129–130, 134n2, 136n42, 140n87, 142n123, 148, 167, 176n12, 180n94
Derrida, Jacque, 7, 10, 16, 29n26, 30n36, 85n43, 140n82, 186n5
destruction, 14, 21, 57–60, 71, 84n29, 101, 110, 135n11, 141n110, 142n113, 150, 155, 182–185; of memory, 135n11
dialectics, 11, 62, 76–80, 84n38, 87n74
Dichtermut (Poet's Courage), 34–37, 40, 45–46, 50, 81n2
Didi-Huberman, Georges, 18, 31n44
dislocation, 49–52, 66; of the mythological, 34; of transience, 66, 109
duration (*Dauer*), 69, 74, 86n49, 90–91, 96, 101, 120, 134n9, 147, 158, 178n62, 180n101
Düttmann, Alexander García, 82n7

Eco, Umberto, 31n52
Eiland, Howard, 141n110, 179n86
Einfühlung (feeling-in), 66–67
Eingedenken (thought, thinking-in), 9, 24, 33, 65–69, 76. *See also* *Einfühlung* (feeling-in)
ephemerality, 22–23, 116, 126, 158, 161. *See also* transience
eternal life, 40, 122, 124, 126
eternal repetition, 16, 24, 59, 124–126, 174
eternal return, 54, 55–57, 59, 69–71, 82n9, 84n31, 108–109
eternity, 126, 155, 170; of God, 156
Europe, 1–3, 27n1, 29n20, 82n9, 85n39, 154, 175

experience: conscious, 93; historicization of, 6; lived, 3, 57, 110; poverty of, 26, 114, 122, 139n71, 174; true, long, deep (*Erfahrung*), 26, 92, 103, 112–115, 120; surplus of, 96

fall of Berlin Wall, 6, 10
Fenves, Peter, 83n12
Ferber, Ilit, 141n106, 142n113
filmmaker. *See* photographer
forgetting: creative, 16–21, 24, 34, 148, 149; universal, 65; work of (*Penelopewerk des Vergessens*), 14, 104
forgottenness of being (*Seinsvergessenheit*), 25, 101, 102, 139n71
Foucault, Michel, 7
fragmentation, 99, 122–123, 130
Freud, Sigmund, 25, 29n24, 43, 90–92, 95–99, 103, 114, 115, 135n13, 136n41, 139n75, 141n106; Benjamin and, 112–115, 164; on memory, 93–108. *See also* death drive
Friedlander, Eli, 82n6, 82n9
Frost, Catherine, 178n56

garbage, 78, 80. *See also Abfall* (garbage); *Müll* (detritus)
Gedichtete (poeticized), 36–38, 40, 81n2
Glazova, Anna, 85n43
Gordon, Peter Eli, 87n74, 179n85

Hansen, Miriam Bratu, 141n110, 179n90
happiness, 22, 30n34, 59, 67, 126, 129, 147, 164, 185
Heidegger, Martin, 25–26, 31n53, 66, 82n7, 83n11, 90–92, 100–120, 130, 136n49, 137n51, 138n67, 139n72, 140n82, 141n101, 160

Hiroshima, 181–186. *See also* atomic bomb
historian, 14, 34, 66–67, 142n113, 168
historical change, 40, 58, 60, 166
historical force, 3, 11
historical time, 11, 28n14, 110
historical truth, 45, 47, 159, 160
history: end of, 10; transcendent ground to, 72
history as *Geschichte*, 2, 65–67
history as *Vergangenheit*, 2, 12, 65, 79, 86n66
Hochschild, Paige E., 178n65
Hodge, Joanna, 83n11
Hölderlin, Friedrich, 24, 34, 36, 45, 47, 49, 52, 60, 75, 81n2, 82n4, 83n11, 161, 165, 171
Holocaust, 1, 18, 28n8, 30n42. *See also* Auschwitz
humanism, 16, 152, 163, 183
Huyssen, Andreas, 3, 8, 11, 28n9, 29n21, 30n30

ideology, 71, 77, 80
image, 1, 10, 14, 18, 65, 67, 72, 73, 81, 82n8, 115, 117, 157, 166, 168; after-, 90; dream, 67, 73–74; memory-, 158, 180n101; mirror-, 69, 83n11, 105; of history, 65, 80, 168; of thought (*Denkbild*), 67; time-, 71, 86n54; wish-, 10, 73
immanence, 40, 45, 62, 85n39
immemorial, 26, 89, 108, 114, 117–134; past, 25, 90, 92, 100, 113, 115, 117, 129, 130, 134n5, 135n10, 174, 180n101
immortality, 27, 54, 59, 126, 151–152, 173, 176n3
impermanence, 14, 17, 92, 98, 101, 106, 120, 122, 126, 127, 132; longing for, 97
injustice, 9, 16, 18, 30n34, 75, 76, 78, 183
interruption, 33, 69, 146; of the passage of time, 16, 128, 146, 152,

153
intervention, 16, 30n34, 85n43, 163; by memory, 3, 9, 122; by thought, 24, 45; divine, 43, 58, 60, 67
involuntary memory (*souvenir involontaire*), 26, 115, 124–129

Jacobson, Eric, 84n34, 87n88
Jay, Martin, 179n86
Johnston, Nicholas, 140n91
Judt, Tony, 1–3, 27n1, 28n7
Jünger, Ernst, 25, 110–112, 140n91, 168; and Martin Heidegger, 110–111, 140n91; and Walter Benjamin, 170

Kafka, Franz, 63–67, 85n40, 151
Kampowski, Stephan, 178n57
Kisiel, Theodore J., 137n51
Kittler, Wolf, 140n91
Koch, Gertrud, 141n110
Koselleck, Reinhart, 6, 11, 28n14
Kracauer, Siegfried, 8, 28n18, 141n111
Krell, David Farrell, 138n68, 140n86

Lapoujade, David, 85n44
Lazier, Benjamin, 84n38
Lebensphilosophie, 24, 57, 69, 83n10, 90
Lebovic, Nitzan, 83n10
Leslie, Esther, 86n66, 88n89
Levi, Primo, 17–18, 30n37
Levinas, Emmanuel, 89, 134n5
life, 9, 16, 18, 23, 24, 26, 34, 45–46, 49, 60, 132, 146, 148–150, 162, 165, 174
Lippit, Akira Mizuta, 186n5
Lyotard, Jean-François, 7

Marcuse, Herbert, 9, 29n24
Margalit, Avishai, 3, 28n9, 29n23
McFarland, James, 84n29
McMullin, Irene, 177n52

memory, 1–2, 3–8, 9–11, 13–14, 18, 23–26, 28n10, 29n20, 50, 66, 69, 73–75, 82n7, 89–97, 103, 104, 111, 112–117, 124–127, 129–130, 134n1, 135n25, 154–155, 157–160, 174, 177n52, 178n65, 178n73, 180n101, 183; and politics of identity, 5–6; and renewed present, 5; and technological evolution, 6; Arendt on, 155–160; Aristotle on, 13, 96, 135n16; as remedy for evil, 9, 29n23; Augustine on, 153–160; Benjamin on, 67–69, 89–92; Bergson on, 69, 89–91; Deleuze on, 85n44, 89, 129; Freud on, 91, 93–101; Heidegger on, 26, 83n11, 91–92, 100–111; history as counterforce of, 12; intervention of, 3; Plato on, 12–13, 93–95, 101, 103; studies, 3–8, 14; tension between and history, 9
Merleau-Ponty, Maurice, 43, 89, 134n5
messianism, 23, 25, 53, 54, 58–65, 67–69, 84n34
metaphor: of mystic writing pad, 93–96; of the child, 145–146, 153, 162, 163, 167; of two arrows, 60; of two opposing scales, 67; of wax and seal, 93–95
metaphysics, 78, 92, 100, 101, 107, 112, 137n51, 140n79
mortality, 27, 151; law of, 146, 150, 155, 156
Mosès, Stéphane, 82n9, 84n34, 85n40
mourning (*Trauer*), 29n26, 98, 120, 123, 141n112
Moyaert, Paul, 99, 135n28, 136n37
Müll (detritus), 78, 80. *See also Abfall* (garbage)
Murphey, Max, 137n51
myth, 34, 43, 43–46, 50, 60, 65, 79, 82n9, 84n31, 86n66, 103, 138n67,

139n71, 141n112; mythic violence, 16–17, 63

Nägele, Rainer, 81n1
natality, 1, 26, 31n58, 146, 150
negation, 24, 25, 40, 54, 55, 57–65, 67, 71, 76–81, 148, 167–172
negative dialectics, 76–80, 87n74
Nietzsche, Friedrich, 13, 22–27, 31n48, 59, 82n9, 84n29, 91, 103, 129, 135n10, 139n75, 145–153, 162, 176n4; and Gilles Deleuze, 54–57, 83n13, 85n48, 86n49; and Martin Heidegger, 107–109, 140n86; and Theodor Adorno, 76–77
nihilism, 23, 25, 34, 53–65, 67, 69, 72, 75, 79–80, 83n28, 92, 98–101, 107–112, 117–120, 136n41, 141n102, 148, 152, 167; and messianism, 25, 54; Benjamin on, 26, 34, 53, 54, 57; complete, 26, 55–59, 62–67, 69–72, 79–80, 98–101, 108, 130, 147, 170, 172; Deleuze on, 54–55; Freud on, 25, 98; Heidegger on, 100–101, 111–112; Jünger on, 110–111; Nietzsche on, 107–110
North, Paul, 85n43
not yet (*noch nicht*), 10, 29n25, 38, 39
Nüchternheit (sobriety), 35, 45, 82n5

oblivion, 3, 8, 11, 17, 23, 103–105, 138n69, 141n107
Oe, Kenzaburo, 183, 186n3
ontology, 90, 100, 107, 122

Passagen-Werk, 27, 53, 65, 73, 75, 84n31, 106, 120, 126
passing-away, 24, 26, 49, 91, 98, 124, 150, 152, 167, 177n35
Pensky, Max, 86n66, 88n89
pessimism, 111, 167
Philipsen, Bart, 82n5
photographer, 38–40

Plato, 3, 12, 30n31, 76, 93, 95, 96, 101, 103, 126, 135n15, 138n67, 184
poetry, 21, 65, 67, 83n11, 120, 121.
   See also Gedichtete (poeticized)
Ponzi, Mauro, 83n28
Proust, Marcel, 14, 26, 92, 114–120, 124–134, 142n119, 185
psychoanalysis, 5, 7, 90, 136n41, 136n50

recollection (*Erinnerung*), 11, 14, 25, 28n8, 50–54, 65, 86n66, 90–93, 96, 111–113, 135n12, 141n103, 155, 157, 160, 171, 176n3, 177n52, 178n65, 183; and representation, 92; as instrument to loosen up the connection with the past, 96
redemption (*Erlösung*), 14, 30n34, 34, 54, 58–62, 81, 84n34, 108–109, 126, 129, 142n113, 175; redemptive images of thought, 67; redemptive intervention, 24, 122, 166; redemptive turning of time, 103
rejuvenation, 40, 60, 67, 126, 129, 148
remembrance, 9, 66, 74, 83n11, 105, 115–117, 151, 155, 179n83, 183
restitutio, 25, 53, 54, 59, 67, 126, 142n121, 165, 166, 171; spiritual *restitutio in integrum*, 54, 126
revolution, 6, 10, 43, 62, 63, 86n66, 168, 174; revolutionary power, 162; revolutionary nihilism, 167
Richardson, William, 137n51
Ricoeur, Paul, 3, 7, 28n17, 95, 135n25
Rieff, David, 27n6, 28n7
room-for-play, 117, 141n111. *See also* space-for-play
Rossellini, Roberto, 72, 145
Rothberg, Michael, 3, 28n10, 29n19

salvation, 33, 129, 142n113, 154
Sanyal, Debarati, 142n115
Sartre, Jean-Paul, 84n30
Schild, Alexandre, 137n51

Scholem, Gershom, 53, 62–65, 78, 84n32; and Theodor Adorno, 78; and Walter Benjamin, 62–65
sense of belonging, 3–5, 116, 117
Sheehan, Thomas, 137n51
Sholl, Jonathan, 85n48
Simmel, Georg, 43, 138n70
sleep, 49–50, 75–76, 81, 124
Sluga, Hans, 139n76
Somers-Hall, Henry, 85n44
Soviet Union, 6, 10, 11
space-for-play, 82n8, 165–167, 179n90. *See also* room-for-play
spiritual: life, 46–49, 52–53; *restitutio in integrum*, 54, 126
Steizinger, Johannes, 179n86
Styfhals, Willem, 85n39
Symons, Stéphane, 81n2, 83n12

Tagebuch (diary), 147, 170–171, 174–175
Tanizaki, Junichiro, 184, 185, 186n6
task: of photographer/filmmaker, 38, 166; of the critic, 38, 39; of the poem, 38; of the translator, 38, 40, 42
technology, 6, 137n54, 139n76, 140n91, 141n110, 165, 168–170, 180n96; mythologization of, 168
temporality, 10, 134n5, 140n82, 155, 172
therapeutic, 96, 99
Thiem, Annika, 83n12
thought (*Denken, Eingedenken*), 24–27, 65–67; Adorno on, 76–79; Arendt on, 153; Benjamin on, 45–49; Deleuze on, 55, 69–72; *ent-sinnen* (de-thinking), 27; Heidegger on, 66
Tiedemann, Rolf, 87n69, 139n71
time: emptiness of, 69, 171; now- (Jetzt-Zeit), 65, 67, 84n29; of death, 172; of the self, 176; passage of, 2, 12–13, 18–22, 27, 30n34, 50, 53, 65–69, 74–75, 98, 101, 108–109, 117, 126, 128, 130. *See also* history as *Vergangenheit*
Todorov, Tzvetan, 3, 9, 29n23
transience, 13–17, 22–24, 49–54, 59, 65, 74–75, 83n12, 90–93, 95–109, 117–130, 132–134, 149, 155–163, 170–175, 184; eternal, 30n33, 59, 97, 120–122, 124, 126; unsurpassable, 158
translator, 38–42, 168
Trauerspiel, 23, 120–127
Traverso, Enzo, 11, 28n13

unforgettable (*unvergeßlich*), 74–75, 86n67, 105
universal equality, 10, 73
unrepresentability, 1, 18
utopia, 10–11, 29n25, 34, 73, 76, 79, 86n66, 126, 141n109, 155, 168, 170; the left as 'thing of the past', 11

van Reijen, Willem, 139n71
violence, 2, 6, 9, 14–21, 30n34, 60–62, 82n9, 84n30, 98, 110, 142n115, 185. *See also* mythic violence
Virgil, 145, 153–157, 160, 176n1, 177n43, 178n56
Virilio, Paul, 186n1
vitalism, 24, 69–71, 90, 130. *See also Lebensphilosophie*

Weber, Samuel, 81n3, 82n4, 141n112
Weigel, Sigrid, 82n4, 141n110, 179n91
Weinrich, Harald, 22, 31n47, 179n83
Widder, Nathan, 86n49
Wohlfarth, Irving, 84n29, 141n110, 142n113
Wood, David, 140n82
Wordsworth, William, 146, 176n3
work, 2–3, 16, 36, 39, 71, 75, 100, 120, 128–130, 185; of memory, 8, 21, 29n20, 42, 50, 54, 65, 75, 92, 93; of thought, 47, 48, 53, 71, 73, 185;

through the past, 22, 30n35, 82n6
Wrathall, Mark A., 137n51, 138n68, 139n76

youth, 96, 146–149, 179n86; and childhood, 40, 147, 160–162; metaphysics of, 27, 160–163, 170

youth movement, 27, 161, 179n86

Zarathustra, 108–109, 140n83, 146, 147, 161, 176n7; nihilism of, 108. *See also* Nietzsche, Friedrich
Zimmerman, Michael E., 137n54
Zourabichvili, Francois, 86n49

About the Author

Stéphane Symons is Associate Professor of Philosophy at the Institute of Philosophy of KU Leuven, Belgium. He is the author of *Walter Benjamin: Presence of Mind, Failure to Comprehend* (2013) and *More than Life: Georg Simmel and Walter Benjamin on Art* (2017), editor of *The Marriage of Aesthetics and Ethics* (2015) and coeditor of *Walter Benjamin and Theology* (2015).

www.ingramcontent.com/pod-product-compliance
Lightning Source LLC
Chambersburg PA
CBHW021827300426
44114CB00009BA/352